The Fundraiser's Guide
to the Law

The Fundraiser's Guide to the Law

Bates, Wells & Braithwaite

Centre for Voluntary Sector Development

DIRECTORY OF SOCIAL CHANGE

CAF

Published by
The Directory of Social Change
24 Stephenson Way
London NW1 2DP
tel.: 020 7209 5151, fax: 020 7209 5049
e-mail: info@dsc.org.uk
from whom further copies and a full publications list are available.

The Directory of Social Change is a Registered Charity no. 800517

ISBN 1 900360 78 0

British Library Cataloguing in Publication Data
A catalogue record for this book is available from the British Library

Cover design by Keith Shaw

Text designed by Sarah Nicholson

Edited by Andrew Steeds

Typeset by GreenGate Publishing Services, Tonbridge

Printed and bound by Antony Rowe, Chippenham

Other Directory of Social Change departments in London:
Courses and Conferences tel.: 020 7209 4949
Charity Centre tel.: 020 7209 1015
Research tel.: 020 7209 4422
Finance and Administration tel.: 020 7209 0902

Directory of Social Change Northern Office:
Federation House, Hope Street, Liverpool L1 9BW
Courses and Conferences tel.: 0151 708 0117
Research tel.: 0151 708 0136

Contents

About the authors

Bates, Wells & Braithwaite

Bates, Wells & Braithwaite is a commercial firm of solicitors with particular expertise in charity law, based in the City of London. It is described in the 1999/2000 Chambers *Guide to the Legal Profession* as 'the leading firm' in this field. The firm contributes to the voluntary sector through an extensive programme of lecturing, training and publications, and many of its staff serve as charity trustees.

Philip Kirkpatrick read English at University College, London before deciding on a career as a charity lawyer. He trained at Bates, Wells & Braithwaite, where he is now a partner. He is a contributor to Jordan's *Charities Administration Service*. He is a trustee of one charity and lectures widely on topics of relevance to charities.

Stephen Lloyd was educated at Bristol and Cambridge universities, reading history and law. He taught English for Voluntary Service Overseas in Sudan and since 1983 has been a partner with BWB, where he heads the Charity Department. He is the author of the *Barclays Guide to Law for the Small Business, The Charities Act Handbook* (with Fiona Middleton), *Charities Trading and the Law* and a contributor to Jordan's *Charities Administration Service*. He is a trustee of five charities and lectures extensively on a range of topics.

Christine Rigby began her legal career as a specialist in intellectual property but, after time spent as a volunteer on a rural project in Africa, she decided to change direction and become a legal adviser to charities. She has been a partner in the Charity Department at BWB since April 2000.

Rosamund Smith read politics at Bristol and is a partner at BWB, where she specialises in charity law. She is a contributing author to *The Non-Profit Sector in the UK* (published by CAF) and to Jordan's *Charities Administration Service*. She was Secretary to the Committee on the Penalty for Homicide chaired by Lord Lane and is Chair of 'Poet in the City'.

The Centre for Voluntary Sector Development

The Centre for Voluntary Sector Development is an independent firm established to advance social enterprise in the UK. Its core concerns are helping smaller charities grow and developing specialist fundraising service companies. It achieves this by delivering consultancy, project management and vital working capital. It has substantial holdings in several charity-fundraising firms with the residue owned by the staff who work in them.

Edward Copisarow graduated in politics, economics and law, became a parliamentary researcher and then moved to Saatchi & Saatchi Advertising. A fundraiser since 1989, he has worked in the senior management teams of a number of agencies and charities. He serves on the ICFM training committee and, as fundraising director of the National Asthma Campaign, instigated legal training for all 24 fundraising staff. He has been chief executive of CVSD since 1998 and is a non-executive director of three fundraising companies.

Katie Martin studied psychology at University of Wales, Cardiff and joined the National Asthma Campaign in 1997, working in the individual supporters team and the corporate and trust team. At CVSD, she focused on helping clients develop their trust and statutory support. A committee member of the ICFM trust group, she is currently fundraising manager at Action on Elder Abuse.

Emma Sambrook graduated in genetics and joined the National Asthma Campaign in 1997 where she managed the National Events Team. At CVSD she worked with clients to develop volunteers as fundraisers and build sustainable corporate revenue streams. She is currently head of events at Whizz-Kidz and is chair of the Events Managers Forum.

Preface

by Stephen Lloyd

This book is the result of a variety of collaborations.

For a number of years Bates, Wells & Braithwaite and the Institute of Charity Fundraising Managers have run a two-day course on fundraising and the law. From these joint sessions – and the evidence they provided of the complex and varied issues that fundraisers face on a daily basis – emerged the idea for a book on the subject which would combine a lawyer's knowledge of the law with a fundraiser's experience of the practice of fundraising.

Conscious of the need to avoid writing yet another legal textbook, we approached the Centre for Voluntary Sector Development, which had the collective experience of the full range of fundraising activities that we felt needed to be covered in the book. In the course of a long weekend away together, the writing team (now comprising Rosamund Smith, Philip Kirkpatrick, Christine Rigby and myself from Bates, Wells & Braithwaite, and Edward Copisarow, Emma Sambrook and Katie Martin from the Centre for Voluntary Sector Development) identified every aspect of fundraising and every point of law to be covered. and began linking the two together. At the end of the weekend, the structure of the book and a detailed skeleton of its contents (down to the majority of the paragraph headings) had been established.

Each chapter of the book was then assigned to a lawyer to write, and the resulting draft was passed around to the other fundraisers and lawyers for additional examples, comments and clarification. All members of the team have thus had the opportunity to comment on each other's work, although the actual authorship of individual chapters is as given on the contents page. The agreed draft was then passed to our editor, Andrew Steeds, whose task it has been to transmute a script that reflected our varying contributions and styles into a single text. We are grateful to him for his patient, careful and constructive editing.

The book has been organised and written with you, the fundraiser, in mind, and the chapters structured in the main around types of fundraising activity rather than points of law. We hope that it achieves our overall aim, which is to help you in the many and varied areas in which you operate.

November 2000

1

Introduction

1.1 This book has been written as a guide for fundraisers to the laws that affect fundraising for charities. It is, necessarily, not a definitive law book. One of the difficulties about the law as it affects fundraising is that there is very little law designed specifically to control fundraising. Instead, a very large number of different laws have an impact on it, and none of these laws is designed to *help* the fundraiser. Indeed, the law may at times seem positively obstructive.

1.2 The summary of the law given in this book is designed to help fundraisers keep within the law. There will be many occasions when fundraisers need to take appropriate professional advice because the information in this book does not deal with their particular circumstances or does not do so in sufficient detail. The book is laid out to follow the varied ways in which charities raise funds. Inevitably, however, this means that there was a risk of duplication between sections because some topics (e.g. contract law) affect many forms of fundraising. These topics are therefore dealt with in isolated detail only once in the generic sections in Chapters 11 to 23. We have made cross-references to the generic chapters and to other relevant pages where necessary in the text.

The United Kingdom has three legal systems: those of England and Wales, Scotland, and Northern Ireland. Some legislation applies in all three systems (e.g. tax and data protection); many legal principles established under common law are also the same in all three (e.g. charity and contract law); but, in some cases, the law is different in each (e.g. on the control of public collections). We have indicated where the law varies; where we have not, you can assume that the law is the same throughout the United Kingdom

1.3 Charity Law and fundraising

1.3.1 Charities can be established in England, Wales, Scotland and Northern Ireland for four separate charitable purposes:

- To relieve poverty
- To advance education
- To advance religion
- For other purposes beneficial to the community.

Fundraising itself is not a charitable purpose. Charities cannot be established just to fundraise. Fundraising is a means to an end. Fundraisers must always understand that their activities are to raise funds so that their charity can achieve its charitable objects. That is not to say fundraising is not vital: fundraising is often the principal means of enabling charities to undertake their work.

1.3.2 Consequently it is crucial that fundraisers understand their charities' objects. The objects are often called 'charitable' or 'primary' purposes. They can be found in the charity's constitutional document, whatever form that may take. If the charity is a company, this will be in the Memorandum of Association; if it is a trust, it will be in the Trust Deed; if the charity is an unincorporated association, it will be in its constitution, and so on. In each type of constitution, there will be a clause setting out the charity's objects.

1.4 Fundraising and trust law

1.4.1 Not only can a charity raise funds only to fulfil its objects, but fundraisers must also always bear in mind the impact of trust law on fundraising. This general principle means that monies raised for a particular charitable purpose are subject, by law, to a trust that the monies raised must be spent on that charitable purpose and 'for no other purpose whatsoever'. This means that the purpose for which the monies raised can be spent is linked to the terms on which these were raised. This may well cut down the general purpose of the charity (e.g. 'to advance education') to something much more specific (e.g. 'to buy 100 text books').

1.4.2 It is therefore essential that fundraisers understand that a trust is created by the way in which the funds are raised. A trust can be created by virtue of the fundraising literature issued at the time (e.g. brochures, appeal documents, etc.) or by what is said when the donor is asked to support the appeal. In all cases, the law takes the interests of the donor as being of overriding importance: the donor's interests are seen as primary. Therefore, the monies may only be spent in accordance with the terms upon which the donor gave the money. These terms are inferred from the fundraising literature.

1.4.3 This general principle means that, if funds are raised for very narrow purposes, then they may be spent on those purposes only. This can cause charities considerable difficulties. Say a fundraising appeal is mounted for a particular purpose – e.g. to rebuild a church roof – but the target is not achieved, and the roof cannot be repaired. What happens to the monies raised, given that they are insufficient to carry out the task in hand? Equally, if more money is raised than the target, can the extra monies be spent on anything else? The answer is that, unless the appeal documentation has made it clear that the charity is free to spend the money raised on purposes other than the roof appeal, then either the insufficient funds or the surplus funds must be returned to the donors, which can be very complicated! Appropriate wording in the appeal literature can prevent this problem arising.

In addition, many charities find it difficult to fund their core costs. The proceeds of a general appeal may be spent on core costs; the proceeds of a restricted appeal may not be spent in this way. When launching a general appeal, a charity should take care to identify clearly any specific project mentioned in the appeal document action as an example of the charity's work.

The two letters on pages 4–5 illustrate this point. Although the first letter implies that the supporter's donation will be applied to the project described, the funding request is general. The wording allows the donation to be applied wherever it is most needed (within the objects of the charity). But beware, there is a fine line between being general and misleading, and while you may be on the side of the law, your supporters will not be too happy if they feel they have been misled.

Funds raised as a result of the second letter *must* be used for the project outlined in the letter. However, the response coupon is sufficiently vague not to restrict funds to *particular items* within the project. Any excess funds raised over and above the cost of the project must be returned to supporters, or their permission must be sought to use them for another purpose. Should the project not go ahead for any reason, donations must be returned or supporters' permission sought to use them elsewhere.

1.4.4   There is a fallback. Under section 14 of the Charities Act 1993 the Charity Commissioners can establish a scheme to handle the proceeds of a failed appeal; classically this applies where it is impossible to trace the donors of money raised from the public because the money has been raised, for example, through street collections or house-to-house collections. If this happens, the charity has to publish prescribed advertisements and make enquiries. No advertisement or enquiry is required where the property in question consists of:

- the proceeds of cash collections made by means of collecting boxes or other means not adapted for distinguishing one gift from another;
- the proceeds of any lottery, competition, entertainment, sale or similar money-raising activity, after allowing for a party given to provide prizes or articles for sale or otherwise to enable the activity to be undertaken.

If the enquiry and advertisements fail to produce a response, then the Charity Commission can establish a scheme that allows the money to be spent by the charity on another activity as close as possible to the one for which the appeal was launched. This is an expensive and time-consuming process, and charities would be well-advised to avoid the need for it by making sure appeal literature is appropriately worded.

Letter sent from the Save the Pig Fund to supporters – to raise unrestricted funds

Dear Supporter

You have been extremely generous in your previous support of our work to protect the world's pigs. I now write to tell you about an important project taking place in southern Borneo to protect the greater-spotted marsh hog from extinction.

You may remember that last time I wrote I told you about a mystery virus which was threatening the future of this unique species. Our field workers in Borneo were sending harrowing reports and shocking photographs of hogs literally losing their spots! This seriously compromises the hogs' safety as they are no longer camouflaged as they wallow away their days in their marshy homes. Our workers reported an alarming decline in the number of pigs in the region.

Good news! I am delighted to report that research carried out at the South Borneo Veterinary School, led by Save the Pig's Professor P. Orker, has isolated the cause of this mystery illness. Not only that, but the team has also developed and tested an effective vaccine against this lethal virus. We now need to begin a programme of vaccination to halt the spread of this terrible disease before it is too late. This is a massive undertaking. We need to hire a team of local trackers to systematically locate and vaccinate the pigs. It is imperative that we find each and every pig, otherwise stray pigs could re-infect future populations. Pregnant pigs must be temporarily restrained in our holding pens until they have given birth – at which time the new-born piglets will be vaccinated.

We rely entirely upon voluntary donations to fund projects like this, and your support is vital to our continued success. Please help us in our fight to protect the greater-spotted marsh hog of southern Borneo – and pigs throughout the world – by sending a donation today.

Ivor Speckle
Director

....

Response coupon
Yes! I would like to support your work in southern Borneo and other projects to protect the world's pigs. Please accept my donation of:
£25   £50   £100   Other amount £_____

Thank you

Letter sent from the Save the Pig Fund to supporters – to raise funds for a specific project in Borneo

Dear Supporter

You have been extremely generous in your previous support of our work to protect the world's pigs. I now write with an urgent request for funding to help us save the greater-spotted marsh hog of southern Borneo.

You may remember that last time I wrote I told you about a mystery virus which was threatening the future of this unique species. Our field workers in Borneo were sending harrowing reports and shocking photographs of hogs literally losing their spots! This seriously compromises the hogs' safety as they are no longer camouflaged as they wallow away their days in their marshy homes. Our workers reported an alarming decline in the number of pigs in the region.

Good news! I am delighted to report that research carried out at the South Borneo Veterinary School, led by Save the Pig's Professor P. Orker, has isolated the cause of this mystery illness. Not only that, but the team has also developed and tested an effective vaccine against this lethal virus. We now need to begin a programme of vaccination to halt the spread of this terrible disease before it is too late. This is a massive undertaking. We need to hire a team of local trackers to systematically locate and vaccinate the pigs. It is imperative that we find each and every pig, otherwise stray pigs could re-infect future populations. Pregnant pigs must be temporarily restrained in our holding pens until they have given birth – at which time the new-born piglets will be vaccinated.

We desperately need your help in this operation. A donation of £28 could purchase sufficient medicine to vaccinate 12 of these pigs; £37 could protect an entire family by enabling us to house a pregnant hog and vaccinate her young; £100 could house a team of trackers for two weeks. Please send whatever you can afford, to help us implement this programme and protect this unique species from extinction.

Ivor Speckle
Director

....

Response coupon
Yes! I would like to help protect the greater-spotted marsh hog of southern Borneo. Please accept my donation of:
£25   £50   £100   Other amount £_____

THE FUNDRAISER'S GUIDE TO THE LAW

If an appeal raises surplus funds, and there is no provision in the terms of the appeal to cover this eventuality, then the Charity Commissioners can make a scheme under section 13 that does not require advertising.

1.4.5 If a charity does raise funds for a specific purpose, these are called 'restricted funds'. The Statement of Recommended Practice for charities' accounts (SORP 2) requires that charities account separately for restricted funds.

Endowment funds are another form of restriction. Fundraisers should be very careful in designing appeal literature for so-called endowment funds: a permanent endowment fund means, in law, that only the income can be spent. The capital must be maintained. An expendable endowment is different: with this the trustees can spend the capital, at their discretion. A charity's account must disclose endowment funds.

1.4.6 Collectors

A very good illustration of the impact of trust law upon fundraising is given by the case of *Johns* v. *Attorney General (1976)*. This concerned payments drawn by individuals who had taken around collecting boxes. Mr Justice Brightman commented that:

'A person who solicits money for a charity is a trustee of the money for the purposes of handing it to the charity. A member of the public who puts money in the box is a donor of his contribution, not distinguishable, in principle, from any other donor or settlor of trust funds. Unless the collector makes known to the donor his intention to retain a percentage of the contribution for himself, it seems to me that he has no possible title to that percentage. If the collector makes clear to all concerned that a specified percentage of the contribution will be retained by him, there can be no objection to the retention of that percentage, however high it may be.'

1.5 Disaster appeals

It is essential to establish from the very beginning of an appeal whether it is for charitable purposes or not. A charitable appeal has to relieve need. Consequently, gifts for the benefit of a particular person or persons or for the benefit of the victim of a particular disaster without reference to their needs will not be charitable. That is because the appeal will be for the benefit of individuals rather than for a public purpose (i.e. the relief of need). This issue became very clear in the wake of the public response to the Penlee Life Boat Disaster in 1982. As a result of that appeal, the Attorney General published guidelines in March 1982 for those concerned with making disaster appeals. These guidelines can be obtained from the Charity Commission leaflet CC40. If you are launching an appeal in the wake of a disaster, you can obtain assistance and guidance from the British Red Cross Society. It may be necessary to consider setting up two appeals: one of which is charitable, and another non-charitable appeal that would allow gifts to be made over and above those which can be made in accordance with charity law.

1.6 Charities and their reputation

In their 1991 report, the Charity Commissioners commented that they considered a charity's name and logo to be a valuable asset. If a charity's reputation becomes tarnished, then fundraising becomes extremely difficult. The Commission also reminded charities that they needed to act at all times to ensure that their name and reputation should not be brought into disrepute. Fundraisers need to be particularly aware of this when considering any fundraising activity. High-pressure fundraising techniques can cause real public opposition. A number of charities have been referred to the Charity Commission by members of the public who have objected to emotional or pressurised fundraising methods, some of which have resulted in the Charity Commission launching enquiries into the charity's affairs. This will cost the charity and its trustees a considerable amount of time and money, and steps should be taken to avoid this.

Equally, having a charity's name linked with a commercial partner through cause-related marketing may expose a charity to risk (see Chapters 8 and 16 for further discussion of this issue). Fundraisers need to be aware of these issues, since criticism of a charity's fundraising techniques will, inevitably, cause trustees to scrutinise and question the fundraisers' activities.

1.7 Registered charity status

Trustees of registered charities with a gross income of £10,000 or more in the last financial year are required by section 5 of the Charities Act 1993 to state, on a range of official documents, that the charity is a registered charity. The documents on which the statement must appear include notices, advertisements and other documents issued by or on behalf of a charity that are intended to persuade the reader to give money or property to the charity. Anybody who issues or authorises the issue of an advertisement in breach of section 5 commits a criminal offence that can give rise to a maximum fine of £1,000.

Consequently all fundraising materials, including static and hand-held collection boxes, must display the fact that the charity is a registered charity (if appropriate). You do not have to state the registered charity number, but it is sensible to do so. The statement can be made in Welsh.

1.8 Fundraising by local charities for other charities

Where a local charity raises funds for another charity, the following points should be borne in mind:

- Prospective donors must be clear which charity will benefit from the funds raised.
- The funds raised belong to the beneficiary charity by virtue of trust law (see **1.4**). The collecting charity can only contribute to the cost of the fundraising if the purpose of the fundraising is within the collecting charity's object.
- Separate financial records should be kept.
- The permission of the beneficiary charity must be sought before its name is used. It is essential that the charity approves copies of any fundraising literature. A local charity aiming to raise money for another charity should check that the beneficiary is a registered charity before it starts fundraising. The reason for this is that section 63 of the Charities Act 1992 provides that a person may be found guilty of an offence if they falsely state that an institution for which they are raising money is a registered charity – unless they have reasonable grounds for believing that the institution was so registered.

1.9 Trustees and fundraising

1.9.1 The degree to which trustees will be involved in fundraising will vary from charity to charity. In small charities without any staff the trustees will necessarily undertake a large amount of fundraising themselves. In a large, international charity with a full-time fundraising department, the trustees will rarely be involved in fundraising except, perhaps, in particular approaches to a grant-making trust or wealthy individual.

1.9.2 However, in either case trustees should first of all lay down their fundraising policies and determine:

- the amount to be raised in each year;
- the particular range of fundraising events or activities designed to achieve that target;
- the resources available to support fundraising;
- the costs of fundraising and the anticipated proportion of gross receipts that will be left after fundraising costs have been met.

Trustees need to monitor these matters as part of their duties. In particular, those charities with fundraising departments need to consider whether or not the trustees should be consulted before new types of fundraising are launched. We would urge fundraisers to obtain the support and sanction of their trustees before launching new types of fundraising. As this book shows, some types of fundraising can incur considerable risks; it would be inappropriate for the staff of a charity to have allowed the charity to begin them without the trustees first having had an opportunity to evaluate and weigh up the benefits and disadvantages. Examples include overseas challenge-type events, activities involving high physical risk (e.g. bunjee jumping) or fundraising by direct marketing.

1.9.3 One aspect of trustee involvement is the degree to which trustees should be asked to sign contracts relevant to fundraising. The Home Office, in its guidance on relations between charities and professional fundraisers and charities and commercial participators, recommends that trustees should sign all such contracts. This may be the counsel of perfection and impossible in the case of large charities with many contracts. Nonetheless, even if the trustees have not signed a particular contract, it is recommended that trustees should be given the opportunity to consider the contractual relationships *in principle*, even if it means that the trustees resolve to delegate the negotiation and signing of any relevant contracts to members of staff.

1.9.4 The Charity Commission recommends that trustees agree in advance the likely proportion of gross receipts that will be spent on fundraising and that actual performance is monitored against the target.

1.10 Refusing donations

1.10.1 Whether or not charities can refuse donations is an interesting issue of fundraising. There are, inevitably, unsolicited donations, like legacies, that come with inherent difficulties for the charity. For example, a charity might be given a small legacy to be received in twelve equal annual instalments, which it is then obliged to divide among five other charities. The cost of administering the legacy might be greater than the value of the legacy itself. Alternatively, a charity might be offered money from a source that is considered to be incompatible with its own objectives. For example, the British Red Cross Society was offered the royalties from the sale of the second edition of Andrew Morton's book on Princess Diana, which was rushed out after her death. The Princess had been a great supporter of the Society's work, and in particular its landmine campaign, but the Society, not wanting to appear to be profiting from her death, turned the offer down.

1.10.2 In certain circumstances, it is possible for a charity to refuse a donation. The trustees must be reasonably satisfied that the damage that will be done to the charity's reputation by accepting the gift – in the eyes of its staff, its volunteers and supporters – will outweigh the benefits that it would receive from accepting. Equally, trustees may reasonably refuse to accept a donation if the cost of collecting the donation outweighs its value. Trustees must make their decision irrespective of any individual or collective personal interest or view, in each and every case. It may be sensible for the trustees to adopt a policy on refusing donations.

1.10.3   The decision to refuse a donation should normally be taken by the trustees, but it is possible for them to delegate this function. Alternatively, it may be resolved by co-ordination between the Chief Executive and the Chairman. In a difficult case, guidance may be sought from the Charity Commission. The Institute of Charity Fundraising Managers (ICFM) has issued a guidance note on 'The Acceptance and Refusal of Donations'.

1.11   Costs of fundraising

1.11.1   Members of the public frequently ask about the cost of fundraising and, in particular, if there is an acceptable ratio of expenditure on fundraising to money received. There is not. Different charities with different objects and beneficiaries will find it more or less difficult to raise funds, with a direct impact on the costs of fundraising. It is much easier, for example, to raise money for children or guide dogs for the blind than for people with Alzheimer's disease or a mental disorder.

The Charity Commission, quite rightly, has always resisted calls to lay down mandatory expenses-to-income ratios.

1.11.2   Nonetheless, charities have to account for their fundraising costs. SORP 2 requires that fundraising costs should be accounted for and brought into account. Charities should not 'net off' expenditure from fundraising income, except in the case of small fundraising events (e.g. where moneys are raised by a local group which remits the net proceeds to the charity). However, in no case should the charity's own staff costs be netted off against the proceeds of any fundraising event. In the case of public collections, charities have to account for their income and expenses to the licensing authority (see Chapter 4) and, in Scotland, expenses of a public charitable collection must not be more than 30 per cent.

Summary

- Note the key distinction between restricted and unrestricted funds.
- Fundraising materials can create restrictions.
- Remember to involve trustees in key decisions about fundraising.

2

Institutional fundraising

2.1 Fundraising from charitable trusts and foundations

Charitable trusts and foundations are an early point of call in many fundraising appeals. Trusts usually give money as grants (donations) but may sometimes give money under a contract. This chapter covers general issues relating to obtaining grants from trusts; for money given under contracts, see also Chapter 8.

2.2 The key elements of a grant are that:

- the grant may be given for a general or specific purpose;
- the recipient is not expected to supply anything material in return to the donor (but see **2.2.9**);
- there may be conditions attached to the way the grant is spent.

2.2.1 Scope of application

In common with all charities, grant-making trusts have a constitution that sets out their objects (see **1.3**). They achieve their objects through the giving of grants, and their constitution therefore sets the limits for their grant making, defining the type of activity and the type of beneficiary they are able to fund.

2.2.2 It is important to distinguish between a trust's *objects* and any *policy* set out by the trustees. The trustees cannot make grants outside their objects. To do so would put them in breach of charity law and make them personally liable for the monies given. However, unlike objects, *policies* are not 'set in stone', and trustees do have power to change their policies or make grants outside their policies, providing the grant is still within the trust's objects. Many trusts are set up with 'general charitable purposes', but within these purposes the trustees have decided to focus their grant making on a particular problem or area. For example, if the 'Notional Charitable Trust' were set up with the broad remit of 'general charitable purposes' and the trustees decided to focus their attention on deprived children, they could have a policy to make grants to charities aiding deprived children. However, if the trustees so wished, they *could* make a grant towards an old people's home or a donkey sanctuary. On the other hand, if the 'Notional Charitable Trust' were set up with the *defined objects* of helping deprived children, it would be illegal for them to make a grant benefiting elderly people or donkeys!

2.2.3 Before submitting an application, a charity also needs to check that any activities covered by its application are within the objects of the charity. If funding is accessible for activities outside the charity's objects, the objects would need to be broadened before funding could be accepted. Amending objects involves a formal process to amend the charity's constitution and requires Charity Commission consent.

Try to avoid applying for or accepting funds for very restricted purposes. Good fundraising practice may be to encourage you to be as specific as possible about the exact way in which you will use the funds, but the legal perspective runs counter to this. Retaining some flexibility means, for example, that you may be able to use some funding towards core costs.

2.2.4 Loans and endowments

In some situations, a trust may offer a loan rather than an outright grant. The loan will usually be repayable over a set period with interest charged. Money lent in this situation should be treated as restricted funds (that is, it cannot be spent for any purpose other than the reason for which the loan was given), and professional advice should be sought before signing any loan agreement.

Some trusts choose to 'endow' funds to a charity for a specific purpose. A permanent endowment means the charity is given a sum of money that it can never spend – it is only the income from the fund that can be used. Generally speaking, it is a good idea to avoid permanent endowments, as they increase the assets shown on a charity's balance sheet without giving the charity any flexibility to spend the money. Where a permanent endowment cannot be avoided, try to retain flexibility for use of the income. If possible, agree a basis upon which your charity might be allowed to spend the capital sum if the purpose for which the funds have been endowed no longer exists – imagine being responsible for endowed funds restricted to research into the prevention and alleviation of smallpox! (See also **1.4.5**.)

2.2.5 Terms and conditions of grants

Since most grant-making trusts achieve their charitable objectives through the giving of grants, the trustees will take reasonable precautions to ensure that grants given are spent as intended. One way they can do this is to make the grant subject to certain terms and conditions. Some standard terms and conditions are described below.

2.2.6 Reporting

There are usually two elements to reporting. The first is an account of the work you have undertaken with the grant, demonstrating clearly that you have carried out the work specified in your application and as amended by the donor in any confirmation of grant. The second element of reporting back is financial. Most charities account for the cost of their activities using SORP (Statement of Recommended Practice for charities) – which means that the overheads associated with an activity are charged to that activity, e.g. rent, utilities, wages and central services such as IT, finance and personnel. You will need to liaise with your accountant/finance department (and refer back to your original proposal) to ensure that you have the necessary financial systems to track this expenditure and that your account of funds clearly identifies the expenditure for which the grant was used.

2.2.7 Claw back

A common term in grants is that the trust can 'claw back' money if:

- the charity has not spent the full grant by a certain date;
- the charity has misspent grant monies.

Always check the terms and conditions of a grant carefully for any unusual 'claw-back' provisions.

Whether or not a trust can enforce the return of money will depend on whether the grant:

- was given outright;
- amounted to a contract;
- was given in such a way that the recipient never owned the money outright but instead held it on trust for the donor, or held it on trust to spend on a specific purpose.

Deciding which of these applies usually requires professional advice. An unjustified refusal to repay grant monies will damage your charity's relationship with that funder and possibly other funders; it could also damage the charity's reputation.

2.2.8 Intellectual property rights

A trust may reserve the right in its terms and conditions to share in the ownership or income generated by intellectual property rights (for a detailed explanation of what intellectual property is, please see Chapter 21). For example, if a grant for medical research leads to a cure for lung cancer, the trust funding the grant may want a share in any resulting income in order to boost its own funds.

The Charity Commission expects grant-giving trusts to have policies on the ownership of intellectual property. The type of policy varies from trust to trust and could include the provision that:

- the trust itself owns all intellectual property rights in work carried out under its grant – this is difficult for recipients to accept, especially if the project is being funded from other sources, because the other funders may also want a share in the rights;
- the recipient owns all intellectual property, but the grant-giving trust has a right to an agreed percentage of any income from exploitation;
- the recipient and trust share ownership of intellectual property. This sounds good in theory, but in practice joint ownership means that neither party can do anything without the other's consent, and this can lead to deadlock. If the trust wants you to agree to this, consider agreeing in advance in what proportions you will share ownership. Also try to agree in advance when the recipient can publish the results of the research and who will pay for any fees needed to protect any intellectual property, e.g. patent applications.

2.2.9 Publicising the source of the grant

Some funders may require a degree of recognition for their support of a project. A condition of the grant may be that their support must be acknowledged in the charity's annual report, and in other ways relating to the funded project, such as in a plaque outside a funded building. You should take care that your obligations to publicise the source of the funds do not amount to providing a VATable service to advertise the donor (see in particular **2.2.12** concerning corporate trusts and also **8.4**).

2.2.10 Enforceability – deeds

If a trust pledges money, what rights do you have if it then fails to pay? If the pledge was just a promise and nothing more, then there is no legal obligation on the trust to pay. This is the case even if the promise is recorded in a letter.

In some situations, you may be able to argue that the pledge did amount to a binding contractual obligation. In this case, you will have a right to sue for breach of contract (see Chapter 11). Say, for example, that a grant-giving trust promised a grant and knew that the proposed recipient had committed itself to something that could be funded only if the grant came through. If the trust subsequently refused to pay the grant, the charity could argue that the trust had acted in such a way as to make the charity rely on the promise and that it was unfair for the trust to be able to change its mind.

If you want to ensure a pledge is legally binding, ask the donor to enter into a deed. This is a legally binding agreement and should be prepared by a lawyer (see **11.5**).

2.2.11 Internal accounting

If a grant has been given for a specific purpose, the grant monies will be 'restricted funds' (see **1.4.5**).

It is not a legal requirement to keep grant monies or restricted funds in separate bank accounts, unless you have agreed with the funder that you will do this. Some charities do keep separate bank accounts for such funds, but this is usually a mechanism to assist them in keeping track of funds held for different purposes.

It is important to keep track of funds raised. It is a necessary function of trust fundraising that you will apply for funds greater than the actual amount you need, and few trust fundraisers will wait for a letter of rejection before applying to the next trust for funding for the same piece of work. What happens if you then find that you have raised more than you need for a particular project and the terms of the grant do not allow you to use the funds for other activities? In this event, your best course of action is to go back to the donor and ask them to apply the funds to other projects that are also within the donor's objects and which are not yet fully funded. If this cannot be negotiated, then you will have to return the unspent money.

Interest earned on restricted funds is treated as part of the restricted fund. It cannot be used for general purposes, unless the grant agreement permits it.

2.2.12 Corporate trusts

Some companies set up a charitable trust as a vehicle for their charitable giving (for example, Boots Charitable Trust). The terms and conditions of a grant from a trust of this kind may include a requirement to publicise the trust's funding, which in turn will inevitably mean publicising the company name. Giving credits or acknowledgement is treated by Customs as providing advertising services, which are VATable. This means that VAT could be payable on the whole grant. You can minimise the VAT by having a separate agreement under which the company or trust pays for the advertising services, so that the grant is then not VATable, but this is something you should take professional advice about (see also **8.6**).

2.2.13 VAT

A grant made with no strings attached is outside the scope of VAT.

2.2.14 Tax

Grant or trust income is not subject to income tax.

2.3 Fundraising from statutory sources

2.3.1   Increasingly, charities are obtaining funding for projects and services from local authorities, government departments, the European Commission and Quangos (such as the Single Regeneration Budget, or SRB). Some of these are statutory services, and the charity delivers the services as sub-contractor for the statutory body: for example, many 'care' charities obtain funding to perform statutory services for local authorities, such as caring for the elderly or education for special needs children. Others are services that the charity wishes to provide and statutory funders exercise their discretion in order to fund them: for example, the Department of Health funds a number of health-related research projects that are carried out by charities.

2.3.2   Statutory funders historically gave grants, but they are now increasingly giving funding under contract (part of what is known as the 'contract culture'). It is important to distinguish between funds obtained as grants and funds obtained under contracts.

- A grant is usually for a restricted purpose. Beyond that purpose, the recipient is free to spend the money as it wishes and does not have to achieve any specified outcomes.
- A contract usually sets specific outcomes that the recipient must achieve.

It can be difficult to tell if a body is offering a grant or contract, and many funders talk about grants when in fact they are offering contracts. You should clarify this before you accept the funding.

2.3.3   Some statutory bodies and sources of income (e.g. SRB) positively encourage bidding by consortiums (i.e. several charities submitting a joint application). Joint applications raise certain legal issues that you should consider.

- What aspect of the overall service or project will your charity deliver?
- Is this within your objects?
- What proportion of the overall funding will you receive?

If the consortium bid includes activities outside your objects, make it clear that your charity has no responsibility for those activities. Ensure that any funds contributed by your charity cannot be used for those activities.

2.3.4   Some statutory funding bodies, particularly the European Commission, make it a condition of payment that matched funding (i.e. an equal amount of funding from another source) must be obtained. It is important to clarify whether matched funding from the charity's own reserves will count.

2.3.5   One additional point to watch out for with EU funding is the effect of currency fluctuations on money received. The grant or contract may require a charity to account for expenditure in a particular currency; this may leave the charity exposed if, as a result of fluctuations in exchange rates between the currency in which the grant was awarded and the currency in which it was spent, money has been 'lost'.

2.3.6　Many of the same considerations for trust fundraising apply equally to fundraising from statutory sources:

- Is the proposed activity or project within the charity's objects?
- Are the funds for a restricted purpose?
- What terms and conditions will be imposed?
- Can funding be clawed back?

2.3.7 VAT implications

If a statutory funder makes a grant with no strings attached, no VAT is payable on the grant monies.

If, however, a statutory funder provides money in return for certain services, whether under a grant or contract, VAT will be payable – unless there is a specific VAT exemption relating to the type of services.

It is always worth checking the VAT position and/or making clear to funders that the funder is liable for any VAT due.

Summary

- A grant may be general or for a specific purpose.
- A grant may be subject to conditions.
- Grant-making trusts frequently adopt grant policies; these may change.
- Make sure that any grant application is to cover activities within the charity's objects.
- Be aware of any possibility of 'claw back' on the part of the grant maker.
- Some grant conditions stipulate that the grant giver has rights in any intellectual property that has been developed.
- Be aware of the need to account properly for restricted funds.

Fundraising from individuals

3.1 Introduction

3.1.1 This section deals with ways of appealing to the public for funds either directly (through, for example, telephone or postal appeals) or indirectly (through media such as television, radio, newspapers or billboards). It does not cover:

- face-to-face direct fundraising through street or house-to-house collections (see Chapter 4);
- tax incentives for giving (see Chapter 19);
- advertising (see Chapter 15).

3.1.2 Much of the law relating to such appeals is dealt with in detail in other parts of this book. Where that is the case, a cross-reference is given.

3.2 Data protection

3.2.1 See Chapter 12 for an explanation of the requirements regarding data protection. See also the Institute of Charity Fundraising Managers' (ICFM's) Code of Practice on Reciprocal Charity Mailing, which contains useful guidance on charity list swapping and terms of reference for a contract between two charities engaged in a swap.

3.2.2 The capture of names and addresses is discussed in detail in Chapter 12. Charities without substantial databases of names and addresses might wish to compile lists from public records such as the electoral roll or the telephone book, although these are very random and not necessarily efficient sources. The electoral roll for each area is a public document and must be kept open for inspection by the local registration officer. The officer must also supply copies of parts of the register at a price of £2.50 per 1,000 names, provided that sufficient copies are available. The government is apparently reconsidering these arrangements, and it may be that restrictions will be imposed.

3.2.3 The telephone directory is a copyright work in the same way as most other lists of names and addresses compiled by private companies. It cannot, therefore, be copied without the consent of the compiler, be it British Telecom, Yellow Pages or another service provider (see Chapter 12 for more on data protection, and Chapter 21 for more on intellectual property). However, from the point of view of data protection law, the data in a published directory is in the public domain and may be captured for fundraising purposes by a charity. How the data may then be processed is dealt with in detail in Chapter 12.

3.2.4 Names and addresses are sometimes taken from raffle tickets sold on behalf of charities. Unless the data subject consents at the time of purchase to their data being used for general fundraising purposes, or is later given an option to opt in or out of the database (see detailed comments on this in Chapter 12), the data can only be used in connection with the raffle.

3.2.5 It cannot be assumed that members of a charity giving their personal data for membership purposes have consented to the use of that data for other purposes, such as fundraising. Consent for different uses must be obtained.

3.3 **Direct marketing houses**

3.3.1 Sometimes charities or their trading companies will wish to rent lists of names and addresses from direct marketing houses or arrange for them to prepare entire fundraising packs, which the marketing house then sends out. In such situations, you should ensure that the charity has a proper contract with the direct marketing house that sets out the basis on which a list is to be used. Such a contract should provide answers to the following questions:

- Is use of the names in accordance with the Data Protection Act?
- Is the list for a single or multiple use?
- Is the charity entitled to capture (and retain for its own purposes without further payment) the data of respondents?
- Can the direct marketing house warrant any degree of accuracy of the data? How can this be checked?
- Can the data be sorted by reference to types of data subjects and so matched to the charity's typical donor profile?
- Who will send the appeal?
- When will it be sent, and how?
- If a full pack-production service is being provided, who will be responsible for ensuring compliance with the British Codes of Advertising and Sales Promotion (see Chapter 15)?

3.3.2 Chapter 11 provides an introduction to contract law. For an explanation of special VAT rules in relation to supplies of advertising services and printed matter, see Chapter 20.

3.3.3 See **3.4** for consideration of whether a direct marketing house is a professional fundraiser.

3.4 **Professional fundraisers**

3.4.1 The use of professional fundraisers is explained in Chapter 17.

3.4.2 Some fundraisers question whether a direct marketing house that prepares and sends a mailshot is a professional fundraiser. Under the usual arrangements with a charity it will be merely the agent of the charity, carrying out the production and/or mailing of materials agreed with the charity, and the recipients of the mailing will not be aware of its existence. Therefore, unless it is also collecting money in response to the appeal, it will not be a professional fundraiser any more than the Post Office, which delivers the letter, or the person who designs the materials.

3.5 **Intellectual property**

See Chapter 21 for an explanation of intellectual property. In relation to the appeals considered here, issues of intellectual property are likely to apply to materials produced in connection with the appeal, and to the compilation and use of databases.

3.6 **Advertising and sales promotion**

Chapter 15 deals with issues such as criminal and civil liability for misleading statements, planning law in relation to the display of public notices, codes of practice for different advertising media, broadcast appeals, political advertising, defamation and the content of appeal documents. You should also refer to Chapter 20, which deals with the VAT treatment of advertising and other fundraising materials supplied to charities.

3.7 **Terms of appeal**

It is important that the wording of an appeal does not create a trust for a particular purpose, unless you have definitely decided to do that (see **1.4**).

3.8 **Incentives for giving**

Fundraisers will often be tempted to offer individuals incentives to give, in the form of goods or services. This can amount to taxable (and VATable) trading, which is discussed in detail in Chapters 6 and 8 and elsewhere in relation to particular types of event. Fundraisers should be particularly wary of such incentives, particularly if donors are being asked to give using Gift Aid or deeds of covenant. Some incentives can prevent the recovery of tax on Gift Aid and deed of covenant payments. See Chapter 19 for a detailed explanation of these rules.

3.9 Payment methods

Payment methods such as credit cards, cash and CAF vouchers are dealt with in Chapter 18.

3.10 Postal appeals

3.10.1 Postal appeals that constitute advertisements (generally they will be advertising or promoting the charity's activities or concerns) will be subject to the British Codes of Advertising and Sales Promotion produced by the Committee of Advertising Practice and policed by the Advertising Standards Authority (the CAP Codes). The CAP Codes are explained in Chapter 15. Note also the VAT rules explained in Chapter 20.

3.10.2 Some charities have been known to use chain letters as a means of raising funds. This practice is discouraged by the Charity Commission and the ICFM, which has published a guidance note on their use. The main difficulties are: being unable to stop or control the letters; the problem of people receiving the same letter many times; bad publicity through press reports; the ease with which chain letters can be used to defraud through the substitution of addresses; and the fact that the letter may continue to circulate even after funds are no longer needed for particular purposes stated in it. Some chain letters (although we are not aware of this applying to any charity appeals) have contained threats about the consequences of not continuing the chain or complying with the letter's request. Such threats could be criminal offences under the Malicious Communications Act 1988. These offences are explained in Chapter 15.

3.11 Telephone appeals

3.11.1 The only statutory requirements relating to ordinary telephone appeals are in the Charities Act 1992 (requirements concerning the refunding of donations are dealt with in **16.5** and **17.8**), and in the Telecommunications (Data Protection and Privacy)(Direct Marketing) Regulations 1999 (restrictions on unsolicited telephone calls for marketing purposes are dealt with in Chapter 12). Statements made are not covered by the CAP Codes. However, if they are conducted using premium-rate services for replies, they will be governed by the Independent Committee for the Supervision of Standards of Telephone Information Services (ICSTIS) (see Chapter 15).

3.11.2 Telephone fundraisers receiving more than £5 per day or £500 per year who are not employed by the charity will be professional fundraisers. As such, they will be required to have a contract with the charity and to make a statement about their payment (see Chapter 17). If they are not professional fundraisers themselves but are employed by one, they must still make a statement about the professional fundraiser's payment.

3.11.3   If a telephone appeal is made by a commercial participator, the usual rules about statements to be made and the refund of donations will apply, as explained in Chapter 16.

3.11.4   If the telephone is being used to recruit collectors, see the ICFM's Code of Practice on Telephone Recruitment of Collectors.

3.12   Fax appeals

3.12.1   Fax appeals that are advertisements will be covered by the CAP Codes. They will also be covered by the ICSTIS Code if they refer to premium-rate telephone services.

3.12.2   They will also be covered by the Telecommunications (Data Protection and Privacy) (Direct Marketing) Regulations 1999 (see Chapter 12).

3.12.3   The same principles concerning professional fundraisers apply, as described in Chapter 17.

3.13   Internet and e-mail

3.13.1   Internet and e-mail appeals that are advertisements will be covered by the CAP Codes (see Chapter 15)

3.13.2   Individuals might use the Internet to browse the charity's website, and this might give them the opportunity to make credit or debit card donations online. You should ensure that the Internet site has proper encryption mechanisms to guarantee that personal details (and particularly credit card details) are kept secure. If donors are not satisfied that safeguards are in place, they may be reluctant to make donations in this way.

3.13.3   One way of attracting potential donors to the charity's website is to incorporate links from other relevant sites. This might include a link from the site of a commercial participator or commercial sponsor who is promoting the charity or their own products on their own site. Ensure that there is an agreement with the other site owner giving permission for the use of such links.

3.13.4   Be careful when putting valuable intellectual property on the Internet, as this will make it freely available to all and available to be copied endlessly. At the very least, if the charity wishes to preserve its rights but nevertheless publish widely, it should include on the website a statement expressly limiting the rights of visitors to copy and further disseminate material from the site. It is particularly important that the charity obtains written permission to publish another person's intellectual property on the Internet. The written permission should specify any restrictions, and the charity should comply with it exactly.

3.14 **Broadcast appeals**

3.14.1 The law relating to broadcast appeals is explained in Chapter 15. Note also the provisions concerning professional fundraisers in Chapter 17. There are special requirements concerning rights of donors to cancel payments made in response to broadcast appeals by professional fundraisers.

3.14.2 If a presenter makes the broadcast appeal but the charity conducts the appeal in all other respects (e.g. *The Week's Good Cause* on Radio 4 or *Lifeline* on BBC Television), the presenter will not be a professional fundraiser.

3.15 **Legacies**

3.15.1 A legacy is a gift in a will. It may be a specific sum or item or a share of what is left of a donor's estate after all the other specific gifts have been made (known as the residuary estate). It may be contained in the will itself or in a codicil, which is a legally valid addition to a will.

3.15.2 The main advantages of legacy income are that:

- it tends to be unrestricted (it is unusual for donors to make gifts to charities in their wills that contain restrictions on how the money is to be used);
- gifts to charities are free of Inheritance Tax (IHT). If a donor has an estate large enough to pay IHT, then they can limit or avoid IHT, which would otherwise be payable on their death, by making a gift to a charity. This allows them to display generosity and direct where they would like the money to go, rather than give it to the state through the tax system (see also **19.6**).

3.15.3 The main disadvantage of legacy income is its uncertainty. A charity cannot usually enforce a promise by a donor to leave money to it in their will, and a will can be changed at any time before a donor's death, provided that the donor is mentally sound. Also, the charity cannot predict the cash flow and so cannot rely on legacy income for day-to-day operations or planned projects.

3.15.4 One way of encouraging legacies is by promoting advice booklets that explain the charity's aims, the advantages of giving by will and how to make a valid will. It is important that such advice booklets are accurate and periodically reviewed by legal advisers. If the advice in the booklet were wrong and a donor's will were invalid as a result (for example because it had not been properly executed), not only would the charity lose its gift but it might also be subject to a negligence claim made against it by another beneficiary under the will whose gift was also invalidated.

3.15.5 See Chapter 20 concerning the VAT treatment of fundraising materials and other printed matter such as legacy advice leaflets.

3.15.6   Another way of promoting wills is to offer free will services by arrangement with solicitors. Provision of such services might lead to claims of undue influence from other disappointed beneficiaries seeking to challenge the gift to the charity. So long as the charity is not itself providing the will-writing service and is doing so only by arranging for solicitors to give independent advice to the donors, claims of that kind should not succeed. However, charities should ensure that their own employees or volunteers promoting the service do not themselves witness the donors' wills, which might invalidate a gift if there is a claim that the charity had exercised undue influence over the donor.

3.15.7   Challenges can also be brought on the basis that the donor has not properly provided for their family and dependants. If any such challenge is brought, the charity should take legal advice; it should not simply accede to demands for repayment of any gift made, and it should take proper action to recover payments that are due. If the trustees do not do that, they may be failing in their duty and be personally liable to the charity. If, on legal advice, the trustees conclude that the costs of obtaining a gift that is due to be paid, or of defending a challenge to the will, would outweigh the value of the gift, they need not take action. The likelihood of success of any action is also a relevant factor. If trustees consider that they have a moral obligation to make a payment to someone out of money they have received (an ex-gratia payment), they should consider Charity Commission leaflet CC7 (*Ex-Gratia Payments by Charities*) and note that the consent of the Charity Commission to the payment will be required.

3.15.8   There are circumstances when a charity might wish to refuse a legacy, and it is possible to do this. One reason might be that the gift comes with costs or liabilities that outweigh the value of the gift itself; another could be that it comes with unreasonable or improper conditions attached. For other circumstances in which a charity might refuse a gift, see Chapter 1.

3.15.9   In general, the executors or administrators of a will will contact a charity if the charity is a beneficiary. Sadly, however, it does not always happen like this, and sometimes the charity needs to take positive action in order to ensure that it receives its gift. Once probate or letters of administration (the right for executors or administrators to deal with the donor's estate) are granted, the will is a public document and can be inspected at the probate registry. Smee & Ford (see 'Useful addresses', p. 244) is a specialist agency that checks every published will and alerts its clients to the existence of a gift. Once the charity has been alerted, it should write to the executors or personal representatives giving full details of how and where to make the payment. The executors must generally wind up the estate and make all the gifts within one year from the date of death. They cannot be required to make any gift before that year is up.

3.16 **Money from members**

3.16.1   One of the main ways of obtaining money from members of a charity or from members of an associated 'friends' organisation is through subscriptions. Donations to charities that do not give the donor any right to receive a benefit do not attract VAT and are not regarded as trading income for the purposes of direct tax. However, that is not necessarily the case with subscriptions. Subscription income will not attract VAT if the only benefits that the members receive:

- relate to the aims of the charity;
- are provided in return for the subscription;
- do not include provision of any right of admission for which non-members have to pay.

It is not clear exactly what will and will not be deemed to relate to the aims of the charity. However, the government's guidance indicates that newsletters, magazines, handbooks and similar publications that provide more than minimal benefits under the current rules will relate to the aims of the charity and therefore be exempt from VAT, in so far as they are not already zero-rated. You should obtain advice from your professional advisers and/or local VAT office in cases of doubt.

3.16.2   If the benefits do not meet those conditions, the subscription income will be liable to VAT, unless the supply of the particular benefit is not already zero-rated. This means that the charity will (if registered or required to register for VAT) have to account to HM Customs and Excise for VAT on the subscription income. Charities will still be able to recover VAT paid in relation to zero-rated supplies as well as to apportion subscription income between VATable and exempt supplies. If you intend to make such an apportionment, you should first discuss it with your professional advisers and/or local VAT office.

For a general explanation of VAT, see Chapter 20.

3.16.3   The provision to members of benefits other than the minimal benefits described above might also amount to the carrying-on of a trade by the charity. Subscriptions or other income from the trade may be subject to direct tax. If you are providing such benefits, you should take advice from your solicitors.

3.16.4   Some members of charities like to pay their subscriptions using deeds of covenant or Gift Aid. Those tax-efficient ways of giving are explained in Chapter 19. If the member receives membership benefits above certain values, they can invalidate the charity's tax reclaim.

The limits on donor benefits (which, from April 2000, are the same for payments under Gift Aid and pre-April 2000 deeds of covenant) are set out in Chapter 19.

3.16.5   Many modern charities are established as limited companies with members and directors, the directors being the trustees. The creation of a membership structure in a limited company has important consequences under company law. First, a detailed register must be kept (including an index, if there are more than 50 members). This register must be made available for inspection by any person on payment of a fee and must be copied and sent to any person requesting it, also on payment of a fee. It is an offence not to comply with these requirements. The courts have held, in a case involving the British Union for the Abolition of Vivisection, that anyone applying is entitled to inspect and copy the register, even if the charity thinks the applicant has an improper purpose (as was the case in this particular instance, since the people requiring access to the register were the pro-hunting lobby). So the names and addresses of all members are open even to opponents of a charity. These problems do not arise with Industrial and Provident Society charities. Although they must maintain registers of members, the registers do not need to be made available to the public. There is no statutory requirement (but obviously a practical one) for unincorporated associations to keep registers of members.

3.16.6   Members of limited companies, Industrial and Provident Society charities and unincorporated associations also have rights to vote at general meetings, to appoint directors (trustees) and amend the constitution. If it is not thought appropriate to give these rights to members or (in the case of companies) to have a publicly open list, it is possible to make separate arrangements whereby the members are not members of the charity itself but rather a separate 'friends' organisation.

3.17   **Trading**

Much charity income is derived from trading, either by charities themselves or their subsidiary trading companies. The legal rules (including tax) on this are complicated. You should consider Chapters 10–15 and 18–22.

Summary

This chapter largely cross-refers the reader to other chapters for a more detailed discussion of some of the legal considerations in this area of fundraising. In particular:

- There are various laws governing the use and storage of data. Refer to Chapter 12 for a full discussion of data protection law as it relates to fundraising.
- Contracts will be required when using the services of suppliers such as direct mail houses and professional fundraisers. Contract law is covered in Chapter 11. The detail of contracts with professional fundraisers is dealt with in Chapter 17.
- The wording of appeals must be considered in light of:
  - codes and laws governing advertising and sales promotion (Chapter 15);
  - creation of restricted funds (Chapter 1).
- Telephone, fax, broadcast and Internet appeals are covered by many of the same codes of practice/laws and some more specific ones.
- Care must be taken in the solicitation of legacies and provision of advice about making a will.
- Membership can give rise to tax and VAT concerns.

4

Collections

4.1 **Background**

Public collections are subject to a variety of different legal controls throughout the United Kingdom. Street collections and house-to-house collections in England and Wales are subject to controls under the 1916 Police, Factories, etc. (Miscellaneous Provisions) Act 1916 and the House to House Collections Act 1939. In Scotland the two types of collection are merged and are regulated under the Civic Government (Scotland) Act 1982. In Northern Ireland street collections are regulated by the Collection in Streets or Public Places Regulations 1927, and house-to-house collections by the House to House Charitable Collections Act 1952. This chapter must therefore consider three different sets of legal controls. (Part III of the Charities Act 1992 proposed scrapping the current system in England and Wales and replacing it with the Scottish system of controls on public charitable collections, whether conducted in the street or house to house. However, that legislation has not been implemented and remains in abeyance.)

All the controls on public collections apply to collections for 'charitable purposes', which has a wider meaning than 'charity'. It covers 'benevolent and philanthropic' purposes, so organisations like Friends of the Earth and Greenpeace (which are not charities) are within the definition. This chapter also refers to 'charitable institutions', i.e. organisations which are charities as well as those which are not charities but are established for 'benevolent or philanthropic' purposes.

Part II Charities Act 1992, which only applies in England and Wales (see Chapters 16 and 17), can also have an impact on public collections in Scotland. The Institute of Charity Fundraising Managers (ICFM) with the Scottish Council for Voluntary Organisations has drawn up the Scottish Code of Fundraising Practice which requires ICFM members to adhere to similar provisions as in Part II Charities Act 1992 when fundraising in Scotland.

4.2 **Static collection boxes**

4.2.1 There are no legislative controls over static collection boxes. The 1992 Charities Act did not extend the proposed controls on public charitable collections to them in England and Wales. The reason for this is that the government at the time considered that the amount of money collected by static collection boxes was usually relatively small and that collection boxes did not cause inconvenience to the public.

Consequently the only control on such boxes is contained in section 5 Charities Act 1993 (see Chapter 1). This requires all registered charities with an income of more than £10,000 to state that they are a registered charity on all advertisements soliciting money for the benefit of the charity.

In the absence of legislative controls, the ICFM has issued a code of practice. The code is based on the controls for house-to-house and street collections and has three key points:

- The conduct and control of static collection boxes shall be the responsibility solely of the charity or fund that is to benefit from the collection.
- The charity or fund will appoint a Chief Promoter who must be an official of the charity.
- The charity shall:
  - obtain the written signed permission of site holders to collect on the premises;
  - issue certificates of authority and identity badges to collectors who are to site and service the boxes;
  - ensure boxes are of a suitable material and are properly labelled, numbered and sealed;
  - maintain records of where the boxes are sited and how much money is collected from each box;
  - keep separate accounting records showing money raised through static collecting boxes and any direct expenses incurred in administering them.

Guidance is set out on: where to site the boxes; who can be collectors; servicing the boxes; remitting the proceeds of the collection to the charity; maintenance of proper accounts.

4.2.2 **Static collection boxes in a street**

Some charities have collecting boxes that are placed on the pavement outside shop premises. These forms of collection are not subject to the controls on street collections (see **4.3**), which apply to collections by individuals and not through a static collection box, even one placed in the street.

4.2.3 Security

The contents of static collection boxes are, of course, the charity's property. Charities therefore need to ensure that they take all reasonable steps to safeguard their property, no matter where the box is placed. Consequently, if, for example, the owner of a public house is willing to put a static collection box on the bar – but subject to being paid 10 per cent of the contents – the fact that that payment is being made must be disclosed to the general public. The general principle of trust law is that monies raised in the name of a charity belong to that charity (see Chapter 1). In this example, the publican would not be considered a professional fundraiser (see Chapter 17), because they are not soliciting money for reward but instead are allowing the static collection box to be placed on their premises in return for a payment to them.

4.2.4 Pin badges as tokens to solicit donations

In recent years it has become increasingly common for charities to arrange for shops to display pin badges (or something similar) next to a collection box. The suggestion is that anybody wishing to take a badge should pay a specified sum as a donation. In some cases these boxes are clearly sponsored by commercial third parties. Fundraisers considering these arrangements need to bear the following points in mind:

- It is perfectly in order to give a small token in return for a donation (see Chapter 8).
- If the charity requires a minimum payment in return for the pin this constitutes a sale by the charity of the pin, which will attract VAT and will not be primary-purpose trading (see Chapter 10).
- The relationship with the sponsor needs to be carefully considered (see Chapter 8).

4.3 Street collections – England and Wales

4.3.1 Street collections are often confused with house-to-house collections. From a legal point of view they are quite distinct.

4.3.2 Collecting money or selling goods for the benefit of charitable purposes in any street or public place in England and Wales is still governed by section 5 of the Police, Factories, etc. (Miscellaneous Provisions) Act 1916 as amended by section 251 of the Local Government Act 1972. This Act allows regulations for street collections to be made by the Common Council of the City of London, the Commissioner for the Metropolitan Police District, and district councils. A model for local regulations is contained in the Charitable Collections (Transitional Provisions) Order 1974, although it is not obligatory on local authorities to introduce such a system of licensing in their area.

4.3.3   Street collections are any collections made in any street or public place. 'Street' includes 'any highway and any public bridge, road, lane, footway, square, court, alley or passageway whether a thoroughfare or not'. 'Public place' is not defined, although according to case law a public place is a place where members of the public go even when they may have no legal right to do so, or a place where they are invited to go (for example, a private field that members of the public were invited to use to watch point-to-point races). In theory, a 'public place' should be wide enough to cover such spaces as a station forecourt, shopping malls and supermarket car parks. However, these areas are generally treated as private and not public place. Collections in these places therefore fall outside the controls on street collections.

4.3.4   Although the Home Office is responsible for overseeing this legislation it does not have a list of those local authorities that have not adopted the model regulations.

4.3.5   The model street collection regulations for the Metropolitan Police District differ in some material ways from those for the rest of the country. For example, a collector may not be accompanied by an animal in London, but may be elsewhere. That said, fundraisers need to bear these key points in mind about the regulations.

- No collection can be made unless the promoter has obtained the relevant permit from the licensing authority. Note that the promoter is not the charity but an individual, e.g. the charity's fundraising manager. It is the promoter who is responsible in law for adherence to the regulations and not the charity that is the beneficiary of the collection. The promoter should consider asking the charity for an indemnity for any losses, costs and expenses they properly incur as promoter. This indemnity cannot extend to any criminal liabilities the promoter incurs.
- A collection can only be made in accordance with the permit.
- Each collector must have received the written authority of the promoter.
- No collector shall 'importune any person to the annoyance of such person'.
- A collector must remain stationary while collecting, and a collector or two collectors together shall not be nearer another collector than 25 metres. No collector may be under 16 (this can be varied in London to 14 with the consent of the Commissioner of Police of the Metropolis).
- Each collection box must be numbered consecutively, and securely closed and sealed in such a way as to prevent it being opened without the seal being broken.
- Each collector shall deliver, unopened, all collecting boxes in their possession to a promoter. Each collecting box must display prominently both the name of the charity that is to benefit and also the fact that it is a registered charity (see **4.2**).

- A collecting box shall be opened either in the presence of the promoter and another responsible person or by an official of a bank.
- No payment shall be made to any collector (in London this is qualified by the words 'by way of reward', which would appear to allow collectors in London to be paid expenses).
- Within one month of the date of any collection (three months in London) the promoter must forward to the licensing authority a statement, as set out in the regulations, concerning the amount received and expenses and payments incurred and certified by that person and a qualified accountant.

4.3.6 Northern Ireland

The controls on street collections in Northern Ireland are similar but not identical to those in England and Wales:

- Permission has to be obtained from the Royal Ulster Constabulary.
- Collectors must be 30 yards apart.
- Collectors must be over 18.
- Collectors must not be accompanied by an animal.
- No payment shall be made to any collector.
- Accounts must be prepared within one month.

4.3.7 Scotland

In Scotland street and house-to-house collections are regulated under the controls on public charitable collections. The key features of these controls are:

- It is a criminal offence to organise a public charitable collection without a licence.
- The licence is obtained from the Local Authority.
- A public charitable collection is defined as a collection from the public of money for charitable purposes taken either in a public place or by means of visits from place to place.

'Public place' is defined under Scottish law as meaning any place (whether a thoroughfare or not) to which the public has unlimited access and includes:

- the doorways or entrances of premises abutting on any such place;
- any corridor, passage, close, court, stair, garden or yard pertinent to any tenement or group of separately owned houses.

This definition differs from the 'public place' contained in Part III of the Charities Act 1992 which, if it is ever implemented, will apply in England and Wales. That Act defines a 'public place' as:

- any highway and
- any other place to which, at any time when the appeal is made, members of the public have or are permitted to have access and which either:
  - is not within a building, or

– if within a building is a public area within any station, airport or shopping precinct or any other similar public area.

There are thus two different statutory definitions of 'public place' in two different pieces of legislation controlling public charitable collections!

Permission to collect in a public place may be refused on the grounds that:

- the date, time, frequency or area of the collection would cause undue public inconvenience;
- another collection is due to take place on the same day;
- it appears to the Licensing Authority that the amount likely to be applied for charitable purposes in consequence of the collection is inadequate, given the likely amount of the proceeds of the collection;
- the organiser has been convicted of an offence under section 5 of the Police, Factories, etc. (Miscellaneous Provisions) Act 1916 or the House to House Collections Act 1939.

The Public Charitable Collections (Scotland) Regulations 1984 impose very similar controls to those in England, Wales and Northern Ireland, but the following key points should be noted:

- Organisers must exercise 'all due diligence' to ensure that any agent they appoint is 'a fit and proper person' to carry out such functions and that any 'agent, collector or other person' is, in the case of street collection, over 14 and, in the case of a house-to-house collection, over 16 and is a fit and proper person to act as a collector. For a discussion of the meaning of 'all due diligence', see **4.4.4**.
- The organiser has to issue each collector with a certificate of authority and all collectors have to retain their certificate of authority and at all times display a badge bearing the name of the funds or organisations that are to benefit from the collection.
- All collections have to be placed by the donor in the collecting box.
- Collecting boxes have to be opened by the organisers or their agents in the presence of another responsible person. If the boxes are delivered unopened to a bank, they shall be opened by an official of the bank.
- There is no ban on payments to collectors.
- There are special controls on envelope collections.
- Organisers of a collection have to submit to the Local Authority accounts relating to the collection within one month of the last date for which they possessed permission to organise a collection. The council may grant an extension of one month if it considers that there are special reasons. The accounts have to disclose particulars of:
  - the amount collected;
  - any other amount attributable to the collection;

- all expenses incurred in connection with the collection;
- the name of the funds or organisations that are benefiting from the collection.

■ The organiser has to retain all vouchers, receipts and other papers relating to the collection for a period of two years from the date on which the accounts are submitted to the council.

■ It is possible to obtain a 'national exemption licence' so that it is not necessary to obtain local licences. An application has to be made to the Scottish Executive Division Department of Justice (see p. 244). The licence will be granted if the charity has been collecting for a period of three years or more from 15 of the 32 local authority areas. Expenses must not be more than 30 per cent of the collection – this relates to both direct costs and overheads. If a national exemption licence is obtained, then annual accounts have to be filed with the First Minister for the Scottish Executive.

■ A breach of the regulations by a collector is a criminal offence with a maximum fine of £25 in respect of each offence. Breach of the regulations by the organiser is a criminal offence with a maximum fine of £50 in respect of each offence.

4.3.8 Summary of the law relating to street collections

Charities engaging in street collections in any part of the United Kingdom should ensure that they:

■ name a promoter ('organiser' in Scotland);
■ obtain a permit;
■ give written authority to each collector;
■ make sure collectors comply with the relevant regulations;
■ do not stray beyond the area of the permit;
■ prepare the return in accordance with the relevant regulations (one month or three months), unless there is a national exemption licence in Scotland.

Charities should make sure they do not:

■ use collectors under 18 in Northern Ireland, under 16 in England and Wales (or 14 in London with special consent) or 14 in Scotland;
■ allow their collectors to be accompanied by an animal in the Metropolitan Police District or Northern Ireland.

Charities may:

■ dress their collectors in an eye-catching way (e.g. with sashes or tabards or in animal costumes);
■ hand out pins and stickers – but beware of the impact of adhesive glue on silk and leather garments; it may be better for the collector to hand over the sticker for donors to put on themselves rather than for the collector to put the sticker on directly.

What happens if you break the law

- England and Wales:
  - breach of the Police, Factories, etc. (Miscellaneous Provisions) Act 1916 is a criminal offence, which carries a maximum fine of £200;
  - breach of the model regulations carries a maximum fine of £2 for a first offence and £5 for subsequent offences.

- Northern Ireland
  - breach of the regulations carries a maximum fine of £2 for a first offence and £5 for subsequent offences.

- Scotland
  - breach of the regulations:
    (a) by collectors – maximum fine of £25 in respect of each offence;
    (b) by the organiser – maximum fine of £50 in respect of each offence.

4.3.9 Borderline cases

- **Collections from pub to pub** – each of these collections takes place on private property but is caught by the house-to-house collections regulations (see **4.4**) in England and Wales and Northern Ireland, and by the public charitable collection controls in Scotland.

- **Collection on a station concourse** – under Part III of the Charities Act 1993 it is clear that such areas are public places and will therefore be within the controls on public collections in England and Wales if Part III is implemented. There is an argument under the existing law in England and Wales that such areas are 'public places' within the meaning of the 1916 Act. They *are* public places in Scotland. However, collections inside a railway station are generally treated as being collections on private land. For such collections, therefore, the charity needs only to obtain the authority of Railtrack to collect on their land.

- **Carol singing in front of a shopping centre** – most shopping centres are privately owned, and there will be a certain amount of space directly in front of the shopping centre that may not form part of the 'street' and will therefore still be private property. If the owner gives permission for a collection to take place on their premises this will be a private collection and not subject to the controls on street collections. If a charity wants carol singers to enliven the proceedings, but the owner refuses this, it would be possible for the carol singers to locate themselves on the public highway and for those responsible for holding the collection tins or buckets to locate themselves on the private property! The act of singing on the pavement would not amount to a collection of money within the 1916 Act or, in Scotland, under the 1982 Act. It might be sensible to request a permit from the local authority and, if they refuse, to notify the police of your intended course of action before the event.

- **Using collecting boxes in one pub** – this would constitute a collection on private property. As such, the only permission needed is that of the landlord or landlady.

- **Collection within a shopping mall but going from shop to shop** – this constitutes a series of collections on private property and is therefore not subject to the controls on street collections. However, this does hinge on the definition of 'public place'(see **4.3.3** and **4.3.7**).

- **Collection at a shop trolley collection point (even outdoors)** – again, this is a collection on private property which will require the consent of the supermarket, although this also hinges on the definition of 'public place'.

4.4 **House-to-house collections**

4.4.1   House-to-house collections in England and Wales are subject to the controls set out in the House to House Collections Act 1939 and the House to House Collections Regulations 1947. Similar provisions apply in Northern Ireland pursuant to the House to House Charitable Collections Act 1952 and House to House Charitable Collection Regulations 1952. In Scotland they are subject to the controls on public charitable collections (see **4.3.7**), but this only applies to collections 'for money' and not to collections for 'other property'. ICFM has issued a useful Code of Practice on House to House Collections, which complements the legal controls.

4.4.2   The two House to House Collections Acts control appeals to the public for charitable purposes 'made by means of visits from house to house, to give, whether for consideration or not, money or other property' (see **4.1** for the meaning of 'charitable purposes'). The Scottish legislation is very similar but only applies to collections 'for money' and not to collections for 'other property'. Hence in England, Wales and Northern Ireland the sale of goods or the solicitation of jumble from house to house for charitable purposes is a collection within the definition. In recent years a number of charities have also sought to obtain pledges of support whether by Deed of Covenant or by standing order from donors through visits from house to house. Some people have argued that this does not constitute a collection of money or other property. This is not a view with which the authors agree. If on the other hand a charity has conducted a series of fundraising appeals by telephone and booked a series of appointments for an individual to go and discuss the possibility of a donation with possible donors, this would not constitute a house-to-house collection. It is all a question of degree. If a charity has sent collectors to knock on a number of doors to arrange appointments, with the appointments taking place almost immediately after, that might well constitute a house-to-house collection.

4.4.3   Just as with street collections, the person who promotes a house-to-house collection has to obtain a licence from the licensing authority: in England and Wales this is the Common Council of the City of London, the Commissioner of Police for the Metropolis, and local district councils; in Northern Ireland it is the County Inspector of Police; in Scotland it is the local authority. The charity is not the promoter; the promoter is always an individual – see **4.3.5** (first bullet point).

4.4.4   Under regulation 5 of the House to House Collection Regulations 1947 for England and Wales, 'Every promoter of a collection shall exercise all due diligence:

■ to secure that persons authorised to act as collectors for the purposes of the collection are fit and proper persons and

■ to secure compliance on the part of persons so authorised with the provisions of these regulations.'

Similar provisions apply in Northern Ireland and Scotland.

The obligation to use 'all due diligence' to ensure that collectors are 'fit and proper persons' is an onerous one. It is thought that many charities honour these obligations in the breach rather than in the observance. It is difficult to believe that a charity that uses telephone recruitment for volunteer fundraisers can have exercised 'all due diligence', bearing in mind, in this case, that of course the charity is technically the agent for the promoter. In order to discharge the duty to use all due diligence, fundraisers should at the very least take up references and, once it is operative, do a search at the Criminal Records Agency on all prospective collectors.

4.4.5   An application for a licence has to be made to the appropriate authority and must specify the purpose of the collection and the locality (whether the whole of an area or part of it) within which the collection is to be made. It is possible to obtain a national exemption licence for England and Wales from the Home Secretary exempting a charity from the need to obtain a licence for collections in specific localities. An application for an exemption certificate in England and Wales is made to the Home Office's Voluntary Service Unit (see p. 244). In Northern Ireland the Secretary of State may grant a similar exemption. In Scotland the exemption is granted by the First Minister for the Scottish Executive. It is normally considered appropriate for the head of fundraising to make the application. To obtain an exemption the Home Secretary has to be satisfied that a promoter is pursuing a charitable purpose 'throughout the whole or a substantial part of England and Wales'. Similar tests apply in Scotland and Northern Ireland. In July 1999 there were 47 such orders in England and Wales. Some local authorities and local charities have complained of what they regard as excessive collections out of local control by charities with exemption orders. If a charity has an exemption licence, it would therefore be well advised to liaise with the local licensing authority in areas where it is proposing to carry out house-to-house collections.

Breach of the obligation to obtain a licence is a criminal offence carrying a maximum punishment in England and Wales of six months' imprisonment or a fine not exceeding £1,000. In Scotland the maximum fine is £50 and there is no provision for a prison sentence. In Northern Ireland the penalty is the same as in England, although the maximum fine is £100.

A licensing authority may refuse to grant a licence or may revoke a licence in England, Wales and Northern Ireland if it appears to the authority that:

- the total amount likely to be applied for charitable purposes as a result of the collection is inadequate in proportion to the value of the proceeds likely to be received;
- excessive remuneration is likely to be or has been retained out of the proceeds of the collection;
- the applicant is not a fit and proper person;
- the applicant has failed to exercise due diligence to ensure that persons authorised by him or her to act as collectors were fit and proper persons.

Fundraisers should be particularly aware that excessive fundraising costs could jeopardise the grant of a licence.

Similar rules apply in Scotland (see **4.3.7**).

4.4.6 Authorisation

In England, Wales and Northern Ireland each collector must be issued with:

- a prescribed certificate of authority duly completed and signed by the chief promoter;
- a prescribed badge;
- a collecting box or receipt book marked with a clear indication of the purpose of the collection and a distinguishing number.

Every prescribed certificate of authority and badge shall be obtained from the Stationery Office. In addition, every prescribed certificate of authority has to be authenticated in a manner approved by the Chief of Police for the area in respect of which the licence was granted. Effectively this means another licence is needed. In reality this provision does not appear to be used, and fundraisers may find it difficult to locate a police station willing to issue the necessary permit.

In Scotland the rules are different: the form of the certificate and badge is not laid down by law. Each collector has to:

- sign their name on the certificate of authority and produce it on demand to any police constable or any occupant of a house visited by them;

- sign their name on the badge issued to them and wear it prominently whenever they are engaged in collecting;
- keep the certificate and badge in their possession and return them to the promoter of the collection on completion of the collection or on demand.

4.4.7 Controls on collectors

- No collector can be under 16 (14 in Scotland).
- No collector shall 'importune any person to the annoyance of such person, or remain in or at the door of any house if requested to leave by any occupant'.
- Monies must be placed only in the collecting box.
- Every collector must return the collecting box to the promoter either when it is full or on completion of the collection or if they wish to cease collecting. The seal must be unbroken.

These rules relating to collectors are similar throughout the United Kingdom.

4.4.8 Inspection of boxes

- On its return, a collecting box shall be examined by and opened in the presence of a promoter of the collection and one other responsible person.
- Where a collecting box is delivered unopened to a bank, it may, in the absence of a promoter of the collection, be examined and opened by an official of the bank.
- As soon as a collecting box has been opened, the contents shall be counted and the amount shall be entered with the distinguishing number of the collecting box on a list.

These rules are similar throughout the United Kingdom.

4.4.9 Envelope collections

An envelope collection requires the specific consent of the Home Secretary (in England and Wales) or the Secretary of State (in Northern Ireland) or the First Minister of the Scottish Executive (in Scotland). The regulations lay down specific rules as to the form of envelope.

4.4.10 Accounts

In England, Wales and Northern Ireland the chief promoter of a collection has to provide accounts to the licensing authority within one month of the expiry of the licence. Similar rules apply in Scotland, although in that case the licensing authority can grant a one-month extension. Charities that organise large-scale house-to-house collections with telephone-recruited volunteers need to remember this and establish a system capable of allowing the charity to produce the required return within the timescales. Charities should also have a system for chasing volunteers who have not returned monies collected. Most local authorities will regard the charity as having abided by its obligations if it sends a reminder letter. Where an exemption order has been made, accounts must be made on a yearly basis to the Home Secretary in England and Wales, the Secretary of State in Northern Ireland, or the First Minister of the Scottish Executive in Scotland.

The accounting regulations will affect charities in different ways. If a charity has independent branches that are separate legal entities, each branch will be responsible for compliance with the statutory controls over its collections. If the Head Office and branches of a charity are one legal entity with one charity number, the trustees should ensure that they have policies in place and that there is guidance for local volunteers. This guidance should cover the scope of their powers and stipulate the arrangements for reporting to the national charity, as well as the regulations that must be complied with. This is especially important where a national exemption order is in force, as a single annual return has to be returned to the relevant minister covering the amount raised by each volunteer. Failure by one branch to produce the necessary data or to conduct its collections properly could thus jeopardise the charity's national exemption order. Failure to produce accounts within the requisite period is a criminal offence. The obligation to produce the accounts is on the chief promoter rather than the charity, but this will be scant comfort to any organisation.

4.5 Non-money house-to-house collections – England, Wales and Northern Ireland

4.5.1 The House to House Collections Acts apply not only to collections for money but also to collections for other property, for example jumble, newspapers, stamps (see **4.4.2**). In Scotland these controls apply only to collections for money: collections for goods do *not* require a licence. The controls in Part II Charities Act 1992 on professional fundraisers and commercial participators apply only in England and Wales.

4.5.2 A charity may employ an agent to carry on a collection from house to house to collect property for the charity. The charity will pay the agent. In England, Wales and Northern Ireland there is, unlike with street collections, no ban on payment to collectors for house-to-house collections. The agent will make clear, as will any materials given out at the same time, that property in the items collected belongs to the charity. Fundraisers in England and Wales need to consider whether such an agent is a professional fundraiser for the purposes of Charities Act 1992 Part II (see Chapter 17). The agent will be considered a professional fundraiser because they will be soliciting property for reward for the benefit of the charity. This means that the charity will need to have an appropriate contract with the professional fundraiser, and a statement will need to be made by the professional fundraiser (see Chapter 17). The charity will be the promoter and will need to obtain the licence.

4.5.3 Collection by a commercial participator – England and Wales

Another form of collection can be carried out by a commercial organisation on the basis that it will give X per cent of the value of the goods received to a named charity. The collector will own the donated items. In this case the collector is a commercial participator and the rules that are set out in Chapter 16 concerning the relationship with a commercial participator need to be considered. The commercial participator will be the promoter of the collection and will need to have the necessary licence.

4.5.4 House-to-house sales

If a charity organises the sale of goods or raffle tickets by means of visits from house to house, this will also constitute a house-to-house collection in England, Wales and Northern Ireland. The definition of a collection is wide enough to include the sale of goods where it is stated that the sale is for 'charitable purposes'. In some cases the goods sold may be sold in fulfilment of the charity's primary purpose (see Chapter 10). This will not alter the position so far as licensing is concerned. Equally, if the goods cannot be sold in the fulfilment of the charity's primary purpose but are sold purely to raise money, then the sales should be carried out by the charity's trading company. The trading company will, however, need to obtain a licence.

The regulations apply equally to the sale of services, for example if a charity's trading company were to dispatch door-to-door salespeople to sell a range of insurance products, armed with the inducement that all profits go to a named charity.

4.6 Rose selling with or without a collection box

In recent years there has been a substantial amount of rose selling in aid of charity. The number of different schemes in operation is too numerous to explain the precise legal status of each. However, the following example illustrates the main legal points.

> **EXAMPLE**
>
> A rose seller goes from pub to pub in England offering roses for sale at £2.00, £1.00 of which she claims goes to a named charity. She also invites further contributions to be made into a collection box.
>
> - The sale of the roses on the licensed premises is a matter between her and the landlord or landlady.

- The fact that she is going from pub to pub means that she is carrying on a house-to-house collection. She will therefore require a licence and must comply with the regulations.
- The claim that £1.00 per bunch sold is also given to charity makes the rose seller a commercial participator. She therefore needs an agreement with the charity (see Chapter 16).

4.7 **Stopping unauthorised fundraising**

4.7.1 Anyone can raise money in the name of a charity without the consent of the charity, provided the collection is carried out lawfully. From time to time it is suggested that charities should have the right to give prior approval to all charitable collections carried out in their name. However, it has been recognised that this could be a major fetter on spontaneous fundraising, and the suggestion has therefore never been implemented. In the example given above (see **4.6**), the simplest and first step would be to report the matter to the police for an investigation of breaches of the criminal law if:

- the collector does not have a commercial participator agreement with the charity (this only applies in England and Wales);
- the collector does not have a house-to-house collection licence (or public charitable collection licence in Scotland).

4.7.2 Under section 62 Charities Act 1992, the court in England and Wales may grant an injunction to stop unauthorised fundraising. An injunction will be granted if the court is satisfied that:

- any person either has solicited/is soliciting money or other property for the benefit of a charitable institution or has represented/is representing that charitable contributions are to be given; and
- this person, unless restrained, is likely to do further acts of that nature; and
- one or more of the following is met:
  – that the person in question is using methods of fundraising to which the charitable institution objects;
  – that the person is not a fit and proper person to raise funds for the charitable institution;
  – that the charitable institution does not wish to be associated with the particular promotional or other fundraising venture.

Before the charitable institution can obtain an injunction it must give at least 28 days' notice in writing to the person in question. The notice must request them to cease fundraising forthwith and must state that, if they do not comply with the notice, the institution will make an application for an injunction. The form of the notice may be prescribed by regulations.

If a charitable institution has given an unauthorised fundraiser 28 days' notice under section 62(3), and the person initially complies with the notice, but then begins to carry on the same activities again, the charitable institution can immediately apply for an injunction without having to serve further notice. This applies only if the application for the injunction is made not more than 12 months after the date of service of a relevant notice upon the fundraiser.

If a charitable institution obtains an injunction under section 62, and the named person acts in breach of it, then that person is in contempt of court. This is a criminal offence and can give rise, ultimately, to imprisonment. It will, however, be up to the charity to prove that there has been a breach of the injunction, which means that the charity will have to consider the expense of hiring a private detective to track the individual concerned.

4.7.3 Charity Commission remedies

The Charity Commission has jurisdiction not only over charities but also over organisations that raise funds for charitable purposes. In their 1998 report the Commissioners refer to the case of a group of companies raising funds for cancer prevention and relief, charity support and equipment for local hospitals. The companies themselves were not charities but the Charity Commission considered that, as the funds were raised for charitable purposes, the Commission had jurisdiction over them.

The Commission's view was contested. However, in a Court case in July 1998 Mr Justice Lightman upheld the Commission's view on the status of the funds raised. He said:

'All monies received are indeed money held on a charitable trust and the Charity Commissioners have full power to institute the enquiries which they have launched. Indeed, on the material before me, it is clear that it is entirely right that they should proceed with their enquiry.'

4.8 Volunteer recruitment for street, house-to-house and lottery ticket sales by telephone

4.8.1 The controls on the use of telephones for 'direct marketing' which, in the opinion of the Data Protection Commissioner includes the recruitment of volunteers, is dealt with in **12.13**. These controls apply throughout the United Kingdom.

4.8.2 Fundraisers will often wish to build up a profile of information on potential collectors or donors by linking the electoral roll with telephone numbers. Although both sets of information are in 'the public domain', the gathering of this information may raise issues under the Data Protection Act 1998 (see **3.2.2** and Chapter 12).

Linking the information on the electoral roll with the telephone directly will create a new database that will be protected by the Database Right (see **21.6** for further consideration). However, the use of the electoral roll and the matching telephone numbers, without consent, will constitute a breach of the database right of the Crown or the telephone operator in that information (see also Chapter 3).

4.8.3　Many charities employ independent agents to recruit potential collectors or volunteers by telephone. That activity in itself is not subject to the regulations set out in Part II Charities Act 1992 on professional fundraisers in England and Wales (see Chapter 17). However, in practice many people, when telephoned by a charity and asked to give some time to become a volunteer fundraiser, decline – but offer to make a donation at the same time. If they make a donation, and the agent processes the gift, then the agent will have become a professional fundraiser for the purposes of Part II Charities Act 1992 (see Chapter 17) – this only applies in England and Wales. That is because the agent is being paid to make the telephone calls and will have solicited a donation, even though the solicitation is implied rather than express. Consequently, unless the agency undertakes not to accept any donations, it would be sensible to ensure that the agreement with the agency complies with the requirements of Part II Charities Act 1992 (see Chapter 17).

In England and Wales the agency will also be required to make the appropriate statement under section 60 Charities Act 1992, and this should be made as soon as possible after the offer to make the donation has been made (see Chapter 17).

4.8.4　If a charity recruits volunteers to carry out fundraising via the telephone, a substantial amount of fundraising materials and/or monies will inevitably be collected that are not accounted for. The charity's primary responsibility in these circumstances is to prevent improper use of its monies and use all reasonable endeavours to recover all materials and funds collected. At the very least, the collector's kit sent out by the charity by post should make an explicit request for the return of monies, and a reminder letter should be sent to those who have not made a return.

4.9　Commercial sponsorship of fundraising envelopes and processing donations

4.9.1　When undertaking house-to-house collections, some charities have succeeded in securing commercial sponsorship of the fundraising envelope. If, in return for the sponsorship, the charity advertises the sponsor's details on the envelope, the charity will have provided advertising services to the sponsor. In this circumstance, the charity will need to consider the implications of this non-primary-purpose trading activity and to reflect on what the VAT position may be. (See also Chapters 8 and 10.)

4.9.2 When undertaking collections on a large scale, charities often contract out the provision of a number of services, including:

- collecting the names of potential supporters;
- processing donations.

In either case the charity should be very clear to stipulate that it owns the property in the databases compiled in this way. It should require the agency to comply at all times with the Data Protection Act in relation to the capture of the data (see Chapter 12) and should insist that all database rights are vested in the charity. As a practical tip, it is well worth requesting that a new electronic version of the complete database is handed over to the charity at least monthly. This can stop the unscrupulous practice (which sometimes happens on termination of an agency agreement) of an agency claiming that it has 'wiped' the database from its records and therefore has nothing to hand over to the charity! Trying to prove the contrary can be extremely difficult, expensive and protracted. It is therefore much better to rely on possession being nine-tenths of the law and to obtain an up-dated version of the database at regular intervals.

4.10 Trading and disabled people

Chapter 10 covers how charities can carry on trade in fulfilment of their objects. One classic example is the sale, by a charity for disabled people, of products created by them in a workshop. The Trading Representations (Disabled Persons) Act 1958 makes it a criminal offence to sell any goods or solicit orders for goods of any description, in the course of visits from house to house, or by post (e.g. catalogue sales) or by telephone, with a representation that 'blind or otherwise disabled persons':

- are employed in the production, preparation or packing of the goods, article or things;
- benefit from the sale of the goods or the carrying out of the business.

The maximum penalty is two years' imprisonment or a £5,000 fine, or both. The Act applies in England, Scotland and Wales. The Act does not apply to businesses carried on by:

- a local authority;
- a company, association or body providing facilities under section 15 of the Disabled Persons (Employments) Act 1944. (A list of these companies may be obtained from the Department of Trade and Industry.)

By this Act, therefore, a charity established to help disabled people and which seeks to sell products or solicit orders (e.g. a printing business run by disabled people) by house-to-house visits or mail order cannot imply that 'blind or otherwise disabled persons' are employed in the business, unless it is registered under the 1944 Act.

The 1958 Act does not apply to sales or representations made in a retail outlet but only representation made by house-to-house visits, by post or by telephone.

If a charity or its trading company is concerned about its position under this Act, it should seek appropriate professional advice.

Summary

Static collection boxes

- There are no legislative controls, but the ICFM has produced a code of practice.

Street collections

- These are distinct from house-to-house collections.
- Controls in Northern Ireland are similar but not identical to those in England and Wales.
- In Scotland street collections are regulated under the controls on public charitable collections.
- A checklist of *do*s and *don't*s is included on page 34.
- A collector cannot be paid in England, Wales or Northern Ireland.

House-to-house collections

- There are both legislative controls and an ICFM code of practice covering house-to-house collections.
- Controls in Northern Ireland are similar to those in England and Wales.
- House-to-house legislation also covers collections for property (e.g. jumble, newspapers, etc.), except in Scotland.
- It is lawful to pay an agent to carry out a collection in England, Wales or Northern Ireland.

Unauthorised fundraising

- Anyone can raise money for a charity without the consent of the charity, as long as they obey the law.
- An injunction can be obtained to stop unauthorised fundraising.

5

Lotteries

The law in this chapter relates to Great Britain and not Northern Ireland. For local law in Northern Ireland, please contact the Department of Health and Social Services Listed in 'Useful addresses'.

5.1   The most important legal fact for all fundraisers to know and digest is that all lotteries are illegal, unless they are the National Lottery or authorised by the Lotteries and Amusements Act 1976 ('the Act'). So if your fundraising venture involves a lottery-type promotion you need to ask yourself the following question:

- Does the promotion constitute a lottery as defined (see **5.2**)?

If your answer to this question is 'yes', then make sure it falls within one of the permitted exceptions (see **5.5–5.7**). If it does not, you, the promoter and others involved with the charity are likely to have committed a criminal offence.

If your answer to the question is 'no', then is the promotion properly structured to avoid illegality, for example as a free prize draw or as a lawful competition (see **5.3–5.4**)?

5.2 Definition of lottery

5.2.1   Defining the essential elements of a Lottery is confusing, because many different and seemingly overlapping terms are bandied about. The terms 'raffles' and 'lotteries' are used interchangeably, but the term 'raffle' has no statutory legal meaning. Both raffles and games of chance, however, may be lotteries if they fall within the definition that Lord Widgery set out in *Reader's Digest* v. *Williams (1979)* 1 WLR 1109. In this seminal case, Lord Widgery held that a lottery has three essential elements:

- a distribution of prizes;
- the fact that the distribution was done by means of chance;
- the fact that participants, or a substantial number of them, make an 'actual contribution' to obtain the chance.

5.2.2 Analysing each of these elements

- **Prizes** – if there are no prizes, what inducement is there for participants to take part? It makes no difference whether prizes are bought by the promoter or donated.

- **Chance** – the key question is what triggers the distribution of prizes. Say, for example, that you structure a promotion with questions of skill, but that there is more than one correct answer; if the winner is ultimately chosen by chance (i.e. the winning entry is pulled out of the hat), you have inadvertently created a lottery. There is obviously no problem if the lottery is structured in such a way as to fall within one of the permitted exceptions. However, this is often not the case, with the consequences that you may well (albeit unwittingly) be promoting an illegal lottery, with attendant criminal sanctions.

- **Actual contribution** – this again has been the subject of much legal debate and indeed case law. The key case *Imperial Tobacco Ltd* v. *the Attorney General (1981) AC718* considered a promotion concerning prize draw cards in cigarette packets. Imperial Tobacco argued that it was not a lottery because no one had to pay to enter the draw; they simply had to pay the normal price for a packet of cigarettes. While there were a small number of cards available for free (0.85 per cent of the total number of cards), this was considered to be negligible, and was disregarded. The House of Lords held that the fact that entrants did have to pay for a cigarette packet was a contribution to enter the lottery. This case explains the reason why many commercial promoters attempt to sidestep lottery law by running lottery-type promotions (e.g. on crisp packets or confectionery) with the strapline 'no purchase necessary'. How lawful such schemes are (see **5.4.3**) has yet to be fully put to the test, particularly where the terms and conditions of entry for non-purchasers is written in very small print.

5.3 Free prize draw

5.3.1 Free prize draws are often attractive to fundraisers, because they give you the opportunity to set up a 'game of chance' type of promotion that legally falls outside the definition of a lottery. A free prize draw is structured on the basis not that 'no purchase is necessary' (see **5.2**) but that no donation, i.e. actual contribution, is necessary. The major plus point is that, because the scheme is not a lottery, it does not have to be squeezed within one of the permitted exceptions to make it lawful. This means that there are no rules about who you can sell the tickets to, at what price, how they can be advertised, and how much can be swallowed up by prizes and expenses. The major downside is that a free prize draw will only be lawful if, instead of selling tickets, you use them to solicit donations: you cannot enforce or impose or demand a minimum sum or indeed any donation.

5.3.2 In order for a free prize draw to be lawful, the following points should be noted:

- Ensure that all marketing and advertising material is accompanied by the words: 'No donation necessary'. Do not use the formula 'Minimum donation £X'; if you do, you will be construed to be selling the tickets (i.e. demanding an actual contribution, the third element of the definition of a lottery) and therefore promoting a lottery. You might be able to use 'Suggested donation £X' alongside 'No donation necessary', but be very careful about how you do this.

- Consider the budget, the cost of the promotion including the provision of the prizes. Can all these expenses be justified as reasonable and legitimate fundraising expenses, given that you just do not know how many donations the promotion will raise?

5.4 Prize competitions

5.4.1 Another way to avoid the restrictions concerning lotteries is to operate a prize competition under section 14 of the Act. The rules concerning competitions are fairly straightforward, but there are two key points to note:

- It is not lawful for the competition to involve predicting the result of a future event or of a past event, the result of which is not yet determined or not yet generally known. For example, do not set a question that asks entrants to forecast which football team will win the Premier League. Make sure that prize competitions do not stray into betting law.

- When framing the questions, be aware that success should 'depend to a substantial degree on the exercise of skill'. What does this test mean in practice? In a 1935 case it was held that identifying certain photographs of famous British landmarks such as Big Ben and Stonehenge did involve 'the exercise of substantial skill'. On the face of this, it seems that the court's view of what is 'substantial' may be different from a more common-sense, practical approach. However, it is as well to remember that in 1935 there was no TV and the general level of education was much lower: what was 'substantial' then may not be substantial now. The key issue to remember is that, if too easy questions are set, it is more likely that more than one entrant will get the answers correct. In this case, it will be necessary to set a tie breaker, in order to avoid the winner being determined by chance.

5.4.2 In structuring prize competitions you should also note the following:

- The marketing and advertising, rules of entry and Judges' panel for the tie-breaker (if there is one) should comply with the Advertising Standards Authority Code of Sales Practice (see Chapter 15).

- Running a prize competition is not a primary-purpose trade. Therefore, if the income from selling tickets is going to be free from income or

Corporation Tax it should be run through a trading company subject to the new thresholds for trading (see Chapters 10 and 22).

- The sale of tickets will be subject to VAT at 17.5 per cent unless they are sold at a qualifying one-off fundraising event (see Chapter 6).

5.4.3   On 10 March 2000 the Home Office announced the members of the Gambling Review body, which is going to consider modernising British gambling legislation, including the law on lotteries. In this respect, it is interesting to note the views of Peter Dean, Chairman of the Gaming Board. In a speech given on 23 February 2000 to the Lotteries Council Annual Conference on illegal lotteries, competitions and promotions, he stated, 'The uncomfortable fact is that there are numerous activities, promoted by commercial organisations, which masquerade as competitions of skill, but are in reality, under the present law, illegal lotteries. Nobody does anything about this, partly (as in the Board's case) through lack of powers, but partly because many of the promotions or competitions seem to be creating no great public mischief. It is, however, unsatisfactory to have laws on the statute book that are routinely flouted. The review body will no doubt wish to look at this issue and perhaps suggest criteria for legitimising the more innocent activities of the sort described.'

5.5 Lawful lotteries (small lotteries incidental to exempt entertainments)

5.5.1   An exempt entertainment is defined in section 3(1) as a:

'Bazaar, sale of work, fete, dinner, dance, sporting or athletic event or other entertainment of a similar character, whether limited to one day or extending over two or more days.'

5.5.2   In order for the lottery to be lawful, the following conditions must be observed:

- None of the prizes can be money prizes. 'Money' is defined in section 23 of the Act as 'cheque, bank note, postal order or money order'. Gift voucher prizes will not fall foul of this rule.
- Not more than £250 of the ticket proceeds can be spent on prizes. A gift can exceed £250 in value if it has been donated.
- Tickets must be sold only on the premises of the entertainment, and the result must be declared on the premises and during the entertainment.
- The lottery must not be the only substantial inducement for the charity's supporters to attend the entertainment.
- All the proceeds of the entertainment must go to purposes other than private gain, except for the lawful deductions that are the expenses of the entertainment (excluding expenses incurred in connection with the lottery) and the expenses incurred in printing tickets for the lottery.

5.5.3 Other key points to note are:

- In respect of alcoholic prizes, Gaming Board Guidance (GBL6) states that, although only the courts can give an authoritative interpretation of the law (the Licensing (Occasional Permissions) Act 1983), it is the view of the Home Office that it is lawful to offer alcoholic prizes.
- You cannot rely on the exemption to sell lottery tickets at a trade fair or promotional extravaganza unless all the proceeds from the entire event, not just the lottery, go to purposes other than private gain.
- The charity can promote these lotteries, as the income is exempt from tax under s505 (1)(f) ICTA 1988.

5.6 Lawful lotteries: private lotteries

5.6.1 The conditions attached to the private lottery exemption in section 4 of the Act are somewhat disappointing for charity fundraisers, making it difficult without ingenuity to raise large sums of money. This is essentially because 'private' does genuinely mean 'private', so the lottery can only be promoted to the following groups of people:

- Members of one society (or any other people on the society's premises), provided that the society is not established for purposes connected to gaming, betting or lotteries. Most charities do not have club-type premises where members meet.
- People who all work on the same premises. This does not mean people who work for the same company (i.e. all the employees of BT or Marks and Spencer); it only relates to people who work on the same premises. It has not been tested by the courts, but it is highly likely that this would be interpreted to mean employees of the same company who work on the same premises, not employees on one site (e.g. Canary Wharf).
- People who all reside on the same premises.

5.6.2 Other relevant points to note are:

- The lottery must be promoted by someone who is within one of the groups mentioned in **5.6.1**, and, if the lottery is promoted for members of the society, the governing body of the society must authorise it.
- The lottery can be advertised only by notice on the relevant premises, whether this is society, work or residential; it cannot be advertised generally. It is a moot point whether a company's intranet could be interpreted as a modern-day noticeboard.

Although there is no requirement to have a ticket, and such a lottery can be run in the manner of a sweepstake, if there are tickets:

- no ticket can be sent through the post, which makes effective promotion difficult;

- the price of all tickets must be the same and must be stated on the ticket;
- the ticket must state the name and address of each of the promoters and carry a statement as to who is eligible to participate.

5.7 Lawful lotteries: society lotteries

5.7.1 Most charity fundraisers are familiar with the society lottery exemption, as it gives the greatest scope for imaginative large-scale promotions. Indeed, following amendments to the Act in 1993, all restrictions governing the number and frequency of lotteries have been removed. In their place, there is a simplified system of two financial limits, which are that:

- the total value of tickets sold must not exceed £1 million in one lottery;
- the total value of tickets sold in lotteries in one calendar year on behalf of one society or local authority must not exceed £5 million.

5.7.2 Definition

The definition of a 'society' in section 5 of the Act concerns a society conducted wholly or mainly for one or more of the following purposes:

- charitable purposes;
- participation in, or support of, athletic sports or games or cultural activities;
- purposes not described above, but which are purposes not related to 'private gain nor purposes of any commercial undertaking'.

5.7.3 The definition of a society includes 'any club, institution, organisation or association of persons, by whatever name called and any separate branch or section of such a club, institution, organisation or association'. A key question is the meaning of 'separate branch or section'. If your charity does not have a 'separate branch or section' and the total value of tickets to be put on sale in any one lottery exceeds a certain threshold, then your charity can only have one registration with the Gaming Board. National charities are caused great administrative difficulties when regional fundraisers unilaterally register lotteries with a local authority.

5.7.4 Registration thresholds with the Gaming Board

A society must register with the Gaming Board if the total value of tickets to be put on sale in any lottery exceeds £20,000, or if the total value of tickets or chances to be put on sale in any lottery, added to the value of those already sold or put on sale in all earlier lotteries in the same calendar year, is to exceed £250,000. Once a society has registered with the Board, it has to conduct all lotteries, whatever their size, under the Board registration until three calendar years have elapsed since the last lottery that would have required Board registration.

5.7.5 Branches

The most recent case to raise the issue of what constitutes a 'separate section or branch' was *R v. Royal Borough of Kensington and Chelsea exp. Sir Adrian Blennerhanet BT and John Evans QB 19:7:96* (unreported). This involved NHT Lotto, which had registered 100 separate branches as society lotteries with the borough and challenged the Borough of Kensington and Chelsea's decision that NHT should register with the Gaming Board. Unfortunately, this case does not take the law much further, because, unlike most charity branches, the sole purpose of the 100 separate branches was to run lotteries. In addition, they all had the same address in London and telephone number; there were no separate numbers or bank accounts; they had identical constitutions, and they had the same promoter.

In this case, it was held that the registrations were unlawful because 'there was no basic reality to or activity in any of the branches'. Gaming Board Guidance (GBL6) states that 'It is clear that "branches" which have identical constitutions and memberships and conduct no activity other than the running of lotteries are unlikely to meet the statutory definition of a society'.

General rules applicable to society lotteries registered with the local authority or Gaming Board

5.7.6 *Promoter*

The trustees of the society under section 11(1) of the Act must nominate one of its members in writing to act as the promoter of the lottery. The Act does not define the term 'member': however, in respect of a society that is a company limited by guarantee, it is likely to mean company law member. If, in your capacity as a charity fundraising employee, you are asked to act as the promoter, you should be aware that criminal offences can be committed for which you will be liable unless you can show that the offence was committed without your consent or connivance and that you exercised all due diligence to prevent it. You might consider asking the charity for an indemnity in relation to the legal costs of any successful defence to a criminal prosecution, but the charity will probably not be able to offer a wider indemnity. Acting as the promoter involves serious legal obligations and responsibilities and the possibility of criminal sanctions for non-compliance.

5.7.7 *Ticket price*

There are various legal requirements concerning the price of tickets.

- The maximum price of a ticket is £1.00.
- No price can depend upon the purchase of more than one ticket or chance, unless the price of the aggregate number of tickets or chances does not exceed £1.00.

- All tickets sold must be the same price (i.e. no discounts on multiple buys).
- No monies can be refunded, and part payment cannot be accepted.

5.7.8 *Ticket particulars*

Every ticket must state:

- the price;
- the name of the society;
- whether the charity is registered with the local authority or Gaming Board;
- the date of the lottery – for instant-win lotteries, the Gaming Board recommends that this should be the last day on which the tickets are to be on sale;
- the name and address of the promoter;
- the fact that the society (if applicable) is a 'registered charity'.

5.7.9 *Prize limits*

In structuring the prizes, you will need to work within the strict limits on prize levels. Generally speaking, this is not a problem for charity lotteries where the promotion is targeted at existing supporters. However, it can cause more difficulties where the lottery is being managed by a commercial manager (see **5.8**) or external lottery managers. A commercial manager will try to promote the lottery through high-street and other national distribution networks. A punter, faced with the extremely low odds of winning millions on the National Lottery and the possibility of winning £25,000–£100,000 on a charity lottery, may conceivably opt for the higher odds of winning a smaller prize.

The limits on prizes are as follows:

- The maximum single prize is £25,000 (Gaming Board Registration required) or 10 per cent of the proceeds, whichever is the greater (i.e. a maximum of £100,000). No single donated prize must contravene this limit.
- The maximum amount to be spent globally on prizes cannot exceed 55 per cent of the proceeds of the lottery (when calculating this figure of 55 per cent, donated prizes will not be taken into account).
- If 55 per cent is appropriated for prizes, this means that the maximum expense ratio is 25 per cent (see **5.7.10** in this respect).

5.7.9.1 Contravening prize limits

If the prize limits are exceeded, then the promoter of the lottery has committed a criminal offence, as has any other person associated with the contravention. However, there is a defence to a charge under section 13(2A), which is that:

- the total value of the tickets or chances sold in the lottery fell short of the sum reasonably estimated;
- there would have been no contravention if the number of tickets sold had matched the reasonable estimation;

- a lesser-value prize could not be given, because this would have breached an unconditional undertaking.

In order to rely on this defence, you would have to show how the 'reasonable estimations' were formulated. This would require hard, scientific data for sales for previous lotteries, market trends and the particular budget and sales forecast for the lottery in question.

5.7.10 Expenses

5.7.10.1 Trying to stay within the expense limits is a particularly thorny issue for society lotteries. The Gaming Board has issued strict guidance about ensuring that all expenses of the lottery are included, even down to a pro-rata calculation for staff time and an apportionment for rent (where it is paid) on premises; VAT is also an expense if it is not reclaimable. A genuine donation towards expenses (e.g. the costs of a postal campaign) does not need to be included.

5.7.10.2 The expense limits are as follows:

- Where the proceeds of the lottery do not exceed £20,000, up to 35 per cent can be spent on expenses.
- Where the proceeds exceed £20,000, then the permitted percentage that may be spent on expenses is 15 per cent, unless authorisation from the Gaming Board is sought to raise this to 35 per cent.
- If 35 per cent of the proceeds is appropriated for expenses, the maximum prize ratio is 45 per cent: see **5.7.9** in this respect.

5.7.10.3 **Contravening expense limits**

If the expense limits are exceeded, then the promoter of the lottery and any other person associated with the contravention have committed a criminal offence. There is a similar defence applicable (section 11(3)) to that outlined for contravening prize limits (see **5.7.9.1**).

The main issue for charities and expense ratios is when an external lottery manager is promoting the lottery. Under the usual contract, they will require the full 35 per cent as remuneration for their services, to include all other expenses incurred. This leaves charities in a difficult position. Strictly speaking, if they agree to this, they can incur no further expenditure or promotional costs in relation to the lottery – for example, staff time or marketing – since all allowable expenditure will have been swallowed up by the external lottery manager. Charity promoters need to beware of the liability for signing off the return and should try to negotiate a better deal with the external lottery manager.

5.7.11 *Age limits and place of sale*

- It is an offence to sell tickets to persons under the age of 16, and it is an offence for persons under 16 to sell society lottery tickets. A common mistake is to think that this age restriction also applies to small lotteries at exempt entertainments and private lotteries. It does not. There is therefore no problem in selling lottery tickets to a 12 year old at the village fete, which is an exempt entertainment.

- You cannot sell lottery tickets in the street: the meaning of 'street' here includes 'any bridge, road, lane, footway, subway, court, alley or passage, whether a thoroughfare or not, which is for the time being open to the public without payment'.
- The Gaming Board Guidance (GBL6) states that the door-to-door selling of lottery tickets is permitted, but it will be necessary to comply with the controls on house-to-house collections (see Chapter 4).
- A person visiting another person at his or her home for an official, professional or commercial function that is not connected with lotteries (for example, an Avon lady) can sell lottery tickets.
- For the time being, lottery tickets can be sold legally in pubs, amusement arcades, licensed bingo clubs and casinos.

5.7.12 *Returns to the local authority and Gaming Board*

5.7.12.1 Local authority

The promoter must send to the registration authority, not later than the end of the third month after the date of the lottery, a return certified by two other members of the society who have been appointed by its Board.

The return must show:

- a copy of the scheme under which the lottery was promoted;
- the proceeds of the lottery;
- sums appropriated on account of expenses and prizes;
- the charity's purposes;
- the date of the lottery.

5.7.12.2 Gaming Board

The return must be submitted to the lottery within three months of the date of the lottery, signed by the promoter and another member of the governing body, and it must give details of:

- the proceeds of the lottery;
- any interest earned;
- sums appropriated on account of expenses and prizes;
- the net proceeds received in respect of each lottery (and a receipt to show this).

If the charity sells more than £100,000 worth of tickets or chances in all its lotteries held in any one calendar year, then it must submit to the Gaming Board accounts in respect of these lotteries, together with a report on the accounts prepared by a qualifying auditor.

5.8 Lawful lotteries: external lottery manager

Commercial bodies frequently approach charities with 'get rich quick' schemes for charity lotteries that they manage. In order to manage a society or local authority lottery lawfully – defined in section 9A(4) as 'managing the promotion, or any part of the promotion of a lottery' – external lottery managers must, if their activities fall into this definition, be certified as lottery managers by the Gaming Board.

The only exceptions to the requirement for a lottery manager to register are where the promotion is not external but carried out by a member of the society, an employee or a wholly owned trading company. It is notoriously difficult to obtain a certificate from the Gaming Board – if a lottery manager should be certified and is not, both the manager and the promoter have committed a criminal offence.

The difficulty is establishing which of the activities of a third-party service provider constitutes the role of lottery manager. The Gaming Board in GBL6 states that 'the degree of management undertaken by both the promoter and the sub-contractor will be crucial factors'. The key factors will be who has control of the funds, who is responsible for the appointment and payment of other sub-contractors, and who controls promotional aspects of the lottery.

5.9 Record keeping

5.9.1 The Gaming Board recommends that the promoters of lotteries keep details of:

- tickets ordered and received from the printer;
- tickets issued, divided into those sold and those unsold – together with details of the reason why any unsold tickets have not been returned;
- all expenses and invoices;
- winners and winning tickets;
- the distribution of the proceeds;
- payment of any agents

5.9.2 All records should be kept for two years unless the Board directs otherwise. Unsold tickets may be destroyed with the prior permission of the Board, provided that the destruction is witnessed by two responsible officers of the society or local authority.

5.10 Tax on society lotteries

Society lotteries can be registered in the name of the charity, because section 505 1(f) ICTA 1988 states that charities will be exempt from tax on the income of society lotteries, provided the income is applied solely to the purposes of the charity.

The Gaming Board will still, however, accept registration of a charity's trading company, if it gives all its taxable profits to the charity.

5.11 Lotteries and the Internet

The 1993 Lotteries Regulations state that no tickets can be sold by means of a machine. In a speech to the Third Annual Internet Symposium on Internet Gambling Law and Management in November 1999, the chairman of the Gaming Board expressed a view on whether this would prevent the sale of tickets via the Internet. He stated that 'the Board's view is that the running of a lottery entirely by computer via the Internet amounts to selling by means of machine, and we have refused to authorise such lotteries.' However, a number of schemes have been approved whereby the Internet is used simply as a means of communication analogous to the telephone.

Therefore, to promote sales of society lottery tickets via the Internet, it is necessary to ensure that there is 'human intervention' and also advisable to obtain the clearance of the Gaming Board. It is also necessary to build safeguards to make sure you are only selling to people over 16 and to make sure you are promoting the lottery in Great Britain only.

In terms of the Gambling Review Body (see **5.4.3**), the Gaming Board is taking the view that, as long as arrangements are put in place to avoid sales to children, there is a sound case for making it easier to sell lottery chances via the Internet, by amending the restriction on sales by machines. However, there may well be restrictions for repetitive, harder forms of lottery, which are more appropriate for a highly regulated gambling environment.

5.12 Gambling Review Body

The Gambling Review Body (see **5.4.3**), which will report in the summer of 2001, is reviewing the entire gambling and lotteries legislation. The Review has been prompted by the potential of the Internet to offer unregulated, unlicensed and low- or no-tax gambling. The Gaming Board has already stated that society lotteries have comparatively lenient treatment compared with other forms of gambling, and that there is unlikely to be a substantial easing of restrictions on such matters as stakes, proceeds or prizes. There is room, though, to lobby, and now is the right time.

Summary

- A lottery involves distribution of a prize by chance to participants.
- All lotteries are illegal unless they fall within one of the express permissions.
- Lotteries and raffles are the same.
- Free prize draws are not lotteries.
- Prize competitions are not lotteries.
- Lawful lotteries include:
  - small lotteries incidental to exempt entertainment
  - private lotteries
  - society lotteries.
- Society lotteries are the most attractive for charity fundraisers.
- Society lotteries are subject to controls on:
  - ticket prices
  - ticket particulars
  - prize limits
  - expenses
  - age limits
  - places of sale
  - returns to local authorities or the Gaming Board.

6

Events

6.1 Introduction

Charities organise a wide range of events and for a wide range of reasons. Some events are part of the delivery of the main objects of the charity; some are purely fundraising events, and many are a mixture of fundraising and awareness raising.

Event fundraising raises two key legal questions:

- Who will be organising the event?
- What activities will take place?

This chapter sets out the legal issues arising from the 'who' and also covers the legal issues for a range of fundraising activities. You can read through the chapter as a whole or use the skeleton checklist on pages 74–5 to see which sections are relevant to any specific event you are organising.

6.2 Who is organising the event?

There are a range of possible answers to this question, and the differences are important. For example, an event can be organised by:

- the charity;
- the charity's trading subsidiary;
- a local group/volunteers;
- a paid consultant/agent/company.

6.2.1 Events organised by the charity

Fundraisers must consider whether organising the event is a charitable activity. Some events will fall within the charity's objects (see Chapter 1), for example a conference to raise awareness of issues covered by the charity's objects. On the other hand, many fundraising events do not fall within the charity's objects. Of these, some small events can still be carried out by the charity as being either ancillary to the charity's objects or covered by the small events exemption (see **6.2.2** and Chapter 10).

Larger events that do not fall into either of these two categories should not be carried out by the charity but should be run through a trading subsidiary. For example, the charity's involvement with arrangements for a challenge event are likely to be non-charitable activities; in such a case, the arrangements should be made through a trading subsidiary (see **6.3** for tax advantages to doing this).

Running large events, such as a concert or a week-long cycle ride, successfully requires a considerable amount of expertise. You should consider whether the charity might be better served by hiring the services of a specialist to run the event (see **6.5** for issues to consider when using specialists).

6.2.2 ## Tax

Fundraising itself is not a charitable activity (see Chapter 1), and therefore the starting point is that all income from fundraising will be taxed. If the income from an event is taxable, the charity could lose a significant proportion of the profits to tax. For example, if the charity were a company, the tax would be a minimum of 20 per cent and could be as much as 32.5 per cent depending on its total profit.

Some events, such as a conference to raise awareness of the charity's objects, would be within the charity's objects, and any profit would therefore not be taxable. However, if awareness raising is only a by-product of an event that is mainly organised to raise funds, then the profit could be taxable.

Tax concessions for events

There are two tax concessions that mean a charity could run an event itself without the income being liable to tax. These are:

- The Extra Statutory Concession 4 (ESC4), which is a concession for certain types of fundraising event. Examples of the type of events that can benefit under this exemption include: balls, dinner dances, concerts, plays, films, fetes, festivals, shows, exhibitions, jumble sales, sporting performances, quizzes, auctions, firework displays. Full details of the concession are set out in **10.9**. In particular, there is a requirement that there are no more than 15 events of the same type in the same location in any one year.
- *De minimis* exception, which is a concession that applies where the overall total trading income of a charity is no greater than either £5,000 or the lesser of £50,000 and 25 per cent of the charity's gross income (see **10.10** for full details).

If an event falls within ESC4 or if its income is below the *de minimis* level, there are no adverse tax consequences of running the event through the charity. You may, however, still want to consider running the event through a wholly owned trading subsidiary, as this helps to ringfence risk from the charity.

6.2.3 Tax – events not within the tax concessions

For events outside the tax concessions mentioned above, the profits or surplus will be taxable. In this situation, there are two ways to minimise tax:

- The event could be run through a trading subsidiary. The trading subsidiary will have to pay tax on its profit, but the tax can be recovered by the charity under the deed of covenant (see Chapter 22).
- The charity can run the event, splitting the entrance fee into a basic minimum charge and voluntary donation. Profits or surplus derived from the minimum charge will still be taxable, but the donation element will not be taxable, provided that:
  - the publicity material and tickets clearly state that anyone paying the minimum payment will be admitted;
  - paying over the minimum payment does not lead to additional benefits such as better seats;
  - the amount of extra donation is left to discretion;
  - for film, theatre, concerts and sporting events, the minimum charge is not less than the usual price for the seats at a normal commercial event of the same type;
  - for dances, dinners and similar events, the minimum charges at least cover the total costs of the event (for example, an admission fee of £5 plus donation for a four-course dinner and dance at the London Hilton would not pass this test).

6.2.4 VAT

Income received by a charity in connection with an event (e.g. admission charges, sale of programmes, sale of advertising space in the programmes, sale of T-shirts or other 'souvenirs') are usually subject to VAT. This means that, if a charity is registered for VAT, it will have to pay 17.5 per cent of the income it receives to Customs and Excise (see Chapter 20).

There is a VAT exemption for some fundraising events organised by a charity or its trading subsidiary. If the exemption applies, all income (including any sponsorship income) is treated as being outside the scope of VAT (for full details, see **10.9**).

In some situations, a charity may be better off not using the VAT exemption. For example, if the attendees at an event are businesses that can recover any VAT paid on tickets, the charity can increase its rate of recovery of input tax by charging VAT.

If the VAT exemption does not apply, a charity can minimise VAT by splitting the entry fee into part admission fee/part donation. The qualifying criteria set out above relating to splitting arrangements (in **6.2.3**) also apply to VAT. Any split between an admission fee and a voluntary donation must be genuine. A charity charging an admission fee of £20 plus a 'minimum voluntary donation' of £30 was treated for VAT purposes as having charged a £50 admission fee.

Special VAT rules relevant to event fundraising

Income raised from 'private' advertisements in an event programme or brochure is treated as a donation, provided that not less than 50 per cent of the total advertisements are 'private'. 'Best wishes from Harry and Joan Brown' would be a private advertisement, but 'Best wishes from Harry and Joan Brown, Butchers, 12 High St, Bath' would not be.

There is no VAT on items donated for a raffle.

6.3 Events organised by the trading subsidiary

6.3.1 A charity's trading subsidiary is not bound by the charity law restrictions that prevent a charity carrying out certain activities. The only restrictions on a trading subsidiary are:

- those set out in its Memorandum and Articles of Association (usually they are drafted with no restrictions at all);
- those arising from decisions of the directors not to do certain things (these would be recorded in minutes of directors' meetings).

Therefore, in a number of situations, if a charity uses a trading subsidiary to run an event, it can avoid the problem of engaging in non-charitable activity, and it can minimise tax. However, since trading subsidiaries tend to covenant all their profits to the charity, this can leave the trading subsidiary with no working capital with which to pay the initial expenses for an event.

6.3.2 Tax

The tax concession ESC4 for some fundraising events (see **6.2.2**) does not apply to events organised by a charity's trading subsidiary. The trading company will therefore have to pay tax on profits made from events, although any tax payable on profits can be avoided by donating the company's profits to the charity (see Chapter 22).

6.3.3 Trading subsidiaries and VAT

The VAT exemption for one-off fundraising events applies to qualifying events organised by a charity's wholly owned trading subsidiary, provided its profits are passed to the charity 'under a deed of covenant or trust or otherwise'. Given the new Gift Aid rules (see Chapter 19), most trading companies will now pass their profits to the charity using Gift Aid.

6.4 **Events organised by local groups/volunteers**

6.4.1   With events organised by local groups or volunteers, the legal responsibilities will depend on whether local groups are part of, or separate from, the main charity.

6.4.2   If groups are part of the main charity:

- the charity is ultimately responsible for events organised by the groups;
- money raised belongs to the main charity;
- the main charity must include income and expenses of the local group in its accounts.

6.4.3   If local groups are separate from the main charity:

- the local group should not be using the charity's registered number unless they have permission to do so;
- the local group is primarily responsible for the event (but see **6.4.5** for ways in which the charity could have some liability) – the legal status and effect of fundraising by local groups is a 'grey' area and the legal position depends very much on the actual circumstances;
- any money raised for the charity belongs to the charity and is held on trust by the local group (see Chapter 1);
- any money raised for the local group belongs to the local group;
- the main charity has to include any income received as part of its accounts, but not expenses.

6.4.4   Whatever way your local groups are organised, it is good practice to issue general guidelines to local groups setting out their authority to fundraise on behalf of the charity and any situations where they must seek specific permission from the charity before continuing.

6.4.5   Some charities also issue guidance to volunteers about different ways to fundraise. There is no legal requirement to do this, but if you do, it is worth bearing these two points in mind:

- Any guidance given about legal issues should be correct and comprehensive; if it is not, the charity may be exposed to a claim for negligence.
- By setting out guidance, the charity could be taken to have approved the fact that volunteers carry out certain types of activity in the charity's name. This is a difficult area for fundraisers: on the one hand, you want to encourage fundraising by volunteers; on the other hand, you do not want the charity to be held responsible. Ideally, any guidelines should be carefully worded to make clear the charity is approving certain activities (although only if carried out in accordance with the guidelines), but that ultimately the volunteers remain responsible for all liabilities.

Fundraisers often ask 'What about those events organised by volunteers that we are not even told about?' In a sense, these events are the best of both worlds – the charity cannot be held responsible (unless its general guidance to volunteers covered this type of event), but the money raised belongs to the charity and must be passed by the volunteers to the charity.

6.4.6 Local groups and tax

A local group is unlikely to have any liability to pay income tax on any surplus raised, unless the local group is 'trading'.

6.4.7 Local groups and VAT

For volunteers or local groups that are part of the charity, the VAT treatment of income is the same as if the charity had organised the event.

Volunteers or local groups that are not part of the charity will be assessed for VAT as a separate legal entity. Specifically, Customs and Excise takes the view that the one-off fundraising exemption does not apply unless the local group or volunteers are a charity or not-for-profit organisation in their own right.

In practice, most local groups would not exceed the £52,000 threshold for VAT (2000 figure), so VAT should not be an issue.

6.5 Events organised by a paid consultant/agent/specialist event organiser

6.5.1 If a company or consultant is involved in an event, there are two possible scenarios:

- The event could be an event run by the charity, with the consultant providing services to the charity to help with the arrangement. As long as the consultant or company is only advising and is not soliciting donations for the charity or selling, say, tickets or advertising space, then the legal, tax and VAT issues for this type of arrangement are the same as for charity events (see **6.2.1**). If the consultant is soliciting donations or approaching any third parties for money or donations for the charity, then the consultant will be a professional fundraiser (see Chapter 17).
- The event is not run by the charity – it is run by the consultant or company with all or some of the income going to the charity.

This latter type of event involves issues about the use of the charity's name and logo (see Chapter 8). The consultant or company is also likely to be a 'professional fundraiser' or 'commercial participator' (see Chapter 16 and 17). There are also tax and VAT issues (see Chapters 8, 10 and 20).

6.5.2   If the company or consultant is a professional fundraiser or commercial participator, there is a legal obligation under the Charities Act 1992 to have a written
contract in place. Section 59 of the Charities Act 1992 sets out the points that
must be covered – these are summarised in Chapters 16 and 17.

6.5.3   It is good practice for a charity to have a written record, if not a signed contract, for all other consultants or companies, which will record what the
consultant is doing for the charity. Particular issues to consider and to cover in
contracts include the following:

- What is the paid consultant responsible for doing?
- What is the charity responsible for doing?
- Who is taking out any insurance necessary for the event?
- What happens on cancellation?
- What are the arrangements for collecting money?
- How much is the consultant paid? If pay is linked to profits, is it clear how
  profits are defined?
- Who is responsible for health and safety issues?
- Does the charity have a right to inspect the consultant's records?
- Has the consultant agreed not to do anything that might harm the charity's
  reputation?
- Does the consultant have permission to use the charity's name and logo?

This list is not exhaustive: specific advice should be taken about important
contracts for unusual, high-income or high-risk events.

6.5.4 Tax

ESC4 does not apply to events organised by a company or consultant. The
arrangements are, therefore, usually best structured by the charity charging a
fee to the company for use of its name and logo for the event. This fee is taxable
(subject to the 'annual payment rule' – see **8.6.4**); any other income for the
charity should be given as a donation under Gift Aid, and thus will not be taxable in the charity's hands and will be tax deductible for the organiser.

6.5.5 VAT

The VAT exemption described above does not apply to an event organised by a
company or consultant unless the event falls within the first example given in
6.5.1.

6.6 Activities

The next section of this chapter covers a range of legal issues that occur
depending not on who is organising the event but on what the proposed activities are.

6.6.1 Venue hire

If an event involves hire of a venue, check the maximum number of people the venue can hold. This number is set by fire regulations, and breach is a criminal offence under the Fire Precautions Act 1971.

Make sure you have a clear contract covering hire of a venue (see Chapter 11). The contract does not have to be in writing, but it is better to record the terms agreed in a letter or an agreement. There are certain clauses to look out for in the contract:

- What is included in the price? Do you have to take out separate insurance cover?
- What rights does the hirer have to increase prices?
- What penalties do you pay on cancellation?
- Are there any limits on the hirer's liability if they cancel?
- Are there any limits on numbers or restrictions on access?

6.6.2 Food safety

Any event involving the production, supply or sale of food must comply with the Food Safety Act 1990, Food Safety (General Food Hygiene) Regulations 1995 and other regulations for specific types of food. More detailed information is available from Environmental Health Departments at local authorities.

There are criminal offences for failing to comply with these regulations, which are punishable by a fine and, in severe cases, imprisonment!

6.6.3 Product safety

New or second-hand products sold at an event must comply with any safety standards set by law. There are safety standards covering, for example, electrical goods, toys, and upholstered furniture – and this is by no means a complete list. Up-to-date details can be obtained from local Trading Standards or Consumer Safety Departments.

There are various criminal offences if goods are sold in breach of the safety requirements 'in the course of business' or 'in the course of trade'.

Volunteer events may not be 'business' or 'trade', but even so most charities would prefer not to sell unsafe goods at all. The best procedure is for the charity to recommend to staff and volunteers that they check with Trading Standards before selling donated goods.

6.6.4 Licensing – alcohol

An alcohol licence is required for any event where alcohol will be provided or sold. If the venue does not have a permanent licence, charities (including local branches) can obtain occasional permission to sell alcohol at up to twelve events in any 12-month period. The Licensing Justices at the Magistrates Court for the area in which the event will take place give this permission. An individual who is a 'member' of the charity must make the application; in practice, the chair, vice-chair, secretary or treasurer of the charity must also countersign the application.

If the event is to be on charity premises, the charity will need to comply with the guidelines set out by the Charity Commission in its booklet CC27, 'Providing Alcohol on Charity Premises'.

6.6.5 Licensing – entertainment

Several different types of licence may be needed for entertainment events:

- A public entertainment licence may be needed for events like dances, sporting events, plays, films. You should check this with your local authority.
- A licence from the Performing Right Society (known as the PRS) is needed for live performances and for playing recorded music. The PRS passes the royalties on to the composers or songwriters (or whoever now owns the copyright). Usually, the obligation is on the owner of a venue to hold a licence. Further details can be obtained from the PRS (see p. 243).
- A licence from Phonographic Performance Ltd (known as PPL) is needed for playing recorded music or music from videos. This is a licence fee collected on behalf of the owners of copyright in particular recordings of music. A PPL licence is not needed if everyone involved in organising the event gives their time free and all the money from an event goes to charity. This is interpreted strictly to mean that money cannot be spent even on expenses for the event (e.g. the cost of hiring the venue). Further details can be obtained from PPL (see p. 243).

6.6.6 Health and safety

Under the Health and Safety at Work Act, 1974 a charity will be responsible for breaches of health and safety legislation at any event it organises, for example failing to ensure that fire escapes are not blocked.

6.6.7 First aid

Under the Health and Safety (First Aid) Regulations 1981 there is a legal obligation to provide first aid to employees. There may also be a legal duty to provide first aid to non-employees, if it might be negligent not to do so.

However, it is good practice to have a first-aid box and a suitably qualified first aider at any event. If the event involves large numbers of people (e.g. a sporting event), particularly members of the public, it is worth contacting St John's Ambulance to see if they will provide first-aid cover. You will usually be asked to make a donation to St John's Ambulance in return.

6.6.8 Advertising

If there will be any advertising for an event, see Chapter 15 on advertising.

6.6.9 Public collections

If donations will be collected at or in the near vicinity of an event, check whether any of the legislation concerning public collections applies (see Chapter 4).

6.6.10 Money collected from events

The Charity Commission has issued general recommendations for money collected at events (see **18.2**).

6.7 Sponsorship

6.7.1 Content of sponsor form

- Under section 5 of the Charities Act 1993, all sponsor forms should show the charity's status as a registered charity.
- As a general rule, a sponsor form must disclose any expenses that the charity is paying the participant or any benefit the participant is receiving. This derives from the Johns case described in Chapter 1, where the court held that a collector should disclose any expenses taken from collected money.
- The wording on the form may restrict the purposes for which the sponsor money can be used (see **1.4.6**). Unless you are sure you want to be restricted to a particular purpose, use wording that is as wide as possible in its meaning.
- Where sponsorship is collected before an event (e.g. challenge events), the sponsor form should make clear whether money will be retained or returned if the person either does not take part or fails to complete the event.

6.7.2 Checking suitability to collect

Strictly speaking, there is no legal obligation on charities to vet collectors, as there is under the house-to-house collections legislation. However, it would be good practice to do so, particularly where collectors are collecting large sums of money (e.g. challenge events) or where collectors are given badges or other materials clearly establishing them as the charity's authorised representative.

6.7.3 Guidance on collecting

House-to-house collection of sponsorship, or collecting sponsorship in the street, falls within the regulations covering house-to-house and street collections (see Chapter 4). Participants in such collections will need licences. (See also the other restrictions that apply to street or house-to-house collections, which are set out in Chapter 4.)

6.7.4 Paying sponsorship by Gift Aid

Anyone other than the participants themselves can contribute to sponsorship by making a Gift Aid payment. Participants cannot pay by Gift Aid because they are getting a 'benefit' from participating in the event (see Chapter 19).

6.7.5 Status of money raised

The money raised is either the charity's or the donor's money – it does not belong to the participant. It is the donor's money if the money was given on certain conditions and the conditions have not been satisfied. If, for example, a sponsor gave £26 to someone running in the London Marathon on condition that they completed the full 26¾ miles, the money is the donor's money until the marathon is completed.

If money is given without conditions, or the conditions have been satisfied, the money is held by the participant on trust for the charity. Failure to pass the money to the charity is a breach of trust. If the participant uses the money themselves for another purpose, it is theft (see **23.6**).

6.7.6 Expenses

A participant can only deduct expenses from collected sponsorship monies if either the charity or the donor has consented to this. For example, the charity might give a participant permission to deduct postage and costs of telephone calls from money collected. Similarly, a participant may seek permission from donors to set off part of the money received against paying for, say, an abseil or parachute jump. However, if consent has not been obtained from either the charity or the donor, the participant cannot deduct expenses.

6.7.7 Money in advance or pledges

Until recently, the tradition has been that sponsorship is collected after an event. However, increasingly, and for larger sponsored events in particular, participation requires the advance collection of a minimum amount of sponsorship.

In these circumstances, there are two options to choose between, which involve balancing risks against having to pay VAT:

- Not collecting any money until after the event leaves the charity with the risk of not receiving anything, since a pledge on a sponsor form will not generally be enforceable. However, all money raised will be tax and VAT free.
- Collecting some money before the event ensures the charity has a minimum income. However, if a charity states that participation depends on a minimum amount of sponsorship being raised, Customs and Excise is likely to treat this as an 'entry fee'. Customs has assessed some entry fees as being subject to VAT, on the basis that the participant is receiving certain supplies,

such as the opportunity to participate in an event, in return for the minimum sponsorship.

VAT treatment of sponsorship income is a complex area: to be clear about the implications for any particular event, you should check with your finance department or take professional advice.

6.8 **Providers of equipment and services**

Fundraisers may buy or hire in equipment for events organised by the charity (e.g. tables and chairs, a marquee, a bouncy castle) and may pay for specialist services (e.g. catering, music, arranging bungee jumps).

There is no legal requirement to have a written contract for this, but it is good practice to do so. In addition to the usual basic terms (see **11.10**), the contracts should cover:

- the safety standards that the provider is agreeing to meet for both services and equipment;
- cancellation by either party;
- insurance.

6.9 **Insurance**

For all events, consider what insurance to have in place. This is particularly important for challenge events, which necessarily involve risks to participants. The following different possibilities should be considered:

- Ensuring that any providers of services or equipment have adequate insurance in place in case of accident.
- If appropriate, offering participants their own insurance policies against their liability to third parties, and cover in case of accident.
- Extending the charity/trading subsidiary's policy to cover any residual risk that may fall on the charity/trading subsidiary.

Chapter 14 covers general insurance issues in more detail.

6.10 **Overseas challenge events**

6.10.1 The Package Travel, Package Holidays and Package Tour Regulations 1992 will apply to any event (in the UK or overseas) lasting more than 24 hours or where overnight accommodation is provided, and where two of the following are included in the event:

- travel (i.e. flights, ferries, bus or train travel);
- accommodation;

- other tourist services – these are not defined but would include the provision of bikes, transport to and from a trek, excursions to tourist attractions.

6.10.2   The main effects of the Package Tour Regulations are that:

- participants in an event must, before departure, be given a 'brochure' covering certain minimum information;
- each participant must be given a contract with the tour operator;
- the participant has rights, set out in the Package Tour Regulations, not to have the tour altered, and a right to compensation or cancellation;
- the tour operator must have security (bonding arrangements) for the protection of pre-payments.

Failure to comply with some of these obligations is a criminal offence.

6.10.3   Where an event includes provision of flights, the Civil Aviation (Air Travel Organisers' Licensing) Regulations 1995 will also apply. The main effect of these regulations is to require anyone offering flights to have bonding arrangements to protect money paid by consumers for flights. These regulations are policed by the Civil Aviation Authority (CAA), which has issued guidance notes setting out its view of what charities organising challenge events must do to comply with the regulations.

6.10.4   Overseas challenge events usually involve having a series of contracts that need to dove-tail together to give protection to the charity. A standard event may involve:

- a contract between the tour operator, the charity and its trading subsidiary which, among other things, sets prices and minimum numbers, and which records what happens in the event of cancellation;
- a booking form, signed by the participant, which creates a contract between the participant and the trading subsidiary, setting terms of entry, minimum sponsorship and giving permission to fundraise;
- a contract between the tour operator and the participant (this is needed to comply with the Package Tour Regulations);
- in some cases, where the participant is a 'professional fundraiser' (see **6.12**), a contract between the participant and the charity.

6.10.5   The legal issues for any events involving travel and accommodation are extremely complex, and the risks to a charity or its trading subsidiary are quite different from any other event. A charity should seek professional advice from a specialist solicitor to ensure that it is protected and that no criminal offences will inadvertently be committed.

The ICFM has issued guidelines for overseas challenge events (see Useful addresses, p. 242).

6.11 ICFM code of practice for outdoor land-based fundraising events

At the time of going to press, the ICFM has two codes of practice for outdoor events:

a The Code of Practice for UK Charity Challenge Events is mainly drafted to apply to events in the UK, such as the Three Peaks Challenge, and includes recommendations to:

– consider the effect the event could have on the environment;

– check with landowners and local communities;

– notify police and mountain rescue teams of the event, proposed routes and number of participants;

– have marshals at key points of the route and good communication arrangements – h.f. (high frequency) radio is recommended.

b The Code of Practice for Charity Challenge Events is aimed at challenge events in the UK and overseas and includes guidance on:

– practical issues to consider;

– tax and VAT implications;

– the requirements of the Civil Aviation Authority for any events including flights.

Both codes are well worth reading before planning any outdoor or challenge event.

6.12 Participants as professional fundraisers

In some situations, participants in challenge events may fall within the definition of 'professional fundraiser' (see Chapter 17) if they receive 'remuneration' (i.e. benefit in kind) that is worth £500 or more. Two examples of participants who would be considered professional fundraisers are:

■ a participant in a cycle ride in India – if the market value of the tour is more than £500;

■ a participant who in the same year runs for a charity in both the London and New York marathons – if the value of the marathon entry fees and any flights or accommodation paid for by the charity are worth more than £500.

6.12.1 Refunding entry fees

Some challenge events are organised so that the participant pays their entry fee themselves, and the charity refunds all or part of the entry fee depending on how much sponsorship is raised.

Payments by the charity of this kind are arguably 'ex-gratia' payments. The charity can only make ex-gratia payments if the Charity Commission has consented to this.

Summary – skeleton checklists

Fete/jumble sale/car-boot sale/coffee mornings

- Who is organising it?
- What are the tax/VAT implications?
- Is there any advertising?
- Will there be music?
- Will food and drink be sold?
- Will new or second-hand goods be sold?
- Will there be a raffle?
- Who is taking out any necessary insurance?
- Are there health and safety considerations?
- Does the choice of venue raise any issues?

Play/concert/theatre first night/gala performance

- Who is organising it?
- What are the tax/VAT implications?
- Is any advertising involved?
- How will the tickets be priced? Will there be a minimum fee plus donation?
- Is there a sponsor for the event (see Chapter 8)?
- Does the choice of venue raise any particular issues?
- Will there be brochures or programmes? Are you selling advertising space in the programme?
- Will food and drink be provided?
- Are licences needed for performances or use of music?
- Will there be a raffle?
- Will any souvenirs be sold?
- Are there any implications for health and safety?

Simple sponsored events

- Who is organising it?
- What are the tax/VAT implications?
- What form will the sponsor forms take?
- Are there any implications for health and safety?
- Will you need to organise insurance?
- Will there be music?
- Will there be food and drink?

Challenge events

- Who is organising the event?
- What are the tax/VAT implications?

- Will there be any advertising?
- What will the sponsor forms look like?
- Are there any health and safety issues?
- What insurance will you need to organise?
- What contracts are needed?
- Does the event conform to Package Travel Regulations?
- Will the event conform to Civil Aviation (Air Travel Organisers' Licensing) Regulations 1995?
- Are participants professional fundraisers?

Participative events (e.g. golf days, go-karting, fishing)

- Who is organising it?
- What are the tax/VAT implications?
- Will there be any advertising?
- How is admission to be priced?
- Will there be a raffle?
- Will souvenirs be sold?

7 Employee fundraising

7.1 Introduction

This chapter is very short: its purpose is to point out to fundraisers the most common types of fundraising activity undertaken by people in the workplace, since employees of organisations frequently engage in a variety of fundraising activities for charities. Apart from payroll giving (see **7.6**), none of these is the subject of particular legal controls.

7.2 Events

If a fundraising event for a charity is being put on, the critical thing for a corporate fundraiser is to be aware of who is actually organising the event. Is it the company, the charity or the individual employees of a company? Once this is clear, the fundraisers should refer to Chapter 6 (for events), Chapter 11 (for contracts) and Chapter 14 (for insurance).

7.3 Raffles and competitions

If a fundraiser is arranging for employees to sell tickets for free prize draws, prize competitions or lotteries at the place of work (or anywhere else) the fundraiser should consider the points made in Chapter 5.

7.4 Nominated Charity of the Year

A company might nominate a charity as its 'Charity of the Year'. This could involve a series of complex relationships such as:

- sponsorship by the company of the charity (see Chapter 8);
- the licence by the charity to the company of the charity's name and logo (see Chapter 10);
- gifts in kind from the company to the charity (see Chapter 9);
- encouragement of staff fundraising through a range of events (see Chapter 6).

7.5 Matched giving

One aspect of employee fundraising may be a commitment by the employer to give to the charity a sum equal to that raised by the employees. This may constitute a straight donation by the company, in which case it can be made under Gift Aid (see Chapters 8 and 19 – refer to Chapter 8 also if the company wants something in return).

If the company genuinely wishes to make a donation, but wants to pay at the end of the series of events (for example), then fundraisers should ensure that the company is obligated to make the payment by a deed of gift (see **8.7.4**).

7.6 Payroll giving

Payroll giving is an important potential fundraising mechanism for charities, even if its take-off has been disappointing in the 12 years of its existence. Anyone who is paid by an employer under the PAYE scheme – in other words, over 24 million UK employees and many pensioners as well – is potentially able to make a tax-free donation from their pay. When someone who pays tax at the current (2000) basic rate of 22 per cent donates £1 to charity via a payroll-giving scheme, it costs them only 78p. Put another way, a donation of £1.28 costs the donor the same as a spontaneous, non-tax-effective donation of a £1 coin in a collection box. There is no limit on how much an individual can contribute via payroll giving. For three years from April 2000, the government will pay charities an extra 10 per cent supplement on payroll-giving donations.

Another reason why payroll giving is attractive to charities is that, once a donation begins, inertia often sets in and donors only infrequently cancel the donation to be made. If this is the case, the donation will continue to be made as long as the employee continues at work.

Almost all the fundraising costs of payroll giving are in the first year, namely promotion, getting donors to sign up, monitoring and thanking them. After that, donors are on the charity database, and are available for further relationship building and fundraising. These factors can make the overall fundraising ratio attractive.

7.6.1 How payroll giving works

Payroll giving requires the employer to sign a contract with an Inland Revenue-registered agency charity. There are currently 15 agency charities registered with the Inland Revenue. The four key players are:

- Charities Aid Foundation (CAF), which operates Give As You Earn
- Charities Trust
- South West Charitable Giving
- The Charity Service.

All of these organisations are registered charities. The agency charity acts as a clearing house, distributing payments to charities nominated by the employee. The employee obtains tax relief by having the amount of their donation deducted from their pay before any tax calculations are made under the PAYE scheme.

7.6.2　The co-operation of the employer is vital for the success of a payroll-giving scheme. There is no obligation on employers to allow their employees to participate in payroll giving. Moreover, of course, employers suffer an additional administrative burden, because they have to deduct the gift from the employees' pay and liaise with the agency charity. The employer gets the tax relief on the costs of administering the payroll-giving scheme.

7.6.3　The agency charity acts as an intermediary between the Inland Revenue, the employer and the employee. In order to become registered as an agency charity, it has to comply with Inland Revenue requirements. This means that it must:

- have a contract with each employer;
- provide written receipts to the employer if requested to do so;
- in no circumstances return to the employer or employees any amounts paid over to it;
- pay over to the nominated charities the amounts requested by the employees, subject to any deduction for charges;
- provide, if requested by the employee, a certificate of the amounts paid over to nominated charities;
- in no circumstances retain money – if it proves impossible to pay over to the nominated charity, it must make payment to another with similar objects;
- notify the Inland Revenue within 30 days of entering into an agreement with an employer;
- notify the termination of an agreement within 30 days;
- make an annual return to the Inland Revenue;
- retain records for three years and make them available for inspection as required.

The employer must:

- pay over to the agency charity the amounts deducted within 30 days;
- keep records for at least three years and make them available to the Inland Revenue when requested to do so.

Most agency charities charge around 5 per cent for their services.

7.7 **Recruiting donors**

Charities may use their own fundraising staff or volunteers or a paid professional fundraising organisation to approach potential donors in the workplace and ask them to sign a pledge form. The ICFM has produced a Code of Practice for Payroll Giving that all fundraisers should consider before beginning fundraising (see **7.10**). Face-to-face canvassing has proven to be the most effective way of recruiting donors, because the fundraiser needs to persuade the donor to provide certain basic information, in particular the amount to be donated when completing the pledge. It is quite possible for the donor to nominate more than one charity as the recipient of their donations. Usually there is a space on the donor form for three or four different charities to be nominated.

7.8 Monitoring by charities

Information on new donors is received either:

- directly, by copies of the pledge form;
- indirectly, via the agency charity when income is first received.

Obviously charities should monitor that they receive the monies pledged. As the agency charges a handling fee, it is best to ensure that employees make their contributions monthly rather than weekly, since the latter results in a higher agency fee.

7.9 Charities Act 1992 Part II

If a charity hires an independent agency to seek donors from employees, the agency will be a professional fundraiser for the purposes of Part II Charities Act 1992 (see Chapter 17). This means that the professional fundraiser will need to have a contract with the charity and make a statement in accordance with section 60(1) Charities Act 1992. The ICFM has issued a standard form of contract for this type of fundraising (see Appendix 2, p. 250). The agency should be aware of the type of statement it should make in order to comply with the Charities Act. One such example is the following:

'*Only if payroll-giving support is generated are we paid a fee by the charities we represent. This fee is X per cent of the first year's donation.*'

7.10 The ICFM Code of Practice for Payroll Giving

ICFM members and affiliated organisations whose fundraising campaigns involve payroll giving agree to abide by the ICFM code of practice. In particular, this provides that all such organisations will:

- abide by the Charities Act 1992 Part II and the relevant regulations under it (see Chapter 17);
- promote, support and require adherence to the code of conduct established and agreed by the Association of Payroll Giving Professional Fundraising Organisations;

- ensure that all payroll-giving canvassers soliciting support on behalf of the charity:
  - do not inflict undue pressure on the potential donors to sign a pledge for payroll giving;
  - do not actively encourage existing donors in any way to change their donation to another charity;
  - act at all times in an honest manner that will in no way mislead existing or potential donors;
  - enable donors freely to select any charity of their choice, without duress, whether represented by the canvasser concerned or otherwise;
  - support those donors who wish to remain anonymous or do not wish to receive further literature or information, by marking the appropriate forms clearly to this effect;

- ensure that all payroll-giving canvassers soliciting support on behalf of their charity will not:
  - knowingly or recklessly disseminate false or misleading information in the course of their fundraising activities nor, where they have responsibility, permit others to do so;
  - imply or state to existing or potential donors that payroll donations are made for a specific, short time span;
  - imply in any manner or state that they represent any organisation other than the organisation they have been authorised to represent in connection with a particular campaign connected to that solicitation;
  - imply in any manner or state that they are a volunteer or paid employee of the charity that they are authorised to represent in connection with the solicitation in question, when this is not the case;

- when payroll-giving solicitation is undertaken by a professional fundraiser, the solicitation should comply with the requirements of Part II Charities Act 1992 – in particular it should ensure that all canvassers connected with them wear visibly, at all times during the course of payroll-giving solicitation, an identity badge (provided by the payroll-giving professional fundraising organisation) that complies fully with the statement required under the Charities Act 1992 Part II section 60(1) and that canvassers, if asked, will describe their role as 'representing' or 'working on behalf of' client charities.

7.11 Some charities have set up consortia to promote payroll giving. Donations to Charities at Work, for example, are shared between Help the Aged, Scope, RSPB, the British Red Cross Society and NSPCC. A consortia agreement helps to reduce costs, because the option of making one donation to support a variety of causes is very appealing to donors. Before attempting to create a consortium, however, fundraisers should consider how the charities involved will co-ordinate the administration, allocate the budgets and share the income. Moreover, producing shared promotional material can be expensive and time consuming and requires careful consideration.

Summary

- Most of what is known as employee fundraising is simply different fundraising methods within the workplace. In this case, the usual regulations covered in other chapters apply.

- Payroll giving is a tax-efficient method of giving directly from a donor's salary. It is administered by the donor's employer and an Inland Revenue-registered agency charity.

- For three years from April 2000 the government is giving a 10 per cent supplement on payroll giving donations.

- The ICFM has a Code of Practice for Payroll Giving.

8
Money from businesses

8.1 Introduction

Charities can receive money from businesses in many different ways. There is a sliding scale from pure donations to straightforward commercial dealings that involve the business advertising its name and logo at charity events or on the charity's products, and the charity licensing its name and logo to the business. Charities need to be very careful in licensing their names to commercial partners (see **1.6** and **16.4**).

Very often the crucial aspect of the relationship between charities and businesses is the degree of recognition the business wants in return for its support.

Many different words are used in this area and it is worthwhile always being clear about their meaning:

- A 'grant' is a form of donation.
- A 'donation' is a payment for which the business supporter expects no or minimal benefits in return.
- 'Sponsorship' involves payment by the sponsor to the charity in return for the charity advertising the sponsor's support.
- 'Cause-related marketing' describes the relationship between a charity and a business supporter whereby the two organisations' names are closely linked for the purposes of promoting the supporter's business.
- 'Commercial participator' is a term defined in the Charities Act 1992 – all arrangements with commercial participators will be a form of cause-related marketing (see Chapter 16 for a more detailed explanation).

8.2 Donations

8.2.1 VAT

A donation is outside the scope of VAT provided that none or only very minimal benefits are accorded to the donor. Any display of the donor's logo or use of its corporate style will transform a donation into the provision by the charity of advertising services to the donor: this will then attract VAT. It is possible for a charity to give public recognition to the donor without triggering an obligation to charge VAT in circumstances:

- where the value of the advertising service rendered by the charity and all other VATable outputs made by it does not exceed £52,000 in any one year (i.e. so that the charity is not registered for VAT – this is the 2000 figure);
- where the donor's name, but not its logo, is printed inconspicuously on an annual report, programme, etc.;
- where the donor's name is placed on the back of a theatre seat.

8.2.2 Tax-efficient gifts made by companies

A company can use a deed of covenant or Gift Aid to make a donation to a charity in a tax-efficient manner (see Chapter 19). A corporate supporter can also make a tax-efficient donation to a charity by means other than Gift Aid or deeds of covenant if it relies on section 577(9) Income Corporation Taxes 1988. This applies if:

- there is some form of advertising accorded to the donor;
- the gift is made for the benefit of a body or association of persons established for educational, cultural, religious, recreational or benevolent purposes, and:
  - the body or association is local in relation to the donor's business activities;
  - it is not restricted to persons connected to the donor;
  - the expenditure is reasonably small in relation to the scale of the donor's business.

Given the advertising element that is necessary in this concession, the charity will need to consider the VAT position. It will have to charge VAT to the corporate supporter if the charity is registered for VAT. This will not, however, be a problem for the business unless it carries on VAT-exempt activities (see **8.6**).

8.3 Taxation – business relationship

The relationship between a charity and a business supporter changes when this support moves from the receipt of a grant or donation to sponsorship or cause-related marketing, and both parties need to be very clear about what is expected of each other. As soon as the business starts looking for publicity for its support beyond that minimal level allowed by the rules regarding Gift Aid, deeds of covenant (see Chapter 19) or VAT (see **8.2.1**), the charity will need to consider how to structure the relationship. The first question a charity should ask in order to ascertain the nature of this relationship is 'From what budget is the business making this payment to us?'

If the payment is coming from the business's charity budget, the business may be willing to make the payment under Gift Aid – in which case, there will be no

VAT consequences because it will have been accorded a minimal level of bene-fits. If, on the other hand, the payment is coming from its advertising or corporate affairs budget, then the business will clearly be regarding the pay-ment as a tax-deductible business expense, in return for which it will be receiving tangible forms of publicity to advertise its support. Publicising the business's name by the charity amounts to a VATable advertising service (see **8.2.1**). Equally, there is a VATable service if a business is granted the right to use the charity's name and/or logo in conjunction with its business in return for payment.

This means that, if the charity is already registered for VAT, it will have to charge VAT on the licence or sponsorship fee. If it is not registered for VAT, but the value of the licence or sponsorship fee – together with any other VATable supplies already made by the charity – amounts to £52,000 in any one year (2000 figure), then it will have to register for VAT and charge VAT on the licence and/or sponsorship fee and/or other VATable outputs.

Important information for negotiations with businesses

When negotiating with businesses, fundraisers should have the following information readily to hand:

- a copy of the charity's objects to show how monies received from the spon-sor will be spent (see **1.3**);
- details about a trading subsidiary, if the charity has one (see Chapter 22);
- clarification of the charity's VAT status (e.g. are the charity and its trading subsidiary registered for VAT, and are they part of a VAT group?);
- some understanding of how the business will publicise its link with the charity;
- explanation of how the charity will publicise its link with the business;
- details of any registered trademarks the charity may have;
- an indication of how likely it is that the charity will receive a surplus as a result of the relationship.

8.4 Sponsorship

Sponsorship is a word used to describe the relationship between a business and a charity where the charity accepts payment from the business in return for advertising the business's support. The advertising can take a variety of forms.

8.4.1 Some examples of sponsorship

- An acknowledgement using the sponsor's name and logo, in its corporate style, on a charity's annual report, on a programme or on its letterhead.
- Hospitality given to the sponsor at an event.

- Display of the sponsor's name and logo at an event put on by the charity which could be for fundraising purposes or in fulfilment of its primary purpose (e.g. a concert by a charitable choral society).
- Putting the sponsor's name and logo on the side of vehicles operated by a charity.

8.4.2 The provision of sponsorship services to business is not within the objects or primary purposes of a charity (see Chapter 10). The sponsorship services provided may be sufficiently small to constitute ancillary trading (see Chapter 10), but, if they do not, then the charity should consider setting up a trading company to operate this service.

8.4.3 The provision of advertising services to a sponsor is a VATable supply, with one exception only. If a sponsor supports a one-off fundraising event that falls within the VAT exemption (see Chapter 6), the sponsorship income is also treated as exempt from VAT. With the exception of this one exemption, sponsorship income is subject to VAT, and charities, or charities' associated trading companies, will have to charge VAT to the sponsor subject to the VAT registration threshold (see **8.3**). This will cause problems for those sponsors who carry on VAT-exempt activities such as banking or insurance services (see **8.6**).

8.4.4 Sponsorship income is usually obtained to underwrite the costs of a particular service or event. It would be unlikely for a charity to make a surplus on sponsorship, although it is possible. If a charity carries on a sponsorship business and makes a surplus from those activities, it may, or may not, be liable to pay corporation tax on any profits. Whether or not tax will be payable depends upon the way in which the profits have been generated. If the profits are part of a primary-purpose trading activity (see Chapter 10), then they will be deemed to be tax free. If, on the other hand, the profits are not derived from a primary-purpose trading activity, then they will be taxable.

8.4.5 This is a complicated area. Charities should not hesitate to take appropriate professional advice on these matters. Those forms of sponsorship income that do not follow a primary-purpose trade should be put through a separate non-charitable trading company, unless the profits derived from the sponsorship after allowing for all reasonable expenses are small and fall within the *de minimis* exemption (see **10.10**).

8.5 Cause-related marketing

Charities are increasingly involved in relationships with commercial organisations that involve licensing their name and/or logo to the commercial partner. The Charities Act 1992 Part II recognised this with the controls that it introduced on commercial participators (see Chapter 16 for further details).

8.5.1 Examples of cause-related marketing

- Affinity Credit Cards, where a charity licenses its name and logo to a credit card operator.
- A charity licensing its name to appear on a commercial product (e.g. a tub of margarine) in return for a statement being made (e.g. '10p per tub sold is given to XYZ Charity').
- A charity licensing its name to a holiday company that states '10 per cent of the price of your holiday will be given to XYZ Charity'.

All these types of activity are called cause-related marketing (CRM). Business in the Community (BitC) has produced a very useful publication that defines CRM as 'a commercial activity by which business and charities or causes form a partnership with each other to market an image, product or service for mutual benefit' (BitC, 1998).

The BitC booklet states that:

'where price and quality are equal, a partnership between a business and a charity or cause can strongly influence purchases:

- *86 per cent of consumers are more likely to buy a product that is associated with a cause or issue;*
- *86 per cent of consumers agree that they have a more positive image of a business if they see it is doing something to make the world a better place.'*

8.5.2 Before entering into a CRM arrangement, fundraisers need to consider a number of key points.

Selecting the partner

You need to be certain that the partnership will be appropriate, that being connected with this particular commercial organisation will not be detrimental to your charity. You therefore need to be very clear in negotiating with potential partners about their objectives, budgets and timing and what you want to get out of the relationship. This may involve not just a CRM arrangement but also employee fundraising, matched giving and other possibilities.

Negotiating the partnership

You need to be very clear that you and your partner share the same objectives. If there are conflicts, how will they be reconciled? BitC recommends that the charity and its commercial partner should audit the potential contribution and support from:

- employees, volunteers, supporters, beneficiaries
- partner organisations
- suppliers
- customers

- government
- other non-governmental agencies.

The contract

A CRM contract will be subject to the controls on relationships with commercial participators analysed in Chapter 16. In addition, the Charity Commission has laid down guidance for charities that are considering licensing their names to commercial partners. Their advice is:

'*The charity's name is a valuable asset. It is the means by which it is identified in the central register of charities and to the public. Before allowing the use of a charity name on a commercial basis, the charity trustees must first consider the needs of the charity, and whether funds could be raised by other methods … . If a charity's name is used commercially it must be shown that the arrangement is:*

- *expedient*
- *in the interests of the charity*
- *on terms which are advantageous to the charity.*

Any such arrangements must be precisely defined by the charity trustees and every detail kept under review.'

(See **16.4.3** on how to ensure that a contract with a commercial partner is drafted so as to protect the charity.)

8.5.3 Cause-related marketing – VAT

Where a charity permits the commercial partner under a CRM deal to use the charity's name and logo in connection with the partner's business, VAT will have to be charged on the fee. This is not a problem for many businesses, which can recover any input VAT charged to them. However, for those businesses carrying on VAT-exempt supplies (e.g. banking or insurance services), VAT is a problem (see **8.6**).

8.5.4 Cause-related marketing – taxation

CRM deals involve a charity licensing its name and/or logo to a commercial partner. This is not a primary-purpose trading activity; it is a form of trade. Therefore, any profits that the charity derives from the activity will be taxed except in certain exceptional circumstances. It is possible for a charity to license its name and/or logo to a commercial partner in return for a fee. If the charity can set the arrangement up as an 'annual payment', then that fee can be received by the charity free of tax of any profits (it will still be subject to VAT). This can only happen if the charity licenses its name and/or logo to the business and does nothing else in return and incurs no expenses whatsoever in conjunction with the licensing: in this way, the income received is 'pure income profit'. The agreement has to be capable of lasting for more than one year. Although the system refers to 'annual payments', it is possible to have more than one payment within a year; in other words, there can be more than one payment per annum and the donation still count as an annual payment.

Annual payments are complex and are rather like deeds of covenant. Any charity that is considering entering into a CRM arrangement with a commercial partner whereby the charity will license its name and/or logo for more than one year would be well advised to take professional advice to ensure that the agreement is set up in the right way.

Where the CRM arrangement requires the charity to provide more than just the licence of its name and/or logo, a charity cannot use the annual payment method. Typical examples of this would involve the charity:

- licensing its database;
- advertising the relationship with the commercial partner and its products.

If the charity undertakes any of these activities it will jeopardise any use of the annual payment method.

In cases where the annual payment route cannot be used, the charity should undertake the CRM contract through a trading company in order to avoid problems with direct taxation. The use of a trading company strains the language of the Charities Act 1992 Part II (to put it mildly), but it is the only way in which the charity can make the arrangements in a tax-efficient manner. Under these arrangements the charity will license its trading company to exploit the charity's name and logo for commercial purposes (see Chapter 22). The trading company will then license the commercial partner with the name and logo and any other rights (e.g. databases, subject to having appropriate clearances under the Data Protection Act – see Chapter 12).

The charity will join in the agreement as well to satisfy the requirements of the Charities Act 1992.

This arrangement will allow the payments for the use of the charity's name and logo to be made to the trading company. The trading company will be able to covenant any profits tax free to the charity (see **22.10**). If this is not done, and the charity licenses its name and logo and makes a profit, the profit will be taxable. That would be very dangerous for the trustees of the charity, as it could be taken as evidence that they have negligently managed the charity. This will in turn expose them to a potential personal liability to indemnify the charity for any loss it suffered in paying tax that could have been avoided by taking appropriate legal safeguards.

8.5.5 Standard contracts

There are standard contracts in Appendices 3, 4 and 5 that deal with situations where:

- a charity licenses its name and logo for more than a year and does nothing else (Appendix 3);
- a charity licenses its name and logo for more than one year, and its trading company agrees to provide other services (e.g. joint marketing) (Appendix 4);
- a charity and its trading company enter into a licensing agreement for less than one year (Appendix 5).

These are useful guides, but you may still need legal advice in adapting them to suit your particular needs.

8.6 VAT and exempt businesses

8.6.1 Some businesses (e.g. banks and insurance companies) that enter into sponsorship or licensing arrangements with charities that attract VAT face problems because the business cannot recover the VAT charged. VAT is effectively a further business expense and reduces the profits of the business. As a result, businesses carrying on VAT-exempt supplies are reluctant to pay VAT. If, in a corporate sponsorship arrangement, the sponsor is told by a charity that VAT will have to be charged, and the sponsor's business is exempt, the sponsor will normally insist that the charity bears the cost of the VAT. This will reduce the value of the sponsorship by 17.5 per cent.

8.6.2 Faced with this, a charity can usually justify making arrangements for the sponsorship or licensing fee to be divided between a charge for the service, which attracts VAT, and a donation. To do this, the charity will need to ascertain the proper market value of the advertising or licensing services that it is providing to the business. Working out what is an appropriate charge for these services is difficult, as there is no ready reckoner. The charge made must be reasonable and justifiable.

The charity's trading company will render a VAT invoice for the advertising/licensing services. The balance of the agreed support can be made as a genuine donation to the charity under Gift Aid by the business.

8.6.3 An example of how to divide a sponsorship sum between a charge for the service and a donation

Without this division, the sponsorship would look like this:

- Sponsorship   £100,000
- Less VAT   £17,500
- Net   £82,500

With the division, it would look like this:

- Advertising charge (inclusive of VAT)   £10,000
- Advertising charge   £8,510
- VAT   £1,490
- Net   £8,510
- Donation   £90,000
- Total   £98,510

8.6.4   If the charity adopts this procedure, it should ensure that the business is contractually obligated to make the donation. A donation is not legally enforceable unless the promise to pay is made by a deed, so the charity should prepare a deed of donation. This may sound excessively cautious, but it is quite possible for a business to agree to make a charitable donation, and for the charity to advertise the fact that it is receiving the donation – only to find that the company is taken over, and the new proprietors refuse to honour the promise. If the promise has been made by a deed, the charity could bring an action for enforcement of the deed. A deed has to contain specific wording to be valid, so it is wise to take professional advice on drafting it.

8.7 **Affinity cards**

8.7.1   Many charities have entered into arrangements with banks and other financial institutions whereby the financial institution issues a credit card that bears the name and/or logo of the charity. Supporters of the charity are encouraged to take out such cards, because the bank pays a fee for every card issued, plus a percentage of the total expenditure on the card, to the charity. The bank will be given access to the names and addresses of the charities' supporters/donors for the purposes of marketing the card. This is a joint promotional arrangement that can benefit both parties.

8.7.2   You need to be aware that arrangements with affinity card companies fall within the controls under Part 2 of the Charities Act 1992, since the affinity card company is a commercial participator (see Chapter 16).

8.7.3 **VAT**

Affinity cards enjoy a unique concession so far as VAT is concerned, but the concession cannot automatically be extended to other areas. Customs are prepared to accept that only 20 per cent of the initial payment is deemed to be payment for the promotional services that will attract VAT. The balance of the initial payment and any subsequent payments (i.e. those linked to use of the card) are treated as outside the scope of VAT. This is somewhat strange because Customs and Excise is effectively treating the licence by the charity of its name as outside the scope of VAT, which it normally does not do! It is essential that arrangements with affinity card companies are structured so that the trading company provides the promotional services and is paid 20 per cent of the initial payment in return for the services.

8.7.4 Direct taxation

The Inland Revenue has accepted the split arrangements that have been negotiated with Customs and Excise. The Revenue has also accepted that payment for the use of the charity's name can be made as an annual payment and therefore received by the charity effectively tax free (see **8.5.4**).

8.8 CAF vouchers

A number of businesses give money under Gift Aid to CAF and receive CAF cheques in return. These cheques are a mechanism to make donations to charities out of funds that have been paid under Gift Aid. A donor who makes a donation under Gift Aid is not entitled to any material benefits in return (see Chapter 19). The CAF vouchers make it very clear that they cannot be used to obtain benefits for the donor.

Nonetheless, many businesses seek to pay for sponsorship arrangements using CAF vouchers. Such a practice is contrary to the Gift Aid rules and the rules of the CAF vouchers. Fundraisers should be aware of this and should draw this to corporate supporters' attention where appropriate.

8.9 Tables 8.1 and 8.2 summarise the different tax and VAT implications of different types of relationship between a charity and a business (pp. 92–93).

8.10 Landfill Tax

8.10.1 Landfill Tax, first introduced in 1996, is payable by all persons who operate landfill sites and is designed to reduce the amount of waste deposited in landfills. The Landfill Tax Credit Scheme was established to encourage environmental activities. Under this scheme, landfill site operators can agree to pay up to 20 per cent of their Landfill Tax liability to an environmental body, rather than to HM Treasury.

8.10.2 An environmental body has to be registered with the government agency Entrust, and a large number of environmental charities have already done so. Any scheme that environmental bodies wish to fund through the Landfill Tax Credit Scheme must be approved by Entrust in advance.

8.10.3 The environmental body can agree with a Landfill Site Operator (LSO) that the LSO will make a payment to the environmental body for an approved scheme.

(continued p. 93)

TABLE 8.1 **Money from business (charity)**

WHAT CHARITY IS WILLING TO DO IN RETURN	CORPORATION TAX	VAT	NATURE OF PAYMENT
Nothing.	Company can use Gift Aid or deed of covenant.	No need for charity to charge VAT.	Donation/grant
Charity just acknowledges gift in its annual report, using the company's name in the same typeface as the rest of the page.	Company can use Gift Aid or deed of covenant.	No need for charity to charge VAT.	Donation/grant
Charity acknowledges gift in its annual report, using the company's name in the company's corporate style.	Company cannot use Gift Aid or deed of covenant. Inland Revenue could refuse charity tax reclaim. Money paid is a business expense.	VAT is chargeable – see option for splitting (8.7.2), if charity is VAT registered.	Sponsorship
Charity acknowledges money in its annual report, using the company's name and logo in its corporate style.	Company cannot use Gift Aid or deed of covenant. Inland Revenue could refuse charity's tax reclaim. Money paid is a business expense.	VAT is chargeable – see option for splitting (8.7.2), if charity is VAT registered.	Sponsorship
Hospitality, e.g. reception where company is invited on condition it makes a donation.	Company cannot use Gift Aid or deed of covenant. Inland Revenue could refuse charity's tax reclaim. Money paid is a business expense.	VAT is chargeable – see option for splitting (8.7.2), if charity is VAT registered.	Sponsorship
Naming event or building after sponsor.	Company cannot use Gift Aid or deed of covenant. Inland Revenue could refuse charity's tax reclaim. Money paid is a business expense.	No need to charge VAT.	Sponsorship
Using company's logo on a banner at a one-off fundraising event.	Company cannot use Gift Aid or deed of covenant. Inland Revenue could refuse charity tax reclaim. Money paid is a business expense.	No need to charge VAT – one-off fundraising event exemption.	Sponsorship

TABLE 8.2 Money from business (company)

WHAT COMPANY IS ALLOWED TO DO IN RETURN	TAX	VAT	NATURE OF PAYMENT
Company publicises its gift in press releases using the charity's name in the same typeface as the rest of the press release.	Company can use Gift Aid.	No need for charity to charge VAT.	Donation/ grant
Company publicises link with charity on products or in advertisements for products/ services.	Cannot be paid under Gift Aid. Licence fee paid is a business expense.	VAT is chargeable – see option for splitting (8.7.2), if charity is VAT registered.	This is cause-related marketing – see Chapter 16 to check if the company is a commercial participator

8.10.3 (cont'd)

EXAMPLE

A charity, which is an environmental body, has an approved scheme with Entrust to plant trees on derelict land within 15 miles of a landfill site. The cost of the project is £100,000.

An LSO agrees to make a contribution of £100,000 to the environmental body.

The LSO will be able to attain a tax credit against its liability for Landfill Tax of 90 per cent of the amount of its contribution (i.e. £90,000). The LSO will therefore have paid £10,000 of its own money towards the environmental body.

8.10.4 In the example, the LSO has had to pay 10 per cent of the contribution to the environmental body. This makes many LSOs reluctant or unwilling to use the Landfill Tax Credit Scheme. However, in some cases it has been possible to arrange for a third party to agree to indemnify the LSO for the lost 10 per cent. Under this scenario, using the example above, the LSO might be reluctant to make the payment of £100,000 to the environmental body (because it will cost them £10,000), but they might well be willing to make the full payment if a third party will compensate them for the £10,000. If that were to happen, the third party's support of £10,000 will have been multiplied in value by ten. Fundraisers for environmental charities may wish to consider using this mechanism to increase spectacularly the value of corporate support for an appropriate charity.

8.10.5　The payment by the LSO to the environmental body, if it is a charity, can be structured as a Gift Aid payment. No VAT will need to be charged on the donation.

Summary

- Donations do not attract VAT.
- Always be clear how a corporate supporter is paying you: is it in the form of a donation or a payment for services?
- Take professional advice where necessary.
- It may be possible to structure arrangements to reduce the adverse impact of VAT on companies carrying on exempt businesses.

9

Gifts in kind

9.1 Introduction

This chapter considers two forms of gifts in kind:

- donation of equipment
- secondment of employees.

Supporters of charities who are asked to make donations in kind will want to know whether they:

- will obtain tax relief on the value of the gift;
- can reclaim the VAT incurred on the purchase of an item that they subsequently donate.

The charity, for its part, will want to be clear about what benefits (if any) it can give the donor in return.

9.2 Business gifts

Tax relief is available on the donation of equipment after 27 July 1999 to charities and educational establishments. The relief is available if:

- the donor donates articles that it manufactures or sells in the course of its trade (and which qualify as machinery or plant in the hands of the educational establishment);
- the donor donates an article that it has used in its trade and against which it has, in the case of a donation to an educational establishment, claimed capital allowances.

Items such as computers, television sets, furniture and some types of laboratory equipment will all qualify as machinery or plant.

The donor is entitled to treat the expenses it has incurred in relation to the donated plant and equipment as having been expended in the course of the business. Provided the donor receives no benefits in return, it will not be considered to have received any taxable income on the disposal of the asset. The fact that it has given the asset away will not expose the donor to a 'claw back' of any capital allowances it has received on the donated plant and machinery. This kind of donation has no tax disadvantage for the donor.

9.3 Charities and gifts in kind

Charities that are offered gifts in kind should give careful consideration to whether or not it is appropriate to accept the gift. A gift may not be without disadvantages: it may bring with it liabilities, and it may pose risks. For example, a charity might be offered the use of a building, rent free, subject to the charity abiding by the terms of a lease. The lease will almost invariably impose obligations concerning repairs, maintenance and so on. It may seem churlish for a charity to quibble about the terms of such a lease, but it should certainly check what obligations it will incur as a result of entering into the arrangement. The liabilities that it might incur for repairs, etc. could well outstrip the benefits it receives in terms of rent-free accommodation. Moreover, the building might be unsuitable for the charity's purposes.

Charities need to weigh up the benefits of any proposed gift and only accept it once they have decided that the likely advantages and benefits outweigh the likely detriments.

Gifts in kind could include:

- rent-free accommodation of a building
- second-hand computers and office equipment
- educational materials
- books
- software programmes
- free use of facilities (e.g. conference rooms, etc.).

9.4 The donor and VAT

A business that donates new equipment to a charity cannot offset the input VAT it has paid when purchasing the equipment against its liability for output VAT, because the equipment has not been used in connection with the business. If the equipment has been used in the business, there are complicated rules about apportioning the amount of input VAT that the business can recover. You should take professional advice on this.

9.5 Secondments

9.5.1 A business's secondment of employees to a charity for a temporary period is another way in which a business can give tax-efficient support to a charity. All the expenses relating to the secondee's employment (national insurance, pension costs, benefits, salaries, etc.) can be allowed as a tax-deductible business expense in the donor's account. There is no definition of what is meant by 'temporary', nor is there a limit set out on the number of employees that any employer can second. The relief does not apply if the employee is seconded to work for the charity's trading company.

9.5.2 Before a charity accepts the secondment it should consider the following questions:

- Is the secondee suitable for the charity's purposes?
- What would the period of the secondment be? If it is too short, this may involve the charity in disproportionate expense in terms of briefing the secondee and integrating them into the charity.
- Who is responsible for discipline? The employer should be – but they should be under an obligation to take steps to discipline the secondee when requested to do so by the charity.
- The charity should make sure the secondee is included in the employer's liability insurance cover.

The charity should ensure that a proper secondment agreement is drawn up with the employer so that all terms of the secondment are clear.

9.5.3 Charities should also be aware of the impact of the Charities Act 1992, Part II on secondees (see Chapter 17). There is a strong argument that a secondee who solicits funds for a charity is a professional fundraiser within the definition in section 58(1) Charities Act 1992. The reason for this is that the secondee is paid to solicit money or other property for the benefit of the charity to which they have been seconded. The secondee is not an employee of the charity – employees of a charity are not professional fundraisers. Therefore, a secondee who does fundraise for the charity to which they have been seconded should give the statement required by section 60(1) Charities Act 1992 (see **17.7**). This can be used to the advantage of the employer who has seconded the employee, because the employer's support of the charity could be made clear as part of the statement.

9.6 **Accounting for gifts in kind**

9.6.1 SORP 2 requires that gifts in kind are brought into account in the charity's Statement of Financial Activities in the following ways:

- Assets given for distribution by the charity should be recognised as income only for the year when they were distributed. Where there are undistributed assets at the year end, a description of the items involved and an estimate of their value should be given by way of a note to the accounts.
- Assets given for use by the charity (e.g. property for its own occupation) should be recognised as incoming resources when receivable.

- Where a gift has been made in kind but on trust for the charity to convert it into cash, it should normally be accounted for in the accounting period when due to be received; in certain cases, this will not be practical (e.g. second-hand goods donated for re-sale in charity shops). In these cases, the income should be included in the accounting period in which the gift is sold.

In all cases, the amount at which gifts in kind are brought into account should be either a reasonable estimate of their value to the charity or the amount actually realised. The basis of the valuation should be disclosed. Where material, an adjustment should be made to the original valuation upon subsequent realisation of the gift.

9.6.2 Where a charity receives assistance in the form of donated facilities, such assistance is referred to as 'intangible income'. Such intangible income has to be included in the Statement of Financial Activities if the charity would otherwise have to purchase the donated facilities, and the benefit is quantifiable and material.

Summary

- Businesses can make gifts in kind to charities without incurring a tax liability.
- The VAT rules on gifts in kind are complicated, and each case should be checked separately.
- A charity can refuse to accept a gift in kind.
- Make sure you have a proper secondment agreement.

10

Charities and commercial trading

10.1 Trading

As a fundamental rule, charities can only carry on a trade:

- if the trade is in fulfilment of the charity's objects (see **1.3**);
- by concession (as outlined in **10.8–10.10**).

Section 832(1) of the Income and Corporation Taxes Act 1988 (the 'Taxes Act') defines 'trade' as 'every trade, manufacture, adventure or concern in the nature of trade'. This is a wonderfully circular definition and a statement of the obvious: Trade = trade = trade! For this reason, the Taxes Act does not assist very much in working out what trade is. Over the years the courts have considered this question on a number of occasions and have developed a number of tests to determine whether or not trading is taking place. These so-called 'badges of trade' are as follows:

- There must be repetition: a one-off transaction is unlikely to amount to trading, but the position is not always so simple. In one case, an individual who ran a cinema purchased and sold a quantity of toilet paper as a single job lot, thereby making a profit. He was taxed on the profits of the sale because there was a profit motive and because of the nature of the goods involved.
- One of the key 'badges of trade' is that there should be a profit motive, and, of course, all charity fundraising activities aim to make a surplus or profit!
- Some form of selling organisation must exist (e.g. a shop or mail order catalogue).
- Items must be acquired for the purpose of being resold (e.g. Christmas cards and T-shirts).

For a trade to be carried out, it is not necessary for a particular activity to display all four 'badges of trade'. If one or more is present, that may be sufficient to establish that there is a trade. The cinema owner who sold a job lot of toilet paper did not repeat the exercise and did not have a specific selling organisation. However, the presence of the profit motive and the nature of the goods bought and resold were sufficient in that case to allow the Inland Revenue to establish that there was a trading activity.

10.2 **Fundraising versus trading**

A charity must be able to decide if particular income-generating activities are merely fundraising or amount to trading. The following list illustrates how the 'badges of trade' test can be applied to particular activities.

Sale of tickets to an annual ball

- Although the ball is run annually, that amount of repetition will not constitute trading.
- There is a profit motive.
- There is no formal selling organisation.

Sale of tickets to an annual ball is therefore fundraising. However, if the ball is run regularly (i.e. more than 15 times a year) in the locality, then the Inland Revenue will regard this as trading.

Sale of Christmas cards

- Unlike an annual ball, the sale of cards is repeated over a period of weeks or months.
- There is a profit motive.
- The goods were purchased with the intention of resale.
- There is a selling organisation, be it through shops, halls or a network of supporters.

Sale of Christmas cards is therefore trading.

Sale of tickets by charitable theatre

- There is repetition.
- There is probably a profit motive (even if the organisation receives a public subsidy).
- The service (spending money on putting on plays and recouping investment through ticket sales) is of a commercial nature.
- There is a selling organisation.

So, sale of tickets by a charitable theatre is trading.

A charitable school running occasional quiz nights to raise money for the building fund

- There is no regular repetition.
- There is a profit motive.

- The nature of the service is not of a commercial nature.
- There is no selling organisation.

This is fundraising.

10.3 Trading by charities

In charity law, a charity can carry on a trade in fulfilment of its main objects or primary purpose (see **1.3.2**). In other words, if a charity is established to run a hospital, it is perfectly legitimate for the charity to charge its patients for the supply of medical facilities, even with a view to making a surplus. The following list illustrates the range of trading activities that charities undertake in the course of fulfilling their primary purposes. It is not comprehensive. The charities have been divided into the four heads of charity (see **1.2**).

(a) The relief of poverty

- **Workshops for the poor** – the sale of goods by the beneficiaries of a charity established in the United Kingdom to relieve poverty.
- **Almshouses** – an almshouse charity may charge maintenance contributions for the services provided to the residents.

(b) The advancement of education

- **University presses and others** – a number of universities have their own publishing arms which carry on the trade of commissioning, publishing and selling books in order to advance education (e.g. Oxford University Press, Cambridge University Press).
- **Musical societies** – societies like choral societies and orchestras charge people to come and hear them.
- **Opera houses and theatres** – such as the Royal Opera House and the English National Opera.
- **Universities and charitable private schools** – universities and other charitable education institutions carry on a primary-purpose trade by providing educational places in return for fees.

(c) The advancement of religion

- **Retreat centres** – many religious organisations run retreat centres, which charge fees for courses, meals and accommodation.
- **Religious publications** – the commissioning, publication and sale of printed matter such as prayer books and religious literature.
- **Coffee shops** – some religious groups run coffee shops as a form of outreach into the community; people can drop in, receive counselling and witness the particular faith in action.

(d) Other charitable purposes beneficial to the community

- **Health services** – fee charging by independent charitable hospitals, e.g. The London Clinic.
- **Care services** – charities that charge local authorities for the provision of care services under contract.
- **Recreational services** – a city farm charging for riding lessons.
- **Environmental charities** – an environmental charity charging for attendance on conservation weekends.
- **Medical charities** – the Inland Revenue sometimes accepts that the exploitation by a medical research charity of patents it developed through its research is a primary-purpose trading activity.

10.4 Tax and charity trading

Charities are exempt from tax in respect of the profits of any trade carried on by the charity if the profits are applied solely to the purposes of charity and either:

- the trade is exercised in the course of the actual carrying out of a primary purpose of the charity; or
- the work in connection with the trade is mainly carried out by beneficiaries.

'Mainly' is taken as meaning 'more than half'. In other words, to fall within this exemption not all the work in connection with the trade has to be carried out by beneficiaries, but only 'a majority of the work'. Examples of where such work is carried out include:

- the sale, by charities established to help disabled people, of goods produced by such people in a workshop;
- the sale of tickets for a play put on by trainee actors;
- the provision of services or the sale of products made by trainees on schemes run for unemployed people.

10.4.1 The reference to 'tax' is to either income tax or Corporation Tax. Income tax is charged on charitable trusts, whereas Corporation Tax is charged on limited companies, other forms of corporation, unincorporated associations and industrial and provident societies.

10.4.2 The reference to a charity is to a charity established in the United Kingdom. The exemption does not apply to the income arising in the United Kingdom of a charity established abroad.

10.5 Sale of donated goods

If the 'badges of trade' are applied to the sale of donated goods by a charity, it is clear that the charity is carrying on a trade. However, the Inland Revenue has accepted that the sale of donated goods does not constitute a trade. Instead, the Revenue regards it simply as the charity converting a donation it has received in kind into cash. Hence the Revenue will not seek to tax the profits that a charity derives from the sale of donated goods, even though the charity has undertaken a trading activity that is not in fulfilment of a primary purpose. The Charity Commission adopts the same view. In paragraph 8 of their 1980 report they stated:

'there can be no objection to transitory and incidental trading by charities, for example, by jumble sales, or *by the running of shops to sell articles given by charitably minded people.*' [author's italics]

Thus the Charity Commission accepts that the sale of donated goods by a charity is a form of 'incidental' trading that *does not* constitute for-profit trading. It is an activity that can be carried out by a charity itself and need not be carried out through a separate trading company. Indeed, charities should guard against operating their sales of donated goods through separate trading companies, as technically the trading company will not be eligible for rate relief (see **10.7**). Moreover, a charity should not give away its assets (i.e. donated goods) to a separate trading company (see Chapter 22 on the relationship between charities and trading companies).

10.6 Trading activities and VAT

There is no general exemption from VAT for charities that undertake trading activities. The trading activities of many charities will fall within the definition of business supplies for VAT, even though charities do not pursue a 'profit motive'. VAT is a tax on turnover, not profit. Whether VAT is payable or not usually depends on the nature of what is supplied and not on the status of the supplier. A charity (like any other organisation or individual) is required to register for VAT if it makes taxable supplies over the VAT registration threshold in any year (£52,000 for 2000). Where a charity is registered for VAT, it must charge output VAT on taxable supplies of goods and services that it makes; however, it can then reclaim input VAT on purchases made in connection with such supplies. The most favourable status for VAT is to make zero-rated supplies. In this instance, the supplier can recover the input VAT but does not have to charge its customers output VAT. Charities enjoy zero-rated status when they sell donated goods.

There is a special VAT exemption for some charity events – see **10.9**.

10.7 Rate relief

Where the rate payer is a charity and property is wholly or mainly used for charitable purposes, the charity will be granted 80 per cent mandatory relief from Unified Business Rate.

A charity that is occupying premises for the purposes of carrying on primary-purpose trading will be using property wholly for charitable purposes. Hence, it will be entitled to the 80 per cent mandatory rate relief; it will also be able to apply for the 20 per cent discretionary relief available under the Local Government Finance Act 1988. The granting of discretionary relief is solely at the discretion of the local authority.

If a charity occupies a rateable property wholly or mainly for fundraising, technically the charity should not receive any rate relief, since fundraising itself is not a charitable activity but a method of raising charitable funds. If a charity occupies a shop for the sale of donated goods, that is accepted as being a charitable activity. If, however, a charity wished to run a shop selling bought-in goods, then the charity will not be occupying the premises wholly or mainly for charitable purposes, because the sale of such goods is not primary-purpose trading – it should therefore do this through a trading company.

10.8 Ancillary or incidental trading

Some charities undertake trading activities which are not in fulfilment of one of their primary purposes, but which are in some way complimentary to or derived from those purposes, for example a museum running a café open to visitors, a canteen at a youth club, a school running a tuck shop.

For the purposes of charity law, a charity does not threaten its charitable status by undertaking such ancillary trading (even though the trading itself is not a charitable activity), provided its constitution gives it the necessary power to do this. This is because the trading is conducted at a minor level and supports the charitable work of the charity. Ancillary trading cannot be or become a major part of the charity's activities. If it were to become so, then the charity would be acting outside its powers, which would in turn expose its trustees to potential risks. Inevitably, it is difficult to discern whether a particular trading activity is ancillary or incidental, or is of a nature or extent that has turned it into non-primary-purpose trading. Each case will depend on particular facts. When it comes to ancillary trading, the Inland Revenue asks two questions:

- Do the profits fall within the Extra Statutory Concession (see **10.9**)?
- Do the profits fall within the *de minimis* exemption (see **10.10**)?

If the answer to both of these is 'no', then the profits are taxable.

10.9 **Tax and VAT exemption for certain events**

Before 1 April 2000, there were exemptions for tax and VAT for certain types of charity events, but the rules for tax and the rules for VAT were different, often leading to confusion.

To improve the position, from 1 April 2000 the government introduced a new exemption for events, which covers both tax and VAT. The detail of how it applies is set out in Customs and Excise Notice 701/59. The exemption from tax arises because the Inland Revenue has agreed that an event falling within the VAT exemption will also fall within a special tax concession called Extra Statutory Concession 4 (ESC4).

The tax and VAT exemptions will apply to all events provided that the following points apply.

10.9.1 **The event is both organised and promoted exclusively to raise money for the charity**. People attending or participating in the event must be aware of its primary fundraising purpose. HM Customs and Excise has produced the following non-exhaustive list of events that they consider will fall within the exemption:

- ball, dinner dance, disco or barn dance
- performance (e.g. concerts, stage productions, and other events that have a paying audience)
- film showing
- fete, fair or festival
- horticultural show
- exhibition – including art, history, science, etc.
- bazaar, jumble sale
- sporting participation (including spectators)
- sporting performance
- games of skill, contests, quiz
- endurance participation
- firework displays
- dinner, lunch, barbecue
- auction
- raffle, lottery.

Street collections, house-to-house collections, etc. are not events for the purposes of this exemption.

10.9.2 **There are no more than 15 events of the same type in any one location within any one financial year**. What constitutes a location is a bit of a moveable feast and will depend on the type of location and kind of event. In some cases, a location will be a town or village and in others it might be a particular building. Individual events held on successive days will constitute separate events, and each will count towards the number of 15. However, an event is not counted towards the 15 if the gross takings from the event are no more than £1,000 per week.

Once the maximum number has been reached, all events of the same kind in the same location in the same financial year will be outside the VAT exemption. The charity will then have to account for VAT on the turnover – hence you will have to keep proper records of all events if there is any danger of breaching the 15-event limit.

10.9.3 **The event does not include the provision of accommodation for more than two nights**. This puts most overseas challenge events outside the scope of the exemption.

10.9.4 What events do not qualify for exemption?

- Any event where 16 or more of the same kind of event are held at the same location during a financial year.
- Events that only form part of a social calendar for members.
- Asking the public for donations through street collections, flag days, etc.
- Selling goods unless at an organised bazaar or similar event. Selling goods through retail outlets is not an 'event'.
- Any events that fall within the Tour Operator's Margin Scheme or where the event includes more than two nights' accommodation.

10.9.5 The exemption covers all the income from supplies of goods and services made by the charity in connection with the event, for example:

- all admission charges
- the sale of commemorative brochures
- the sale of advertising space in those brochures
- other items sold by the charity at the event (e.g. T-shirts) *Note:* zero rating can be applied to items sold, if applicable (e.g. children's clothing)
- sponsorship payments directly connected with the event.

10.9.6 The exemption does apply to events organised by a charity's wholly owned trading company.

10.9.7 At the time this book went to press, the legislation implementing the changes had not been published – the summaries above are based on guidance issued by Customs and Excise and the Inland Revenue. You should check up-to-date guidance in case the legislation contains any changes.

10.10 *De minimis* **exemption**

If a charity carries on trading activities that are not in fulfilment of a primary purpose or are not eligible for exemption under the Extra Statutory Concession (perhaps because they are undertaken 'regularly'), any profits resulting from that trade will be liable to be taxed.

With effect from April 2000, charities have been given a new tax relief to exempt all profits of small trading and other fundraising activities carried on by charities. The relief will apply where the charity has a reasonable expectation that the turnover will be no greater than either:

- £5,000 or
- the lesser of £50,000 and 25 per cent of the charity's gross income.

Note that this applies to turnover and not profits.

> EXAMPLES
>
> - A charity has a gross income of £150,000
>   The maximum turnover of non-primary-purpose trade it can put through the charity is 150 × 25% = £37,500.
> - A charity has gross income of £2 million
>   The maximum turnover of non-primary-purpose trade it can put through the charity is £50,000

10.11 **What happens if a charity's trade is not primary purpose or within the ESC or *de minimis* exemption?**

If a charity carries on a trade that is neither primary purpose nor within either the ESC or *de minimis* exemption, then the charity will be liable to pay tax on the profits of the trade. If this happens, there is a very real risk that the trustees could be held personally liable for any tax that the charity has to pay. That is because the trustees are under a duty to act in the best interest of the charity and to organise its affairs so as to maximise its income and minimise its liabilities. Allowing the charity to be managed in a way that exposes it to a tax liability that can be avoided is an example of negligence by the trustees. If trustees of a charity are negligent and the charity suffers loss as a result, then the trustees can be made to compensate the charity from their own resources for the loss it has suffered. Fundraisers who have allowed this to happen may find themselves looking for another job!

The following are examples of trading activities that a charity should not undertake:

- Licensing its name and logo to appear on merchandising, unless this falls within the ESC4 or is an annual payment (see **8.6.4**).
- The sale of charity Christmas cards, unless it can be argued successfully that this promotes the charity's primary purpose (e.g. an art therapy charity selling Christmas cards designed by its clients).
- Sale of merchandising by catalogues; this can only be carried out by a charity if the items sold through the catalogue are in fulfilment of its primary purposes (e.g. a charity established to help deaf people selling appropriate aids). If the catalogue contains other items (e.g. T-shirts, tea towels, ties, etc.), this will amount to for-profit, non-primary-purpose trading.
- Large scale fundraising not within ESC4 (see **10.9**).
- Licensing its name and logo to commercial partners unless such licensing lasts for more than a year (see Chapter 8).

All these activities must be put through a separate trading company (see Chapter 22 for further guidance on establishing and operating a trading company). However, there is a big risk that the Inland Revenue will seek to tax any profits made on the trading activity. So the first step is to calculate carefully the profits attributable to the trading activity. In doing this, the charity should make sure that all costs and expenses attributable to the trading activity are offset against the profits generated. It should take professional advice on this. It may find, when all the direct and indirect costs are taken into account, that there is only a small, or even no, taxable profit.

Summary

- Charities can only trade if it is in fulfilment of their objects or if there is a relevant tax exemption.
- There are tests to determine whether or not trading is taking place, the so-called 'badges of trade'.
- Charities are exempt from tax on the profits of primary-purpose trading.
- Ancillary trading (e.g. a canteen at a youth club) is permissible as long as it does not become a major part of the charity's activities.
- ESC4 means that Corporation Tax is not due on some forms of fundraising events.
- *De minimis* exemption exempts profits on non-primary-purpose trading if turnover is under £50,000 or 25 per cent of the charity's gross income (whichever is the lowest).
- If a trade is not in fulfilment of a primary purpose or is carried out by beneficiaries, and if it does not fall within the ESC4 concession or *de minimis* limits, it must be put through a separate trading company.

11
Contracts

11.1 What is a contract?

A contract is a legally binding relationship between two or more parties. A contract can give you rights, for example the right to be paid a certain amount or the right to use a name or logo or expect a certain level of service. It can also impose obligations and restrictions.

Contracts are called by a number of names: agreements, arrangements, deeds, service agreements, licences, assignments.

11.2 Why contracts are important

It is a necessary part of fundraising that charities enter into contracts all the time, whether this be booking a venue, commissioning artwork from a designer or selling tickets for an event.

There are also situations where the law requires a charity to have a written contract, for example to record arrangements with 'commercial participators' and 'professional fundraisers' or to give permission to companies to use a charity's name and logo (see Chapters 16 and 17).

Such contracts protect the charity's interests – whether from deliberate misuse of its assets (such as its logo) or from general bad service.

11.3 For a contract to be created:

- there must be 'consideration' from each party – this means each party must be giving something or doing something in return for the promises the other party is making;
- the detail of the contract (known as 'the terms') must be reasonably clear – if everything is uncertain there will be no contract – and it is vital that the terms be brought to the other party's attention before the contract is finalised, otherwise the terms will not apply;
- each party must have intended to create a legally binding relationship – this is not usually a problem, but see **8.6.4** about promises to give donations;

■ there must be an 'offer' to enter into a contract (e.g. 'I would like to buy some T-shirts') and 'acceptance' ('OK').

11.4 Common myths about contracts

Contrary to popular misconception, a contract does not have to be in writing or signed by the parties. This means contracts can be created by verbal agreement or by exchanging letters or, most importantly, by each party going ahead and doing what they have agreed to do. A contract can also be part written, part oral: for example, a contract to commission a design could be partly set out in a letter to the designer and also contain terms discussed by telephone. The advantage of having a written contract is that the terms are clearly set out.

Another misconception is that contracts have to be fair. As a general rule, there is no law against a bad bargain. For example, if you agree to pay over the odds for a fundraising consultant's fees, then you will usually be bound by that. The law does treat some terms as unfair and therefore unenforceable; this is particularly the case with terms that restrict or exclude liability. The legislation dealing with exclusion clauses is the Unfair Contract Terms Act 1977, and the Unfair Terms in Consumer Contract Regulations 1994 (see **11.7**).

11.5 Deeds

A deed is a special type of contract, usually entered into where one or more of the parties is not providing any consideration (see **11.3**). For a document to be a deed, it has to contain specific wording: this is something you should take professional advice about.

The other difference between a deed and a contract is that you have six years to sue for any breach of contract, but twelve years to sue for breach of a contract made under a deed.

If you want a promise to give a donation to be legally binding, ask the donor to sign a deed recording the promise (see **8.7.4**).

11.6 Implied terms

The law implies some terms into particular types of contract.

11.6.1 Terms implied into contracts for services include the following:

■ Any services will be provided with reasonable care and skill.
■ If the time for performance of the services is not fixed in the contract, the supplier will carry out the service within a reasonable time.
■ If the amount to be paid is not fixed in the contract, a reasonable charge will be paid.

What is 'reasonable' is a question of fact and varies depending on the circumstances.

11.6.2 Terms implied into contracts to buy goods include the following:
- The seller has the right to sell the goods.
- The goods are of satisfactory quality (i.e. they are fit for their normal expected use, bearing in mind the description of the goods, the price and all other relevant circumstances).
- The goods are fit for any specific purpose that the purchaser has told the seller about.
- The goods meet any agreed description or sample.

These implied terms derive from the Sale of Goods Act 1979, the Supply of Goods and Services Act 1982 and the Sale and Supply of Goods Act 1994.

11.7 Excluding or limiting liability

Many contracts contain clauses limiting liability: for example that the organiser of a parachute jump is not responsible if anything goes wrong, or that liability is only accepted to a maximum of £250,000.

The law makes certain exclusions unenforceable – and the rules for contracts with consumers are different from those for contracts with businesses.

11.7.1 Contracts with consumers
- Sellers cannot avoid liability for death or personal injury arising from their negligence by any contract term or notice. For example, the Youth Hostels Association cannot avoid liability should a youth hosteller be injured at a youth hostel because of its negligence.
- Sellers cannot exclude their obligations under the Sale of Goods Act 1979 and the Supply of Goods and Services Act 1982 to sell only goods that they own. Hence, a charity shop cannot sell stolen goods without being in breach of the Acts.
- Sellers cannot exclude their liability under the Sale of Goods Act 1979 and the Supply of Goods and Services Act 1982 to sell goods that are of satisfactory quality, fit for a particular purpose or as described. In the case of the sale of second hand-goods, the standard of care will be lower than for new goods.
- Sellers can exclude liability for misrepresentation, if this is 'reasonable', as laid down in the Unfair Contract Terms Act 1977.
- Under the Unfair Terms in Consumer Contracts Regulations 1994, any term in a contract that the consumer can show to be 'unfair' will not be legally binding on the consumer. These regulations are policed by the Office of Fair Trading, which can obtain injunctions to prevent the continued use of the unfair term.

Some examples of terms that have been held to be unfair are:

- a health club's term that 'membership fees are non-returnable';
- a residential outdoor activity centre's term which limited its liability if it failed to provide all appropriate services;
- a university's terms and conditions for adult learning courses which excluded liability for death or injury on field trips.

11.7.2 Contracts with businesses

These terms apply, for example, to the purchase of goods or services by a charity or its trading company:

- Sellers cannot avoid liability for death or personal injury by any contract term or notice.
- Sellers cannot exclude the obligation under the Sale of Goods Act 1979 to sell goods for which they have title.
- Sellers can exclude their obligation to sell goods that are:
  - as described or as samples
  - of satisfactory quality or fit for a particular purpose

  provided that it is 'reasonable' to do so.

This limitation only applies if the contract is made on standard written terms of business. If a charity or its trading company negotiates an individual contract with its business customer (or vice versa), then the Act does not apply, and the parties can contract out of these various obligations, even if it appears 'unreasonable' to do so.

- Sellers can exclude liability for misrepresentation, again if this is 'reasonable'.
- Sellers can exclude any other liabilities arising from a breach of the contract (e.g. for delay, distress or economic loss), if this is 'reasonable'.

The general test of whether a term is reasonable involves looking at the circumstances when the contract was created and considering what each party knew or ought to have considered at the time of making the contract. Specific factors are:

- the strength of the parties' bargaining positions;
- whether the goods were made specifically for the customer;
- whether the customer actually knew about the term;
- the availability of insurance to cover the risk.

11.8 Contracts made by mail order, telephone and the Internet

In order to enhance consumer confidence in distance sales, new regulations have been introduced to regulate certain aspects of distance-selling contracts. These are the Consumer Protection (Distance Selling) Regulations 2000. A distance contract is one where the supplier and consumer do not come face to face up to and including the moment at which the contract is concluded (e.g. mail order, telephone sales, electronic commerce).

The most important provisions of the regulations are the following:

- The consumer must be provided with certain information in good time before the conclusion of the contract. The information is fairly basic and includes the name and address of the supplier, the main characteristics of the goods and services, arrangements for payments, price and the consumer's right to withdraw from the contract.

- The information above must be confirmed in 'writing or another durable medium'.

- The consumer is notified of their right to withdraw from the contract within seven working days after receipt of goods or the conclusion of the contract (in the case of services) without penalty. The period of rejection is increased to three months if written confirmation of the information has not been made available to the consumer in full at the time of the delivery of the goods. If the supplier subsequently provides the information during the three months, then the consumer has only seven days to withdraw from the date of the receipt of the information.

- If the consumer exercises their right to withdraw, then the supplier must reimburse all sums paid by the consumer except the cost of the return post in the case of goods. The right to withdraw does not apply to certain contracts, e.g. contracts for personalised goods.

- The supplier is required to execute the contract within 30 days. If the supplier fails to do so, then the consumer has a right to a refund within 30 days.

- The supplier is restricted from using 'automated calling machines' or faxes without the prior consent of the consumer to solicit sales or to make contracts.

- Under the regulations, it is a criminal offence not to provide the consumer with notice of their cancellation rights and not to reimburse the consumer in the event that they exercise their right to withdraw from the contract. The maximum fine is Level 4 on the standard scale (£2,500 at the time of going to press). This liability extends to persons other than the principal offender, i.e. directors and managers.

11.9 Checklist for negotiating a contract

- Start negotiating well before the contract is due to start.
- Avoid creating a contract before you are ready – using the words 'subject to contract' on correspondence makes it clear you are still negotiating.
- Keep written notes of telephone calls to discuss the contract so that you can refer back to these to clarify what certain terms were intended to mean or cover.
- Should you get the final contract checked by a lawyer or should a lawyer be involved with negotiations from the beginning? Some relevant factors to consider here are:
  - potential liabilities under the contract – what could the charity be sued for if it goes wrong? What would the charity lose if the other party fails to perform? Are the potential liabilities significant even if the projected income is fairly low?
  - value of contract – how important is it to the charity in terms of both money and reputation?
  - timescale – how quickly does the contract have to be concluded?
- Have clear internal procedures for negotiating, approving, signing and monitoring contracts.

11.10 General guidelines for reviewing a contract

- Is the contract within the charity's objects? Or should the contract be with the charity's trading subsidiary?
- If someone else has prepared a draft contract, read it carefully – it may not say what you are expecting.
- Check the parties to the contract, and get some information about them (e.g. carry out a search at Companies House, take up references, carry out credit card checks). The level of information you seek to obtain will depend on the importance of the contract.
- Check that all schedules or appendices are attached. If the contract refers to any other documents or policies, make sure you have read them.
- Are important words defined?
- Does it make sense? Are any parts ambiguous?
- Establish what the key issues are for you – have they been covered?
- What is the worst that could happen and what would the contract allow the charity to do in that situation?
- If any unusual losses would arise from a breach of contract, add wording to say that the other party acknowledges that it is a foreseeable risk.
- Check the termination provisions.
- Check that the payment provisions are correct and clear.

- Water down your obligations, but not the other party's!
- Make clear if any deadlines are crucial and cannot be changed.
- As well as looking at what is in the contract, think about what might be missing.

As a very minimum, the basics for any contract are:

- the parties
- the date of the contract
- the duration of the contract
- the obligations on each party
- payment detail
- what rights either party has to terminate
- use of the charity's name and logo and protection of the charity's reputation.

(For other terms you should include in specific types of contract, see **3.3**, **6.5.3**, **6.6.1**, and Chapters 16, 17 and 22.)

11.11 When things go wrong

When things go wrong with a contract, the two questions most frequently asked are:

- Can I terminate the contract?
- Can I claim damages?

11.11.1 Termination

The first thing is to check what the contract says about termination. Common problems here are that you:

- have no rights to terminate in the first year;
- have to give a minimum of three months' notice;
- have to give the other party at least three warnings before terminating;
- can only terminate on the anniversary of the agreement.

If there is no easy way to terminate by notice, you will have to try to argue that the other party's actions are so serious as to breach the whole contract. This is called a 'fundamental breach'. It is often difficult to assess if a breach is 'fundamental', and you would be well-advised to take legal advice. In general terms, a fundamental breach is one so serious that it goes to the root of the contract. One such example might be when a professional fundraiser fails to raise any money for a charity in a year and there is compelling evidence that they have failed to carry out their other contractual duties with reasonable care and skill.

11.11.2 Claiming damages

A right to damages is triggered if the other party breaches (or 'breaks') the contract. Some breaches entitle you to treat the whole contract as terminated, in which case you can both terminate and claim damages. With other breaches, however, you can claim damages, but the breach does not give you the right to terminate. Take the case of a charity that has a contract with a publisher to print 12 editions of its monthly newsletter for supporters. If the publisher fails entirely to deliver the first edition, this is likely to be a fundamental breach entitling the charity to terminate and claim damages. If the publisher delivers the first editions, but 10 per cent of the newsletters are blank on one side, this is unlikely to be a fundamental breach: the charity can claim damages, but the contract is not automatically terminated.

This is often a grey area, and telling the difference is difficult. If in doubt, you should seek professional advice.

11.11.3 What can you claim for damages?

The way the law calculates damages for breach of contract is to calculate the amount needed to put you in the position you would have been in had the contract been performed properly.

> **EXAMPLES**
>
> - You order some Christmas cards. The printer fails to meet the agreed delivery date in August and says they will not be ready until late November – too late for you to distribute them. Your damages would be calculated as the loss of profit on the cards – but see mitigation below.
> - You hire a venue to hold a gala performance. The hirer has double-booked and cancels your booking at the last minute. Your claim would be for the lost profit on the gala.

As a general rule, the law does not allow you to claim for:

- hassle and worry;
- what might have gone wrong, rather than what actually did;
- anything where you could have taken steps after the breach to 'mitigate' your loss. This means that, if another party breaches the contract, you cannot sit back, do nothing and let the damages mount up. You must take any reasonable steps you can to limit the damages. In the two examples above you should mitigate your loss by:
  - trying to buy replacement cards at short notice – your claim will then be for any extra cost of the replacement cards rather than for your loss of profit;
  - looking for an alternative venue – your claim will then be for costs associated with arranging the event at another venue.

Summary

- A contract is a legally binding relationship.
- A contract can be written or oral.
- Contracts do not have to be fair.
- The law implies some terms into contracts for services and the sale of goods.
- You can exclude or limit liability under a contract by an appropriate clause in certain circumstances.
- Some types of exclusion clause are unenforceable.
- Distance selling (e.g. contracts by telephone, mail order, etc.) is covered by specific regulations.
- Compensation (damages) can be claimed for breach of contract.

12

Data protection

12.1 **The Data Protection Act 1984**

The Data Protection Act 1984 imposed some controls on charities and fundraising, but it did very little to promote good practice in the use and management of personal data. The 1984 Act basically allowed a data user to use data for any purpose, provided the data user had registered in very broad terms what it intended to do with the data. There were limited controls on data capture.

12.2 **The Data Protection Act 1998**

The Data Protection Act 1998, which came into force on 1 March 2000, is a far more demanding piece of legislation. It gives effect in the UK to the EC Data Protection Directive (95/46/EC). Its origins are European and reflect European concerns about centralised holdings of personal data. These concerns often run counter to the desires of fundraisers to build up detailed information about donors and to use that information to raise funds from them.

While the 1984 Act applied only to computer-held records, the new legislation applies to both computer and manual records. The transitional period exempts existing manual databases until 24 October 2007. A new manual database that is created after 1 March 2000 is subject to the Act.

12.3 **'Personal data'**

The Act is concerned with 'personal data'. This refers to data about **individuals** who are **identifiable** and **living**. It does not therefore apply to information about companies or organisations, although it could apply to contact names within organisations. It does not apply to information about people who have died.

Examples of personal data include:

- membership records
- newsletter mailing lists

- lists of supporters
- details of delegates at a conference
- notes prepared by counsellors.

12.3.1 Personal data is divided into two categories:

- personal data (i.e. all information that is not sensitive)
- sensitive personal data.

Sensitive personal data is information about:

- the racial or ethnic origins of the data subject
- their political opinions
- their religious beliefs or other beliefs of similar nature
- whether they are a member of a trade union
- their physical or mental health condition
- their sexual life
- their criminal record.

Information about an individual's financial position is not sensitive personal data!

The controls are imposed on the 'data controller' who will be either the company itself (if a charity is a company) or the trustees or members of the management committee (in the case of a trust or unincorporated association).

12.3.2 Notification

If an organisation holds personal data on computer, it must notify the Data Protection Commissioner. The Data Protection Commissioner will register trusts and unincorporated associations as the data controller in the name of the organisation. (If personal data is held manually, then there is no need to notify, but the data controller is still subject to the Data Protection Principles.)

Failure to register is a criminal offence. The prosecution will be brought, in the case of an unincorporated organisation such as an association or trust, against the individual trustees. In the case of a charity that is incorporated, proceedings may still be brought against the trustees personally. Under section 61, if it is proved that an offence has been committed with the consent or connivance of any director, manager, secretary or similar officer of a body corporate, or is attributable to any neglect on their part, they can be found guilty of the offence and can be punished.

12.4 Data capture and processing – non-sensitive personal data

The First Data Protection Principle states that data must be processed 'fairly and lawfully'.

'Processing' is defined very widely. It includes holding, capturing, using or transmitting personal data.

Non-sensitive personal data can be processed 'lawfully' if any one of the following applies:

- The data subject has given their consent.
- It is necessary for the performance of a contract to which the data subject is a party.
- It is necessary to ensure compliance with a legal obligation.
- It is in the data subject's vital interests.
- It involves a criminal investigation.
- It is necessary for the legitimate interests of the data controller.

In most cases, it will be best for charities to assume that they need the consent of an individual in order to process their personal data. Therefore, when capturing data it will be necessary to obtain the data subject's consent for the charity to use the data for any other purpose than that for which it is to be used at the point of capture.

12.4.1 Three examples of using personal data

- Newspaper advertisement soliciting donations
- Telephone calls soliciting donations
- Telephone answering services receiving donations

In all these cases, the charity will need to obtain the data subject's consent for the right to use the personal data for any other purpose (e.g. to add to the charity's mailing list of supporters). This is easy in the case of a newspaper advertisement – a suitable consent form can be included. In the case of the telephone calls, it is necessary to ensure that the persons who make or receive the calls seek and obtain the verbal consent of the data subject and note this down in writing. It may be advisable to record the telephone call, but in this case it is necessary to inform the caller first.

12.4.2 Relationship with trading companies

Under the 1984 Act, the Data Protection Registrar accepted that it was an obvious use for a charity to disclose details of its supporters to its associated trading company. There was no need to seek prior consent from the data subject. This has now changed. It will be necessary to obtain the data subject's consent for a charity to pass personal data to its associated trading company. This means that charities wishing to pass personal data they have captured to their associated trading company must seek consent at the point of capture.

12.4.3 List swaps or disclosure to third parties (other than trading companies)

If charities wish to engage in list swaps of their supporter database, or disclose their database of supporters to third parties, it will be necessary to have the consent of the data subject. If charities wish to do this, they will need to obtain consent at the point of data capture. The ICFM has issued a Code of Practice on Reciprocal Charity Mailings.

12.4.4 Examples of opt-out and opt-in notices

The following notice could be put on a newspaper advertisement soliciting funds, to be returned with the donation. This could be suitably adapted for use on the telephone.

Opt out

XYZ Charity

We would like to use your information:

☐ For use in connection with our charitable activities and fundraising appeals.

☐ To pass to our associated trading company, XYZ Trading Limited.

☐ To pass to other organisations with similar objects.

Please tick the appropriate box(es) if you object to any of these disclosures.

This allows supporters to opt out from the charity's database. There is some dispute as to whether or not data controllers should, in fact, obtain the specific consent through an opt-in system. An opt-in system could have a major impact on direct market fundraising for charities. It is currently thought that an opt-out system is acceptable, provided all reasonable steps are taken to give the data subject the chance to opt out. This means that Data Protection notices need to be clear and well presented and not given in thin grey type among a mass of information.

Opt in

XYZ Charity

Please tick the following boxes:

☐ I would like you to send me fundraising materials and information about your charity.

☐ I would like you to pass my personal details to your associated trading company XYZ Trading Company.

☐ I would like you to pass my personal details to other organisations with similar objects.

Please tick the appropriate box(es) to signify your consent.

12.4.5 Capture of non-solicited data

Volunteers or donors may contact a charity themselves, by letter or by telephone, rather than in response to a formal appeal. Under the 1984 Act, it was clear that the data controller's duty was to tell the data subject at the earliest possible opportunity of all possible non-obvious uses of the personal data that the data controller had in mind. Normally this means the point of data capture. The 1998 Act makes this obligation clearer. For example, a charity wishes to use a donor's personal data where that donor has written in with a donation out of the blue. The charity can use the personal data to process this donation. But if it wants to use it for other purposes, it should send out an opt-out notice along the lines set out in **12.4.4**, in order to comply with the requirements of the 1998 Act.

12.5 Fair Processing Code

The 1998 Act provides that any use of personal data must be 'fair' and 'lawful'. The Act gives guidance on what constitutes 'fair' processing, and this has been dubbed 'The Fair Processing Code'. Under 'The Fair Processing Code', the data subject must not be deceived or misled as to the purpose or purposes for which the personal data is to be processed.

As a result, the data controller is obligated to ensure 'so far as practicable' that the data subject has been provided with information about:

- the identity of the data controller (e.g. XYZ Charity);
- the purpose or purposes for which it is intended that the data be processed (e.g. fundraising);
- any further information that is necessary, taking into account the specific circumstances in which the data is to be processed to enable processing in respect of the data subject to be fair.

Our view is that, when data is captured (e.g. from a newspaper coupon or telephone call), provided the steps outlined in **12.4.4** above for an opt out are taken, the Fair Processing Code will have been complied with. However, there are other areas in which the Fair Processing Code could have a major impact on fundraising. For example, charities may build up detailed information about target individuals whom they may wish to approach for support. The charities may obtain information from a variety of sources: the electoral role, the telephone directory, *Who's Who*, newspaper articles, etc. The charity will argue no doubt that all this is information in the 'public domain'. So far as the Data Protection Act is concerned, this is personal data, and under the Act the charity should advise the data subject as soon as it has obtained sufficient information about that individual for them to be identifiable. This is subject to a proviso that the data controller does not have to advise the data subject if this would involve 'a disproportionate effort' (see **12.8**). It could also be argued that this activity is in the charity's 'legitimate interests'.

12.6 Existing data

The examples considered above have dealt with capturing new personal data and the steps to be gone through under the 1998 Act. However, the position with existing personal data also needs to be considered. Given the changes in the law introduced by the 1998 Act, it is necessary for charities to renew their authority from the data subject to use personal data held on computer in good time before 24 October 2001. At the very least, this means that charities should send a mailing to their existing supporters/members/donors with an opt-out notice similar to that in **12.4.4**. The information should be printed clearly and, in addition, use such wording as 'Data Protection Act 1998: we would like to use your personal data for the following purposes. If you wish to object, please return this coupon to Freepost address (XYZ address) or telephone Freephone number 000000 within 40 days.' The charity must do all it can to show that it has acted reasonably and has given data subjects an easy and simple way of exercising their rights. It is unclear whether or not the Data Protection Commissioner or the courts will accept that this is a fair practice. However, in the circumstances it appears to be the most sensible way of proceeding.

12.7 Sensitive personal data

Many charities will hold sensitive personal data (see definition in **12.3**) in their fundraising database. For example, some cancer charities will distinguish those persons on their database who they know to be suffering from cancer from those who are not. They will deliberately not send out certain information (e.g. fundraising materials) to those persons suffering from cancer. The information about someone's medical condition is sensitive personal data. That information can only be used with the 'explicit consent' of the data subject. 'Explicit consent' is not defined in the Act but it must mean an informed consent for a particular use of that data. Consequently, charities that hold sensitive personal data on their fundraising databases should consider whether or not it is necessary to get explicit consent from those individuals about whom they do hold sensitive personal data in order to use that information. It may be possible for some charities to use an exception to the requirement for explicit consent set out in Schedule 3 to the Act. This requires that explicit consent will not be required when processing is carried out 'in the course of its legitimate activities by any body or association which:

- is not established or conducted for profit, and
- exists for political, philosophical, religious or trade union purposes'.

In addition, the processing has to be carried out with appropriate safeguards for the rights and freedoms of data subjects, must relate only to members or regular supporters and must not involve disclosure of the personal data to a third party without the consent of the data subject. This will clearly be of benefit to religious charities in relation to their members or regular supporters. However, this exception begs the question of what is meant by a 'philosophical' organisation. Is a charity established to relieve suffering in the developing world established for a 'philosophical' purpose? This question will have to be resolved in the courts. In the meantime, charities will no doubt want to take a broad interpretation of this provision to allow them to use sensitive personal data in relation to their members or regular supporters without obtaining explicit consent.

12.8 Exchanges and rentals of data

The 1998 Act does not prohibit list swaps or exchanges but it imposes far greater controls than the 1984 Act. Where a data controller obtains data from someone other than the data subject (e.g. via a list swap or purchase), then the data controller has to give the data subject the 'Fair Processing Information' (see **12.5**) before the time when the data controller first processes that data. Given that 'processing' includes 'use', technically the act of using the data to send the information required to the data subject is breach of the Act!

The information that has to be disclosed to the data subject is:

- the identity of the data controller
- the purpose(s) for which the data is intended to be processed
- any further information that would make the processing fair.

There is an exception, which is if compliance with the Act would have a 'disproportionate effect'. This phrase is not defined in the Act. However, the Data Protection Commissioner will take into account a number of factors including:

- the costs incurred by the data controller in providing the information (e.g. postage and/or staff/employee time);
- the length of time it will take the data controller to provide the information, again weighed against the benefit;
- how easy/difficult it is for the data controller to provide the information.

It is understood that the Data Protection Commissioner is currently of the view that it would be disproportionate to expect a charity to provide the fair processing information to new names obtained under a data swap. Charities should remember, however, that, if they wish to sell or swap data, they must have obtained the data subject's prior consent.

12.9 Rights of data subjects
12.9.1 Information

By section 7(2) of the 1998 Act the data controller is obliged to supply the following information in an intelligible form and, if requested, in writing:

- whether or not personal data is being processed by or on his or her behalf;
- a description of the personal data, the purposes for which it is being kept or processed and the recipients or class of recipients to whom it is or may be disclosed;
- the appropriate fee (to be fixed) to be paid by the data subject.

12.9.2 Right to stop processing

According to section 10, an individual is entitled at any time to require a data controller to cease processing personal data if it is causing or is likely to cause 'substantial damage to him or another'.

There is no obligation, as there was under the 1984 Act, for the data subject to establish that the information held is inaccurate.

12.9.3 Direct marketing

Section 11 of the Act entitles an individual to require a data controller to cease or not to begin processing personal data for the purposes of direct marketing. 'Direct marketing' is defined as 'the communication (by whatever means) of any advertising or marketing material which is directed to particular individuals.' Clearly this will cover individually addressed fundraising appeals. This means that charities may be faced with demands to stop sending fundraising letters; charities have, however, already been participating in the Mail Preference Service, so in reality this should not make much difference.

12.9.4 Advertising Standards Authority

Direct marketing rules in the British Codes of Advertising and Sales Promotion cover the obtaining, compiling, processing, management and use of data for the purpose of marketing products and services. The Advertising Standards Authority can request that the data controller clean its files or suppress data.

12.9.5 Damages and compensation

An individual who suffers damage because of the data controller's breach of any of the requirements of the Act can seek compensation. The data controller will be either the trustees (in the case of an unincorporated charity) or the corporate entity (in the case of a charity that is a limited company).

12.10 Controls on data processing by third parties

Charities frequently sub-contract the task of managing their databases to a commercial organisation: such an organisation is called a 'data processor'. Charities need to consider their relationships with data processors, because the Seventh Data Protection Principle requires that 'appropriate technical and organisational measures shall be taken against unauthorised or unlawful processing of personal data and against accidental loss or destruction of or damage to personal data'. In order to comply with the Seventh Principle, the data controller must:

- choose a data processor providing sufficient guarantees in respect of the security measures they take;
- take reasonable steps to ensure compliance with those measures;
- ensure that there is a written contract made, under which the data processor is to act only on instructions from the data controller – the contract must require the data processor to comply with obligations equivalent to those imposed on the data controller by the Seventh Principle.

Accordingly, charities that arrange for data bureaux to manage their databases of personal data should ensure that such contracts comply with the obligations imposed by the Act.

12.11 Transfers outside the European Economic Area

The European Economic Area (EEA) comprises the European Union, Iceland, Liechtenstein and Norway. The Eighth Data Protection Principle requires that personal data must not be transferred to a country outside the EEA unless that country can ensure an 'adequate' level of protection for personal data. It is currently estimated that only two countries in the world outside Europe reach this standard: Hong Kong and New Zealand. These restrictions can be over-ridden by:

- the subject giving consent or
- the transfer being made on terms that are of a kind approved by the Commissioner as ensuring adequate safeguards for the rights and freedoms of data subjects.

This latter exception is currently the subject of negotiations with the Data Protection Commissioner to establish a form of contract, acceptable to the Commissioner, that will allow data controllers to export personal data in accordance with the terms of such an agreed contract.

Pending that clarification, charities need to review any contracts for the export of personal data for processing to countries outside the EEA (e.g. India).

12.12 Criminal sanctions

12.12.1 The Data Protection Act imposes a number of criminal offences including:

- processing personal data without having notified the Data Protection Commissioner;
- failure to tell the Data Protection Commissioner of changes to notification of a register entry;

- failure to comply with a written request for particulars from a data subject;
- failure to comply with an enforcement notice from the Data Protection Commissioner;
- knowingly or recklessly obtaining or disclosing personal data, or procuring the disclosure to another person of personal data, without the consent of the data subject.

Any breach of the Data Protection Principles by a data controller can result in an enforcement notice being served by the Data Protection Commissioner.

All the above offences can give rise to a maximum fine of £5,000 upon conviction in a Magistrates Court or an unlimited fine in the Crown Court. (See also **12.3.2.**)

12.13 **Telephone privacy regulations**

The Telecommunications (Data Protection and Privacy) (Direct Marketing) Regulations 1999 came into force fully on 1 March 2000. They derive from a European Union Directive concerning the processing of personal data and the protection of privacy in the telecommunications sector. They regulate the use of faxes and telephone calls for 'direct marketing', which is defined as 'the communication of any advertising or marketing material on a particular line'. The legislation is enforced by the Data Protection Commissioner. She has indicated that she believes that telephone fundraising by charities and volunteer recruitment by charities are forms of 'direct marketing' and are within the scope of the regulations.

As far as faxes are concerned, the regulations provide that unsolicited direct marketing materials cannot be sent by fax where:

- the called line is that of a subscriber who is an individual or a corporate subscriber, and
- the subscriber has previously made a notification that they do not wish to receive unsolicited communications by fax, or
- they have registered with the Telephone Preference Service (see below).

As far as telephones are concerned, the regulations provide that unsolicited direct marketing calls cannot be made where:

- the called line is that of a subscriber who is an individual, and
- the subscriber has made a previous notification that they do not wish to receive unsolicited calls, or
- they have registered with the Telephone Preference Service.

The distinction between unsolicited faxes and unsolicited telephone calls is that the controls on faxes apply to both individuals and corporations, while the controls on telephone calls apply only to individuals. An individual is defined as 'a living individual and includes an unincorporated body of such individuals'.

That means, for example, that partnerships of solicitors or accountants fall within the regulations, because they are unincorporated bodies of individuals. Therefore, they have the right to use the opt-out system as well.

Regulation 27 provides that, where a direct marketing call is made, the name of the caller must be given and, on the request of the recipient, their address or telephone number.

Under regulation 35, a person who suffers damage by reason of any contravention of any of the requirements of the regulations shall be entitled to compensation for the damage.

Breach of the regulations is a criminal offence.

The Telephone Preference Service (TPS) is operated by the Direct Marketing Association (DMA, see p. 239) under appointment by Oftel. Every 28 days the DMA issues new information on the subscribers who have exercised their rights to opt out. This means that fundraisers who are fundraising or recruiting volunteers via telephone or fax will need to check the subscribers to the TPS lists every 28 days.

Summary

- The Data Protection Act 1998 is far more extensive than 1984 Act.
- Be aware of the distinction between sensitive and non-sensitive personal data.
- Consider the terms upon which you capture new personal data.
- Consider the purposes for which you use existing personal data, and renew data subjects' consent.
- Consider the degree to which you transfer personal data to others (including your trading company).
- Consider if personal data is being transferred overseas.
- Are you fundraising via fax or telephone? If so, are you checking numbers with the Telephone Preference Service?
- The Telecommunications (Data Protection and Privacy) (Direct Marketing) Regulations 1999 came fully into force on 1 March 2000. They regulate the use of faxes and telephone calls for 'direct marketing'.
- The distinction between unsolicited faxes and telephone calls is that controls on faxes apply to both individuals and corporations, whereas telephone calls apply only to individuals.
- If an individual (or corporation, if using faxes) has subscribed to the Telephone Preference Service, or made it known that they do not wish to be contacted in this way, unsolicited approaches cannot be made.

13
Liabilities and claims

13.1 Introduction

From time to time fundraisers will have to consider whether the charity has any kind of claim against another party, and also if third parties could have any claim against the charity. Claims can arise in many different ways, but the most common are:

- claims arising under a contract;
- claims arising under the law of negligence;
- statutory claims (i.e. claims arising because liability is created by legislation).

13.2 Claims under contract

See Chapter 11.

13.3 Claims arising under the law of negligence

13.3.1 There is an area of law, known as tort, that creates liabilities for negligence in certain situations. As an example of how this works, say that A wants to bring a claim for negligence against B. Liability will only arise if the following three tests are satisfied:

- B owed A a 'duty of care';
- B acted in breach of that duty of care;
- A has suffered loss, and A's loss was reasonably foreseeable as a result of B's actions.

13.3.2 The case that founded the law of negligence concerned a bottle of ginger beer that contained a decomposing snail. The court held that the manufacturers owed a 'duty of care' not just to anyone buying the drink but also to any eventual consumer of the drink. The key thing is that this liability can arise in situations where there is no contract between the parties.

13.3.3 Examples of other situations where a duty of care has been held to arise are: schools having a duty of care to look after pupils, professionals such as accountants, solicitors and doctors owing a duty of care to their clients. A fundraising example would be that a company supplying a bouncy castle to use at a charity's ball would owe a duty of care to anyone using it.

13.3.4   Here are some examples of situations where fundraising may give rise to a duty of care:

- If a charity sells pin badges, it has a duty of care to ensure they are safe.
- If a charity runs a gala dinner, it has a duty of care to ensure the food does not cause any stomach upsets.
- If a charity runs a sponsored abseil, it has a duty of care to ensure all equipment is safe and the event is properly organised.

13.3.5   What does this mean in practice?

- For any fundraising activity you should consider, and take professional advice about, any ways in which the charity could be held to be negligent. If the charity could be exposed, take professional advice about what steps the charity should take to discharge its 'duty of care'. Also, and this is just as important, take out insurance to cover the risk. (See Chapter 14 for ways to insure against negligence.)
- If you think the charity itself may have a claim for negligence, take professional advice. Before instructing a solicitor, gather together:
  - any documents relevant to the claim (e.g. letters, receipts for expenses);
  - written statements from any people involved;
  - the charity's own insurance documents.

13.4 Statutory claims and liabilities under Health and Safety legislation

Two particular pieces of legislation create potential liabilities for charities.

13.4.1   The Health and Safety At Work Act 1974 and all the regulations deriving from it set up a regime for regulation by enforcement to prevent unsafe and unhealthy practices connected to the working environment (in its widest possible sense). Criminal liability kicks in after an accident or incident has occurred, but criminal responsibility is also linked to taking steps to prevent situations that give rise to harm.

13.4.2   The general duties are set out in sections 2 and 3 of the Act. Section 2 sets out general duties of employers to their employees. Section 3 sets out the general duties of employers and self-employed persons to persons other than their employees. It is worth looking at the specific wording of section 3(1), which states:

'*It shall be the duty of every employer to conduct his undertaking in such a way as to ensure, so far as is reasonably practicable, that persons not in his employment who may be affected thereby are not thereby exposed to risks to their health or safety.*'

13.4.3   This section is drafted extremely broadly and means that a charity's duties under the Health and Safety Legislation extend not just to employees but also to:

- volunteers who work at the Head Office or in any branches;
- volunteers who participate in any charity-organised fundraising activities ;
- members of the public who attend any charity-organised events or activities.

13.4.4   Section 3 does say that the employer needs take only such steps as are 'reasonably practicable'. This means that the risks need to be measured against the steps necessary to eliminate the risks, and reasonable steps taken.

There is a vast array of sub-regulations relating to particular risks, but of overall relevance are the Management of Health and Safety at Work Regulations 1992. These place obligations on employers to assess the risks to employees and anyone else who may be affected by the work activities being undertaken. Risk assessment should include five key stages:

- Look for hazards.
- Decide who might be at risk from these hazards, and in what way.
- For each hazard, evaluate the chance of harm actually being done and how big this chance is, then decide whether existing precautions are adequate, or whether more should be done.
- Record the significant findings of your risk assessment (e.g. the main risks and the measures you have taken to deal with them).
- Review your assessment, and revise your practice if necessary.

Two useful books on health and safety issues are *Charity and Voluntary Workers* (HSE and the Charities Safety Group, 1999) and *The Health and Safety Handbook* (Hinde and Kavanagh, 1998).

13.4.5   Some examples of ways in which health and safety need to be considered for fundraising activities are:

- ensuring that staff have proper training to deal with any risks that may arise in the course of their work;
- ensuring that guidelines are issued to volunteers if there are any health and safety issues for an event they are participating in.

13.4.6   Liabilities for defective products

The main source of liability is the Consumer Protection Act 1987, which imposes 'strict liability' on the producers and importers of defective products. Strict liability means that the producer of a product is liable for any damage that is caused by a defect in that product, irrespective of whether the producer has been negligent. All the consumer has to do is prove that:

- there was a defect – this is defined to mean that the safety of the product was not such as persons are generally entitled to expect;

- the defect caused damage – you can claim damages for death, injury and damage to property, but you cannot claim 'economic loss' (i.e. loss of profits).

13.4.7   Under the Consumer Protection Act the persons who may be liable for defective products are:

- the producer
- any person who puts their name on the product
- any person who imports the item from outside the EU.

13.4.8   Charities could be liable under the Consumer Protection Act, for example, for:

- selling any defective products made by the charity
- supplying goods imported from outside the EU
- being associated with the sale of defective products on which the charity's name appears (e.g. cause-related marketing arrangements).

If there is any risk that the charity could be liable, make sure that you take out adequate product liability insurance (see Chapter 14).

13.4.9   Liability can also arise under government regulations for specific products, for example:

- The Children's Clothing (Hood Cords) Regulations 1976 (SI 1976/2)
- The Nightwear (Safety) Regulations 1985 and 1987 Amendment Regulations (SI 1985/2043 and SI 1987/286)
- The Toys (Safety) Regulations 1995 (SI 1995/204)
- The Furniture and Furnishings (Fire) (Safety) Regulations 1988, 1989 Amendment Regulations and 1993 Amendment Regulations (SI 1988/1374, SI 1989/2358 and SI 1993/207).

The detail of these regulations is outside the scope of this book – explanatory booklets and a full list of safety regulations can be obtained from the Health and Safety Executive (see p. 240).

Summary

- Claims against charities can arise under contracts, through negligence or under legislation.
- For contract claims, see Chapter 11.
- Be aware of the risks of acting negligently, and take professional advice.
- The Health & Safety legislation is very important.
- The Consumer Protection Act (which deals with defective products) is equally important – be aware of the detailed regulations issued under it in respect of a variety of products.
- Liabilities may be covered by insurance (see Chapter 14).

14

Insurance

14.1 Introduction

Insurance is rather like the mythical Dutch boy with his finger in the dyke. It is supposed to hold back the flood waters of physical destruction or liabilities from swamping a charity. Fundraisers need to be aware of the extent of their charity's insurance policies, because fundraising, and in particular fundraising events, can result in a charity incurring liabilities, whether in contract or through negligence (see Chapters 11 and 13).

Law lurks behind everything in insurance, be it the legal complexities of the relationship between the insurer and insured, the meanings of the risks or perils insured against, or the legal liabilities that the policy is designed to cover.

Charities can arrange insurance policies by either:

- going straight to an insurance company or
- going to the insurer via a broker.

Whether or not your charity uses a broker or deals directly with an insurance company does not affect the advice given in this chapter. The charity needs to check with the appropriate person (insurer or broker) about the inter-relationship between the charity's fundraising activities and its insurance policies.

14.2 Utmost good faith

Insurance contracts are different from normal contracts (see Chapter 11). They are contracts of the 'utmost good faith'. This means the insured has a duty to act with the 'utmost good faith' towards the insurer. In particular, you must advise the insurer of all material facts relevant to your application for insurance. You must reveal anything that would influence a prudent insurer in their decision either to take on the risk or to determine the premium. If you fail to disclose all material facts, the insurer can escape *all* liability. It does not matter that you thought the fact was irrelevant: if it might have affected the mythical prudent insurer, you have broken the duty to act with 'utmost good faith'. So beware. Fill in proposal forms with care and keep the insurer up to date with all changes in your activities and practices.

14.3 Who is covered?

You should check that the charity's insurance policies extend to cover the activities of the charity's trading company, if appropriate. A charity's trading company is not automatically covered by the charity's insurance policy. It has to be expressly extended to include the trading company.

14.4 Planning

You should review all your fundraising activities and the insurance cover for them at least once a year. If necessary, do not hesitate to take legal advice. Insurance contracts are legal contracts, and it is true to say that many insurance brokers and insurance companies do not always understand the exact meaning of the policies that they sell! It would be unusual for a fundraising department to be responsible for renewing or reviewing the charity's policies of insurance, but fundraisers should liaise with whoever is responsible within the organisation to ensure that appropriate insurance cover is taken out. A lot of time and effort can be saved if a schedule of proposed fundraising activities for the next insurance year is supplied to the insurer at the time the policy is renewed. But bear in mind the obligation imposed by the duty of 'utmost good faith', which means that you must update the insurer during the course of the year about any developments that could affect their decision to insure the charity or the premium charged.

14.5 Compulsory insurance – employers' liability

The Employers' Liability (Compulsory Insurance) Act 1969 requires that every employer who carries on a business trade or profession in Great Britain (separate legislation applies in Northern Ireland) has to take out and maintain insurance with an authorised insurer against liability for any bodily injury or disease that their employees might sustain as a result of their employment. The minimum indemnity is usually £5 million per employee.

- A certificate of insurance has to be displayed at the employer's premises.
- The premium is usually based on the estimated amount of annual wages and salaries.

The insurance cover applies to employees only and not to independent contractors, volunteers or secondees. However, it is recommended that any charity that uses volunteers extends its employers' liability insurance policy to include volunteers. If it has no employees at all, the charity should take out appropriate insurance to cover volunteers against the risks of bodily injury or disease sustained in the course of their volunteering.

The policy does not cover any liability incurred as a result of the loss by employees (or volunteers) of their property in the course of employment or volunteering. If the employer wishes to cover this risk, then the employer needs a separate policy.

14.6 Compulsory insurance – motor insurance

Section 143 (1) of the Road Traffic Act 1988 requires:

'*every person who uses, or causes or permits another person to use a motor vehicle on a road, to have a policy of insurance to cover any liability which may be incurred as a result of the death of, or bodily injury to, any person or damage to property caused by, or arising out of the use of the vehicle on a road in Great Britain.*'

Similar legislation applies in Northern Ireland. Fundraisers need to be aware that, if they are requiring employees or volunteers to use their cars for fundraising purposes, the individuals' motor insurance policies are extended to cover the risk. This is because the doctrine of 'utmost good faith' can result in what you thought was a valid insurance cover being invalid. For example, a policy that specifies the insured use as 'social, domestic and pleasure purposes' does not cover a trip by the owner of a business to negotiate a business contract.

14.7 Public liability insurance

The purpose of taking out public liability insurance is to cover the charity against its liabilities to third parties for causing death, personal injury or damage to their property. The public liability policy excludes risks covered by other types of policy such as employers' liability and road traffic insurance. The two broad areas covered by a public liability policy are:

- risks arising from the ownership, occupation or management of premises – **premises risks**;
- risks arising from the activities of employees or volunteers to third parties – **activities risks**.

Both of these liabilities can derive from the law of negligence (see **13.3**).

14.7.1 Premises risks

- Escape of dangerous things from the charity's land or buildings: for example, a sponsored kite-flying contest that results in a kite becoming tangled in a light aircraft, with a resulting crash.

- Premises: under the Occupiers' Liability Act 1957, the occupier of any premises owes a duty of care to their visitor to see that the visitor is reasonably safe in using the premises for the purposes for which he or she is invited. If premises are not safe and someone is injured or their property is damaged, the owner can be sued.

> EXAMPLE
>
> A marquee company is contracted by a charity to put up a marquee.
> Someone trips over a guy rope and breaks a leg. They may then have a claim against the charity as the occupier of the land.
> If a claim is successfully brought against the charity, the charity may have a claim itself against the marquee company for having put up the marquee negligently.

14.7.2 Activities

The charity's liability for risks arising from the activities of employees and agents (including volunteers) is known by lawyers as 'vicarious liability'.

An employer is liable for the negligent acts or omissions of employees or volunteers that cause death, bodily injury or damage to property during the course of the employees' employment or the volunteers' volunteering.

It is best to ensure that a charity has a decent level of indemnity under the public liability insurance. A million pounds' worth of cover is the very minimum that a charity should think of.

14.8 Product liability insurance

Chapters 11 and 13 considered the obligations imposed on producers or importers of certain types of goods under the Consumer Protection Act 1987, the Sale of Goods Act 1979, or under the common law rules of negligence. Claims under these Acts or in negligence could put a charity into insolvent liquidation.

> EXAMPLES
>
> A charity sells for 20 pence a booklet which is held together with a staple. The purchaser cuts himself on the razor-sharp exposed edge of the staple, develops blood poisoning and dies.
> The estate of the deceased makes a claim against the charity.
>
> A charity licenses its name and/or logo to a manufacturer of a certain type of good. Under the Consumer Protection Act 1987, the charity could be held liable for damage caused by such a product if it turns out to be defective (see 13.4).

To cover against these risks, a charity can take out product liability insurance. Such insurance is not cheap. Fundraisers should consult their colleagues with responsibility for insurance and consider whether or not items the charity sells or the risks associated with endorsement of products are such that the charity should have a product liability insurance policy.

14.9 Professional indemnity insurance

By the Supply of Goods and Services Act 1982 and common law, suppliers of services are under obligations to use reasonable skill and care in carrying out their duties (see Chapter 11). Failure to do so can give rise to a claim in contract. Professional indemnity insurance is designed to insure a supplier of services against liabilities incurred in the course of his or her business. The title 'professional indemnity' insurance is a misnomer. The insurance is available not only for what are usually termed 'professionals' but also for plumbers, electricians and brokers.

A charity should consider whether or not it is engaging in any services where it could be sued for breach of duty. For example, a charity may supply services as part of primary-purpose trading (see Chapter 10), and some charities have trading companies that supply fundraising services in addition to other organisations. In such cases, a charity should consider whether or not it needs professional indemnity insurance cover. It is possible that, under the terms of the contract whereby the charity or its trading company supplies services, it is required to have professional indemnity insurance cover.

14.10 Defamation

Charities and their trading companies frequently publish materials. The publisher is responsible for the contents of any publication. If the materials are defamatory, then the publisher can be sued. You cannot avoid liability for defamation by printing a disclaimer. Charities should consider whether or not they run any risk of publishing defamatory material and, if so, whether they need to take out defamation insurance. The insurance is normally a separate policy or can form part of a trustee's indemnity insurance policy.

14.11 Trustees' indemnity insurance

Trustees' indemnity insurance is designed to cover the trustees of a charity against liability for breach of their duties as trustees. In the case of a charity that is a limited liability company, it can also include liabilities incurred as a result of wrongful trading.

Wrongful trading applies only if a limited company has gone into insolvent liquidation. A director can be ordered to pay money into the company to help pay the creditors if the director is found guilty of wrongful trading. Broadly speaking, it means allowing a company to go on trading and racking up debts when a reasonable director would have called a halt and realised that continuing to trade would only make matters worse.

If a charity does not have the legal capacity set out in its constitution to take out trustees' indemnity insurance, it is necessary to obtain the Charity Commission's prior consent to a constitutional amendment. The Charity Commission has laid down procedures as to when they will agree to give consent.

One particularly crucial area for trustees can be a Charity Commission investigation into a charity's fundraising methods. The Charity Commission would certainly challenge the use by the charity of its funds to pay for the trustees' legal expenses and accounting fees in resisting any such investigation by the Charity Commission. If, however, the charity has a trustees' indemnity insurance policy, the policy wording is normally wide enough to cover indemnifying the trustees for professional expenses incurred by them in connection with such an enquiry.

Trustees' indemnity insurance policies often contain a number of other types of insurance, such as defamation and professional indemnity. Therefore, if a charity does consider taking out a trustees' indemnity insurance, it is imperative that it considers the precise terms of the policy to see whether or not that policy covers risks that are already insured by the charity under other policies.

14.12 Money

Most standard business policies include a provision for cash on the premises. However, you will not be able to claim unless you can show how much you have lost. You must therefore have an agreed procedure with your insurer on how the amount will be reckoned.

You cannot usually insure unbanked cheques, because they are a promise to pay rather than an actual payment. However, you may be able to insure against the 'additional cost of working' involved in asking donors to write fresh cheques. Again, you will need to be able to show what you have lost, so it is essential to record all cheques as you receive them.

Unopened post poses the biggest risk for money, as it is usually not possible to demonstrate what is inside any unopened post that is destroyed.

Most charities 'self-insure' against their risk (i.e. they bear the risk themselves) but limit the risk with procedures to ensure money is banked on the day they receive it. If you have a sudden and huge surge of donations and cannot open the post the same day, it may be possible to insure 'the expected value' of each sack of mail and just count the sacks.

The costs of recovering money raised by fraudsters without the authority of the charity is not insurable.

14.13 Special events

When undertaking a fundraising event, a charity will be exposed to a number of potential risks, in particular the dangers of a wash-out or cancellation. If this is the case, the charity should consider taking out pluvial insurance cover. The precise cover will depend upon the risks, for example whether tickets have been sold in advance or whether they are all to be sold on the gate. If the latter is the case, the bad weather risks are far higher.

14.13.1 Dangerous or high-risk activities

Charities are increasingly involved in using so-called high-risk activities as a fundraising mechanism (e.g. bunjee jumping, parachute jumping, challenge events, marathons, etc.).

In such circumstances, fundraisers should consider very carefully whether or not the charity's public liability insurance policy affords sufficient cover for the risks involved. Fundraisers should certainly discuss these methods with the charity's insurers to check whether any additional cover is needed.

Don't forget the principle of 'utmost good faith': you might invalidate the whole charity's policy if you fail to notify them of planned activities of this kind.

Fundraisers may think that it is possible to limit the charity's liability by putting an appropriate exclusion clause in the booking conditions so that participants waive any claim they may have against the charity if they suffer bodily injury or death as a result of participation. However, any such exclusion clause is unlawful under the Unfair Contract Terms Act 1977 (see **11.7**). This means that the disclaimer is no defence if a claim is brought.

14.14 What happens when a third party puts on a fundraising event for a charity?

A number of charities engage the services of specialist organisations to put on fundraising events for them like parachute jumping and outdoor concerts. Whether it is the charity or the organiser that is liable in the event of an accident will depend on the circumstances. If the event is put on by an independent organiser, the organiser will probably be responsible to the injured person under the law of negligence (see **13.3**). However, the injured person could also no doubt argue that the charity had effectively endorsed the organiser and therefore also owed the participant a duty of care.

When negotiating with third-party organisers, charities should consider the following points:

- Check that the organiser has public liability insurance (remember this is not compulsory).
- If so, what is the amount of insurance cover?
- Who is the insurer? Are they a reputable company?
- Is the insurer aware of the activities undertaken by the organiser?
- Is the policy wording wide enough to cover the participants?
- Is there a need for special event insurance (e.g. against loss through rain, etc.)?
- Is the organiser handling the charity's money? If so, what insurance is in place/necessary?
- What is the excess?

14.15 Events organised by volunteers

Fundraisers responsible for liaison with branches, and volunteers who fundraise in the charity's name, should consider producing guidelines on what activities volunteers may undertake in the name of the charity and what they may not undertake without the prior consent of the charity's head office and its insurance brokers.

Volunteers can organise events in different ways. If they organise an event in the name of the charity, the charity will be responsible to the participants for the conduct of the event. In the event of any accident, a claim can be made on the charity's insurers.

You should clarify with the insurer whether the activities of your volunteers are covered or whether insurers require the charity to dispatch a letter of authorisation in order to trigger the policy cover.

On the other hand, an event may be put on by an independent group of volunteers, without any liaison with the charity. The only link with the charity may be when a cheque is paid to it at the end of the event. In this case, the event will have been put on by the volunteers in their own name, and it will be they who owe a duty of care to the participants and they who, in the event of any accident, will be sued. Independent volunteers should therefore ensure that they have appropriate insurance cover. From a charity's point of view, it is important not to endorse such activities, even over the phone, without being clear on the liability implications.

Summary

- Charities can arrange insurance either through a broker or directly with the insurance company.
- Insurance contracts are contracts of 'utmost good faith' (i.e. the insurer must know the full facts about what is to be insured).
- Trading companies are not automatically covered by a charity's insurance policy.
- Employer's liability insurance is compulsory, as is motor insurance if driving is a requirement for employees or volunteers.
- Public liability insurance covers the charity against risks to third parties causing death, personal injury or property damage.
- Product liability insurance is expensive and should be considered only if the risk to the charity is great enough to justify the expense.
- A charity should consider whether it is engaging in any services where it could be sued for breach of duty – in which case, it might need to take out professional indemnity insurance.
- Defamation insurance may be required if a charity publishes materials.
- Trustees' indemnity insurance is designed to cover the trustees against liability for breach of their duty.
- Money insurance covers cash on the premises.
- Insurance is required for high-risk activities. If the activity is organised by a third party, the charity must check they have public liability insurance. If volunteers organise events, it is wise to check with your insurers.

15

Advertising

15.1 Misleading advertisements

Making misleading statements in advertising can give rise to criminal offences as well as civil (non-criminal) liabilities.

15.1.1 The Trade Descriptions Act 1968

The Trade Descriptions Act 1968 makes it an offence to:

- apply a false trade description to goods;
- supply or offer to supply goods to which a false trade description is applied;
- knowingly or recklessly make false statements about services, facilities or accommodation.

The maximum sentence for an offence of this kind is an unlimited fine and/or two years' imprisonment.

The statements must be made in the course of a trade or business. For these purposes, you should assume that both fundraising and the general activities of a charity would be regarded as a trade or business.

A description will be false if it is false or misleading 'to a material degree': a minor inaccuracy would not be an offence.

It is a defence to show that the offence was due to a mistake, or reliance on information supplied to the offender, or the act or default of another person, an accident, or some other cause beyond the offender's control. However, the offender must also show that they took all reasonable precautions and exercised all due care to avoid the offence. The defences are very hard to establish, which should give cause for concern, especially if you do not have total knowledge of the goods or services you may be advertising. For example, a false trade description might be attached to goods donated to and sold on by a charity shop.

There have been numerous prosecutions of holiday companies for statements in their brochures and advertisements; this might affect charities (or more usually their trading companies) that advertise overseas challenge events (see Chapter 6).

15.1.2 **The Consumer Protection Act 1987**

The Consumer Protection Act 1987 makes it an offence to give misleading indications as to the price at which any goods, services, accommodation or facilities are available. The maximum sentence for this is an unlimited fine and/or two years' imprisonment. One example of the effect this could have is a brochure that states the minimum amount of sponsorship required for participation in a challenge event: if paying the minimum amount in fact gives no right to take part, and the event literature does not make this completely clear, then the charity will have committed an offence. Guidance is available in the DTI Code of Practice for Traders on Price Indications.

15.1.3 **Package Travel, Package Holidays and Package Tours Regulations 1992**

If you are organising challenge or other events involving travel, you will commit offences if you omit information from the charity's brochures that is prescribed by the Package Travel, Package Holidays and Package Tours Regulations 1992 (see Chapter 6 for more details).

15.1.4 **Control of Misleading Advertisements Regulations 1988**

Under the Control of Misleading Advertisements Regulations 1988, the Director General of Fair Trading may consider complaints about misleading advertisements and bring court proceedings for injunctions to prevent them. His powers cover all advertisements except those for investments or financial services and those broadcast on television or radio. The regulations allow the Independent Television Commission (the Welsh Authority in the case of SC4) and the Radio Authority to hear complaints about misleading advertisements in those media. These bodies then have powers to require broadcasting licence holders to exclude certain advertisements. They may also require any person who appears to them to be responsible for the advertisement to provide evidence of the accuracy of any statement made in the advertisement. All three bodies and the Director General must give reasons for their decisions. Advertisements for investments and financial services are controlled by the Financial Services Authority.

15.1.5   These powers allow the relevant bodies to control false advertising claims by people who claim to be raising funds for your charity but are not in fact authorised by it to do so. Persuading the relevant body to take action could spare a charity in England and Wales the expense of bringing its own proceedings for an injunction under section 62 of the Charities Act 1992 (see **4.7**).

15.1.6   The Control of Misleading Advertisements Regulations 1988 will soon be amended to deal with comparative advertising. Among other things, the regulations will limit the ways in which rival products can be compared, prohibit the denigration or discrediting of competitors, and permit the Director General of Fair Trading to bring proceedings for injunctions. The Director General, as well as the Independent Television Commission and the Radio Authority, will also be required to consider complaints about misleading comparative advertising.

15.1.7 Misrepresentation and breach of contract

Misleading statements about goods or services can give rise to liabilities for misrepresentation or breach of contract. A statement might lead someone to make a purchase, or it might amount to a contractual term; anyone relying on such a statement and suffering loss as a result might be able to sue the charity for that loss (see Chapter 11 for more information about contracts).

15.1.8 Defamation

Some advertising statements can lead to claims for defamation (libel, slander and malicious falsehood). There are various defences to such claims (not least that the statement is true or justified), but you should always seek legal advice before making any statement that might give rise to a claim. The obvious example of such claims in charity advertising is political advertising in which another person or organisation might be denigrated (but see the comments on political advertising in **15.17**).

15.1.9 Other civil law matters are dealt with under the various codes of practice applicable to particular types of advertising that are discussed below.

15.2 Other relevant criminal offences

15.2.1 The Charities Act 1992 section 60

In England and Wales, section 60 of the Charities Act 1992 makes it an offence (with a maximum fine of £5,000) for a professional fundraiser or commercial participator to solicit donations for a charity or other philanthropic or benevolent institution without making the statements required by the Act about their payment and about entitlement to refunds (see Chapters 16 and 17 for a more detailed explanation of this requirement). This applies to advertising and promotional literature. There are no current reported cases of prosecutions.

15.2.2 The Charities Act 1993 section 5

In England and Wales, section 5 of the Charities Act 1993 requires all charities with a gross annual income exceeding £10,000 to include a statement that they are registered charities on all notices, advertisements and other documents soliciting money or other property for their benefit. Failure to comply is an offence punishable by a maximum fine of £1,000.

15.2.3 **The Trade Marks Act 1994**

The Trade Marks Act 1994 makes it an offence to use another person's trade mark in connection with the sale of goods (including advertising goods for sale). It is a defence to show that the user had reasonable grounds to believe that the use did not infringe the trade mark. A case involving the Teletubbies in June 1999 decided that ignorance of the registration of a trade mark is no defence. The maximum sentence is an unlimited fine and ten years' imprisonment. The legislation is aimed at counterfeiters, but it is wide enough to catch the inadvertent use of trade marks on charity merchandise and the sale of donated goods in charity shops.

15.2.4 **The Trading Representations (Disabled Persons) Act 1958**

Except in Northern Ireland, it is an offence under the Trading Representations (Disabled Persons) Act 1958 to make out that blind or disabled people have been involved in the production of goods offered for sale, or that they will benefit from the proceeds of sale, unless the business is carried on by persons excepted under section 15 Disabled Persons (Employment) Act 1944, or by order of the Secretary of State. This applies even if the representation is true. The authors are not aware of any attempt to enforce this legislation, and it is highly unlikely to be enforced against charities that make truthful statements that their goods are manufactured by disabled people or that the sale of goods would otherwise benefit disabled people. The organisations excepted under section 15 of the 1994 Act are those contracted with the Employment Service under the supported employment programme (see p. 240).

In order to seek exemption under the 1958 Act, by order of the Secretary of State, you should apply to the Department for Education and Employment's Adult Disadvantage Policy Division (see p. 236), explaining:

- that you have charitable status (you will need to provide evidence, e.g. registered number);
- what you intend to sell, to whom and how;
- whether disabled people are employed in the making of the goods or benefit from their sale (or both).

15.2.5 **The Financial Services Act 1986**

The Financial Services Act 1986 makes it an offence (maximum sentence an unlimited fine and/or two years' imprisonment) to issue or cause to be issued an advertisement about regulated investments, unless the advertisement is issued or approved by an authorised person under the Act. The definition of advertisement is very wide and could cover the mention in newsletters of commercial-participator arrangements with financial services institutions. The authorised institution should always be asked to approve such copy in advance and to confirm that it complies with the law. One of the types of regulated investment that charities might encounter in the fundraising field is long-term life insurance. If fundraisers have any doubts about whether a commercial participator's product is a regulated investment under the Act, they should ask the commercial participator; alternatively, they should speak to their solicitors or the Financial Services Authority (tel.: 0845 606 1234; see also p. 240).

It is an offence under the Financial Services Act to 'make arrangements' for anyone to buy a regulated investment unless you are either authorised under the Financial Services Act or formally appointed by an authorised person as its representative. The Act contains a very wide definition of the phrase 'making arrangements', which includes endorsing an investment. The Financial Services Authority has indicated that merely licensing a commercial participator to use the charity's name and logo in connection with a statement by the commercial participator that the charity will benefit from a sale is not, on its own, making arrangements. However, if the charity gives the commercial participator access to its database of supporters, or itself promotes the arrangements to its supporters, or the statement made implies the charity's endorsement of the investment itself, the Financial Services Authority would regard this as making arrangements. In such cases, the charity should be formally appointed as the commercial participator's authorised representative.

15.2.6 The Banking Act 1987 and the 1988 Advertisements Regulations

The Banking Act 1987 and the 1988 Advertisements Regulations issued under it control the way in which bank-deposit advertisements are issued. A deposit advertisement includes any means of bringing to a person's attention information that might reasonably be presumed to be intended to lead directly or indirectly to the making of a deposit. This is wide enough to cover information in newsletters notifying supporters of certain commercial-participator arrangements with banks. All copy relating to such arrangements should be cleared with the relevant bank to ensure it complies with the regulations.

15.2.7 The Building Societies Act 1987

The Building Societies Act 1987 does not contain similar restrictions, although the Building Societies Commission has power to issue directions in relation to particular building societies or advertisements and advertisements generally, and may require modifications to advertisements.

15.2.8 The Consumer Transactions (Restriction on Statements) Order 1976

It is an offence under the Consumer Transactions (Restriction on Statements) Order 1976 to try to include in a contract certain terms that are void under the Sale of Goods Act 1979 and other Acts, and to try to exclude certain consumer rights. The Order also makes it an offence to supply information about a consumer's rights against a supplier without stating that the consumer's statutory rights remain unaffected.

15.2.9 The Unsolicited Goods and Services Acts 1971 and 1975

The Unsolicited Goods and Services Acts 1971 and 1975 make it an offence for any person in the course of any trade or business to make demands or threats about payment for goods sent unsolicited. Any person receiving unsolicited goods is entitled to treat them as if they were a gift. See also Chapter 4 concerning consumers' rights to cancel certain contracts concluded after unsolicited visits.

15.2.10 The Malicious Communications Act 1988

The Malicious Communications Act 1988 makes it an offence (maximum fine £2,000) to send letters containing:

- a message that is indecent or grossly offensive,
- a threat,
- information that is false and that the sender knows or believes to be false,

if the sender intends that it should cause distress or anxiety.

It is unlikely that fundraisers will fall foul of this provision, but they should take care with distressing advertising material. These provisions might also apply to certain types of chain letter (see Chapter 3). The Malicious Communications (Northern Ireland) Order 1988 creates the same offences in Northern Ireland. The legislation does not apply to Scotland, although the distribution or display of obscene material can be prosecuted under the Civic Government (Scotland) Act 1982.

15.2.11 Post Office Act 1953

It is an offence to send a postal packet that has on it anything that is grossly offensive or of an indecent or obscene character.

15.2.12 Post Office Act 1953 Business Advertisements (Disclosure) Order 1977

Advertisements for goods sold in the course of a business (which would include most sales of goods by charities) must make it reasonably clear that they are being sold in the course of a business. This does not apply to auctions.

15.2.13 The Consumer Credit Act 1974 and the Consumer Credit (Advertisement) Regulations 1989

You are unlikely to be involved in offering credit to consumers. If you do, however, you should be aware that the Consumer Credit Act 1974 and the Consumer Credit (Advertisement) Regulations 1989 control advertisements that indicate that credit is available. There are criminal offences for breaching the Act and regulations.

15.3 Planning law and flyposting, etc.
The Town and Country Planning Act 1990

15.3.1   The Town and Country Planning Act 1990 and the 1992 Control of Advertisements Regulations issued under it contain detailed requirements as to the display of public notices generally. It is an offence to display such a notice in contravention of the regulations. It is not only the person who displays the notice who commits the offence but also (unless they can prove that they did not know or consent) the person on whose land it is displayed and the person whose goods, trade, business or other concerns are publicised by the advertisement.

15.3.2   The regulations establish a system for obtaining consent from the local planning authority, although certain types of advertisement are permitted without express consent. If you are unsure about whether you need express consent, contact the local authority and ask to speak to the planning department.

15.3.3   The following standard conditions apply to any consent:

- the advertisement and site must be kept clean and tidy;
- any hoarding must be maintained in a safe condition;
- the site owner's permission must be obtained.

15.3.4   General consent is granted for many types of advertisement, of which the following may be relevant to fundraisers:

- **Advertisements announcing any local event of a religious, educational, cultural, political, social or recreational character**, as long as this is not an event promoted or carried on for commercial purposes. There is no definition of commercial purposes, so the consent may not cover some fundraising events carried on by charities or their trading companies. If in doubt, speak to the local planning authority. The advertisements: must not exceed 0.6 m²; must not be displayed earlier than 28 days before the first day of the event; and must be removed within 14 days after the event.

- **Advertisements for the sale of goods displayed on the land where the goods are situated or the sale is held**, as long as this is not land normally used for holding such sales. Only one advertisement may be displayed at a time; it must not exceed 1.2 m²; no character or symbol may be more than 0.75 m high; no part of it may be more than 4.6 m above ground level; illumination is prohibited; it must not be put up more than 28 days before the sale, and it must be removed within 14 days after the sale.

15.3.5 Special provisions apply in relation to certain areas that have been declared areas of special control, such as conservation areas. Contact the planning department at the local authority to find out whether the area is one of special control.

15.3.6 The local planning authority can serve notices that discontinue express or general consent and require advertisers to comply with the regulations. Breach of the regulations is an offence punishable by a maximum fine of £1,000 and, in the case of a continuing offence, £100 per day. The local planning authority can also charge to the offender its costs of removing the advertisement.

15.3.7 Private landowners can bring prosecutions: British Telecom, for example, has brought prosecutions in relation to prostitutes' calling cards in telephone boxes. Presumably, fundraisers will not be adopting this form of fundraising.

15.3.8 Scotland and Northern Ireland have similar planning laws: fundraisers there should contact their local planning authorities for more details.

15.3.9 The Highways Act 1980

The Highways Act 1980 makes it an offence to paint or otherwise inscribe or affix any picture, letter, sign or other mark on the highway or on any tree, structure or works on the highway without the consent of the highway authority. The maximum fine is £2,500, which is potentially per poster or mark.

15.3.10 Flyposting might also constitute the offence of criminal damage, but prosecutions are more likely to be brought under the above Acts.

15.3.11 Private landowners could also sue for trespass (a civil law claim) and recover their costs of removing posters.

15.4 Intellectual property

Advertising can infringe other people's intellectual property rights. Before advertising, consider, for example, whether you have a right to publish someone else's photographs, drawings, designs or text. Are you using the trade mark of another person or organisation? If so, is that permitted either by the owner or under the Trade Marks Act 1994? That Act permits the use of another person's trade mark to identify their goods or services in accordance with honest practices and as long as the use does not without good cause take unfair advantage of, and is not detrimental to, the distinctive character or repute of the mark. (See Chapter 21 for more information about intellectual property rights.)

15.5 General trust law

See Chapter 1 about the creation of trusts for particular purposes and restricted funds through appeals for funds. Ensure that all appeal literature takes account of the law described in that chapter.

15.6 **The British Codes of Advertising and Sales Promotion**

15.6.1   These two codes are produced by the Committee of Advertising Practice (CAP) and enforced by the Advertising Standards Authority (ASA). New codes came into force on 1 October 1999. They cover the vast majority of print media advertisements such as those in newspapers, magazines and billboards and also:

- cinema and video commercials;
- advertisements in non-broadcast electronic media such as computer games;
- view-data services;
- marketing databases containing consumers' personal information;
- sales promotions;
- advertisement promotions;
- advertisements sent by fax and e-mail and posted on the Internet.

15.6.2   They do not cover, for example:

- radio and television advertisements;
- oral communications, including telephone conversations and advertisements on premium-rate telephone services (although they do cover advertisements for such services);
- press releases and other public relations material;
- editorial communications;
- flyposting;
- packages, wrappers, labels and tickets unless they advertise a sales promotion or are themselves visible in an advertisement;
- most point-of-sale displays;
- party political advertisements.

15.6.3   The essential requirements are that all advertisements and sales promotions must be legal, decent, honest and truthful. The codes elaborate on these requirements: fundraisers should read them in detail if they are not employing an advertising agency. Copies can be obtained free from CAP or from their website (see p. 238). Some of these elaborations are as follows:

- If there is significant division in informed opinion about any claims made, they should not be represented as universally agreed.
- Advertisements should not contain anything likely to cause widespread offence, although this is judged in the context of the advertisement. Advertisements may be distasteful without necessarily conflicting with that requirement.
- Advertisements must not mislead by inaccuracy, ambiguity, exaggeration, omission or otherwise.
- Advertisements should not cause fear or distress without good reason.

Shocking claims or images should not be used merely to attract attention.

- Other businesses and their products should not be unfairly attacked. Comparisons should be clear and fair.
- Compliance with the Codes will be judged on the context, medium, audience, product and prevailing standards of decency.
- Advertisements should not portray people unfairly or refer to them in an adverse or offensive way.

15.6.4 The Sales Promotion Code, which regulates the nature and administration of promotional marketing techniques, contains specific rules about certain types of promotion and claim, including charity-linked promotions. It goes further than the requirements under Part II of the Charities Act 1992 (see Chapters 8 and 16) and states that all promotions claiming that participation will benefit registered charities or good causes must:

- name each charity or good cause that will benefit, and advertisers must be able to show the ASA the formal agreement with those benefiting from the promotion;
- when it is not a registered charity, define its nature and objectives;
- specify exactly what will be gained by the named charity or cause and state the basis on which the contribution will be calculated;
- state if the promoters have imposed any limitations on the contribution they will make out of their own pocket;
- not limit consumers' contributions – if an amount is stated for each purchase, there should be no cut-off point for contributions; if a target total is stated, any extra money collected should be given to the named charity or cause on the same basis as contributions below that level.

In addition, advertisers must:

- be able to show that any targets set are realistic and should not exaggerate the benefit to the charity or cause that will be derived from individual purchases of the promoted product;
- if asked, make available to consumers a current or final total of contributions made;
- take particular care when appealing to children.

15.6.5 The requirement to specify *exactly* what will be gained by the charity is more onerous than the requirements under the Charities Act 1992. This is particularly important if an advertiser intends to make a statement that complies technically with the Act but does not really tell the public how much the charity will receive. If there is any doubt, seek advice from the CAP Copy Advice Team. A statement that 'all net profits' will be paid or donated to the charity is frowned on by the Charity Commission and the Home Office, although it complies technically with the Act. However, the Copy Advice Team has indicated that it would comply with the codes, so long as net profits are reasonably expected. If there is any real doubt about whether a profit might be made, the phrase 'any net profits' should be used. The concern of the Charity Commission and Home Office is that 'all net profits' might (and often do) amount to £0.00.

The importance of saying exactly what will be gained by the charity is illustrated by a complaint that was upheld against SWALEC. Their advertisement stated in the small print that some of the money (which the large print stated was to be paid to the NSPCC) would be retained in order to cover 'tightly controlled' costs of SWALEC. No percentage was given, nor other information that would explain or limit those costs.

15.6.6 The timing and placing of advertisements is also important. For example, a complaint was upheld against the British Red Cross Society for scheduling an advertisement on the Cartoon Network that showed children and adults with diseases and injuries. Only two complaints were made, in one case involving a three year old said to have run from the room in distress at the pictures.

15.6.7 Other rules that may be particularly relevant to charity advertising concern promotions with prizes (see Chapter 5), advertisements addressed to or featuring children, environmental claims such as 'environmentally friendly', distance selling, and list and database practice (see also data protection in Chapter 12). The rules affecting database owners and users are a gloss on the charity's obligations under the Data Protection Act 1998, but they are essential reading for those compiling and using or selling the charity's database of supporters.

15.6.8 Consumer protection is an essential element of the Sales Promotion Code. In particular, promoters must ensure that their products (and adventurous activities are specifically mentioned) are safe, and must respect the right to a reasonable degree of privacy and freedom from annoyance. Promoters must also be able to demonstrate that they have made a reasonable estimate of the likely response and that they are capable of meeting it. Using the phrase 'subject to availability' is not enough. This may be particularly relevant to those organising challenge events.

15.6.9 Before placing an advertisement, the advertiser must hold (and be able to send to the ASA almost immediately, if requested) all relevant evidence to substantiate any claim made in an advertisement.

15.6.10 The ASA needs to receive only one complaint before it begins an investigation, which it will do if it considers the complaint has some justification. Complaints must be in writing and should include a copy of the advertisement or a note of where and when it appeared. The identities of individual members of the public who complain and have no commercial interest in the complaint are not revealed without their consent. The identities of complaining competitors are revealed.

15.6.11   Once the ASA has conducted its investigation, it will publish its adjudication. There is then an appeal to the ASA's chairman. A leaflet explaining the full complaints procedure can be obtained from the ASA (see p. 000). One vitally important aspect of the complaints procedure is that the codes are interpreted and applied in the spirit as well as the letter. They cannot be circumvented on technicalities, and a strict legalistic approach is not taken when adjudicating on complaints.

15.6.12   If the ASA upholds a complaint, it can lead to bad publicity. In addition, the ASA can effectively ban an advertisement by bringing pressure to bear on the organisation carrying the advertisement. This would have a big financial impact on the charity: many charities have fallen foul of the codes, with just such consequences. Rather than risk this, it is possible to obtain free and confidential advice in advance from the CAP Copy Advice team (see p. 238).

15.6.13   Any ruling the ASA makes can be judicially reviewed. After 2 October 2000, it may also be challenged in the UK courts under the Human Rights Act 1998 as an infringement of the right to freedom of expression.

15.7 Independent television

15.7.1   Television advertisements and programmes are regulated by the Independent Television Commission (ITC), which licenses commercial television in the UK under the Broadcasting Act 1990. All licensed stations must comply with the ITC codes including:

- the Code of Advertising Standards and Practice
- the Programme Code (which also covers broadcast appeals)
- the Code of Programme Sponsorship.

Because of the high cost, any charity intending to advertise on television or make broadcast appeals would engage an advertising agency which would advise on the codes. Brief details only are given here, but copies of the codes can be obtained from the ITC (see p. 241).

15.7.2   The ITC Code of Advertising Standards and Practice contains detailed requirements about charity advertising, religious advertising, politics and public controversy (see also **15.11**), lotteries (see also Chapter 5), and mail order and direct response advertising, among other things.

15.7.3   The ITC also publishes guidance notes that should be read alongside the codes. Those that may be particularly relevant to charity advertising are:

- No 6 Religious advertising (re-issued December 1998)
- No 7 Lotteries, pools and bingo (re-issued December 1998)
- No 9 Children and young people (re-issued December 1998)
- No 11 Services ancillary to programmes (re-issued December 1998).

This last one deals with, for example, information that backs up programme or advertising material such as supplementary educational material, invitations to viewers to take part in future programmes and details of events featured in programmes designed to assist viewers' understanding of the programmes.

15.7.4   The code does not permit advertisements soliciting donations for, or promoting the needs of, bodies whose activities are financed wholly or mainly from donations, unless those bodies are either officially recognised in the UK as charities or are non-UK-based charities. The peculiarities of UK charity law and the fact that many non-UK bodies may be granted 'charitable' tax concessions in their own jurisdictions (but would not have charitable status if established in the UK) make this illogical, and it will certainly be open to challenge by UK non-charities under the Human Rights Act 1998.

15.7.5   Before accepting advertisements from a charity, a licensed station must satisfy itself that the charity is registered with the Charity Commission or is otherwise officially recognised (e.g. by the Inland Revenue) and obtain assurances from the charity:

- that it does not involve itself in transactions in which trustees or staff have a financial interest;
- that all donations will be applied solely for the purposes specified or implied in the advertising (this would nevertheless permit reasonable administrative overheads);
- that it will not disclose the names of contributors without the contributors' consent and will otherwise comply with data protection law (see Chapter 12).

15.7.6   Advertisements for charities must:

- handle with care and discretion matters likely to arouse strong emotion;
- not suggest anyone will lack proper feeling or fail in any responsibility if they do not support the charity;
- respect the dignity of those on whose behalf the appeal is made;
- not address any fundraising message specifically to children;
- not contain comparisons with other charities;
- avoid exaggeration, for example by illustrating a message with non-typical, extreme cases;
- not mislead as to the activity of the charity or the use to which donations will be put;
- not be scheduled immediately before or after programme appeals or community service announcements;
- not feature presenters who regularly present on the same station.

15.7.7   If a commercial participator promotes a charity in a television advertisement, the following conditions apply in addition to the requirements under Part II of the Charities Act 1992 (see Chapter 16):

- The advertiser must provide the licensed station with evidence of the charity's consent.
- If sale proceeds are to be donated, the basis on which the donations will be calculated must be made clear; conditions such as sales reaching a particular level before donations are made are not acceptable.
- Offers in relation to medical products are not acceptable.

15.7.8   There are special rules on religious advertising.

15.7.9   The ITC Code of Programme Sponsorship covers programmes that are paid (or part paid) for by an advertiser with a view to promoting its own or another's name, trade mark, image, activities, products or other commercial interest. Although this is an area dominated by commercial interests, a charity might be able to justify such an activity with particular programmes and might do so with commercial partners. The code contains specific requirements applicable to sponsorship by charities and religious bodies (which may or may not be charitable). One provision applicable to charities is that the sponsored programme must not promote the charity itself or its activities, even if it addresses issues within the charity's field of activity.

15.7.10   Any body whose objects are wholly or mainly of a political nature is prohibited from sponsoring programmes. This will not affect charities (see also Chapter 5).

15.7.11   The ITC Programme Code covers the content of programmes including broadcast appeals by charities, the giving of publicity to charities in programmes and the coverage of fundraising events.

15.7.12   UK-based non-charities may not make a broadcast appeal unless it is in response to an emergency. In such a case, a 'responsible public fund' must have been established to deal with it. There is no definition of a 'responsible public fund', but it would probably include a fund established under the supervision of, or with the guidance of, the broadcasters, or a fund established by a consortium such as the Disasters Emergency Committee.

15.7.13   All charities wishing to make broadcast appeals must be able to demonstrate that they can fulfil an established need and achieve a stable position in the charitable world. They must also be able to show that they need funds for specified purposes that cannot reasonably be provided from income or reserves. In relation to broadcast appeals, see also the details of the Broadcast Appeals Consortium (**15.10.1**) and the explanation of the creation of restricted funds and trusts for particular purposes in Chapter 1.

15.7.14   The Programme Code also contains provisions about free community service announcements that publicise local voluntary and community organisations and are transmitted between programmes. These must be confined to appeals for volunteers and giving information about the service; there must be no appeal for funds.

15.7.15   Advertising copy can be cleared in advance by the Broadcasting Advertising Clearance Centre (BACC, see p. 237). BACC must view all advertisements before transmission is approved. The ITC can require a licensed station to withdraw advertising that it believes infringes the code. Advance clearance by the BACC does not prevent the ITC from banning an advertisement. The ITC is subject to judicial review and will be required under the Human Rights Act 1998 to comply with the European Convention on Human Rights, in particular the right to freedom of expression.

15.7.16   The ITC complaints procedures are set out in ITC Guidance Note No 8.

15.8   Independent radio

15.8.1   The Radio Authority (RA) licenses commercial radio stations under the Broadcasting Act 1990 and controls radio advertisements using the same powers as the ITC. The RA Code of Advertising and Sponsorship and its Programme Code contain very similar requirements to those in the ITC codes. (Copies may be obtained from the RA: for details, see p. 244.)

15.8.2   The RA reserves the right to temporarily suspend advertising on the radio by individual charities soliciting funds in connection with a disaster when a free appeal has been organised by the Disasters Emergency Committee on behalf of charities pooling their activities to deal with the disaster.

15.8.3   Advertisements for charities must not be broadcast immediately before or after programme appeals for donations or community service announcements.

15.8.4   Advance clearance of all charity advertising must be obtained from the Radio Advertising Clearance Centre (see p. 243).

15.8.5   As with the ITC, the RA is subject to judicial review and will have to comply with the European Convention on Human Rights, particularly with respect to freedom of expression.

15.9   BBC Television and Radio

15.9.1   The BBC is governed by its charter and is not permitted to carry advertisements as such. However, its programmes frequently cover the activities of charities, and there are regular broadcast appeals in *The Week's Good Cause* on

Radio 4 and *Lifeline* on BBC Television. The BBC Producers' Guidelines (copies are available on its website at www.bbc.co.uk) specify how programmes must deal with charities. The guidelines are principally concerned with upholding the balance and integrity of BBC journalism and other programme making, but they also seek to ensure that some charities or causes are not given prominence over others. Programmes should not, for example, be seen as endorsing any particular charity.

15.9.2 Charity appeals are advised on and co-ordinated by the Appeals Advisory Committee, which aims to spread appeals as widely and fairly as possible among suitable charities. Appeals for emergencies abroad are usually only given on behalf of the Disasters Emergency Committee, a consortium of aid charities. There are separate Appeals Advisory Committees for Scotland, Northern Ireland and Wales.

15.9.3 The BBC has also published its appeals policy. Copies are available from the BBC Appeals Office (see p. 236). The general policy is summarised as follows:

- Organisations should be concerned directly, or indirectly through preventative work, with the alleviation of human suffering, or they should aim to promote social, physical, cultural, mental or moral well-being.
- This remit may be widened to include animal charities and charities concerned with preservation of the national heritage, the general aim being to achieve a catholic range of interest over a period.

15.9.4 The policy is elaborated by working principles that may be summarised as follows:

- The organisation must be a recognised UK charity.
- The charity should have; or be likely to gain, public support.
- The charity should have attained, or have a good prospect of attaining, a record of achievement and should be financially viable.
- The charity must demonstrate a need for funds beyond its income or reserves.
- Religious charities are eligible if funds are to be used for the relief of suffering, etc.
- Repair of architectural heritage is permitted.
- Memorial funds are generally not recommended unless charitable and of great national interest.
- Educational charities are only permitted in limited circumstances.
- Appeals are not permitted if a trade or professional organisation's benevolent fund would normally provide the benefits.
- Medical or other research appeals should be able to show that the research is of national significance, of the highest quality and for the public benefit.
- The applicant's work must either be national or international in scope, or have some national or international significance.

■ Most charities may generally not apply for an appeal more than once every three years, or two years if the previous application was turned down.

15.10 **Broadcast appeals**

15.10.1   The main requirements of the ITC and the RA under the Broadcasting Act 1990, and the BBC under its charter, are set out above. In addition, fundraisers making appeals on radio and television may wish to consult the Charter and Recommendations of the Broadcasting Appeals Consortium, which was established by a number of charities and the Broadcasting Support Services. For copies, contact Broadcasting Support Services (see p. 237).

15.10.2   If the appeal is in response to an emergency or disaster, you should consult the Attorney General's Guidelines for Disaster Appeals (Charity Commission leaflet CC40) and Chapter 1 concerning the terms of appeals and the creation of trusts for particular purposes and restricted funds. It is particularly important to word the appeal properly, so that surplus funds that are not needed to deal with the immediate crisis can be put to similar use within the charity's objects or form part of the general funds of the charity.

15.10.3   See also Chapters 16 and 17 concerning the requirements of professional fundraisers and commercial participators making such appeals, including certain rights to refunds, and the exclusion of actors, etc. from the definition of professional fundraiser when they are paid to make broadcast appeals on behalf of charities.

15.11 **Broadcasting Standards Commission**

15.11.1   The Broadcasting Standards Commission (BSC) was established under the Broadcasting Act 1996 and publishes a Code on Fairness and Decency and a Code on Standards. These codes apply to both state and independent radio and television and give guidance on matters such as violence, sexual conduct and general standards of taste and decency, whether in programmes, appeals or advertisements. The BSC considers and adjudicates on complaints from the public about these matters and about unfair or unjust treatment. If a complaint is upheld, the BSC can require the broadcaster concerned to publish a summary of the complaint and the BSC's findings. The BSC has no power to punish.

15.11.2   Only people or organisations affected by the relevant programmes can make complaints about unfair or unjust treatment and infringement of privacy. Such complaints must be made in writing (a complaint form can be obtained from the BSC) within three months after a television broadcast or six weeks after a radio broadcast. The Commission can extend the time limits.

Anyone can make a complaint about matters of taste and decency. Complaints must, again, be in writing (using the complaint form) and must be made within two months of a television broadcast and three weeks of a radio broadcast. Once a complaint has been received, the BSC will investigate. If it considers it appropriate that the complaint be pursued, it will generally require the broadcaster to respond in writing. The BSC can hold oral hearings. Personal details of a complainant are not included in public information.

15.11.3 There is no appeal against the BSC's adjudication, although it can be judicially reviewed.

15.11.4 Contact details for the BSC are given on page 237.

15.12 Cinema

All cinema advertisements must be approved by the copy panel of the Cinema Advertising Association. If advertisements last 30 seconds or longer, they must also be submitted to the British Board of Film Classification.

15.13 Telephone, faxes and e-mail

15.13.1 Advertising Standards Authority

Oral communications are not covered by the British Codes of Advertising and Sales Promotion, but faxes and e-mails are. See Chapter 12 about data protection and restrictions on direct marketing.

15.13.2 Premium-rate telephone services

Premium-rate services are regulated by the Independent Committee for the Supervision of Standards of Telephone Information Services (ICSTIS). The ICSTIS Code of Practice defines a premium-rate service as one 'where the overall charge paid by a customer to the network operator for the service … is passed by the network operator … to the service provider'. Fundraisers might provide premium-rate telephone services for supplying information about events or for other purposes such as competitions with prizes.

15.13.3 If a charity or its trading company wishes to provide a premium-rate service, it must do so through a network operator registered with ICSTIS. However, it is the service provider itself that is responsible for compliance with the code, and before starting a service the code and guidelines issued by ICSTIS should be considered carefully. Copies of these, as well as an application form for registering a service, can be obtained from ICSTIS or from its website (see p. 241).

15.13.4 The code has detailed requirements as to the promotion and content of services, the first three being that they must be legal, decent and honest.

15.13.5   There are detailed requirements about price indications:

- Promotional material must clearly state the price per call in the form of a numerical price per minute inclusive of VAT, or the total maximum cost of the complete service.
- The information must be legible, prominent, horizontal and presented in a way that does not require close examination.
- If the service is advertised on television, the pricing information must be spoken and displayed if the cost can exceed £2 per call.
- If a caller is unlikely to have seen or heard a promotion containing the pricing information, the service provider must include such information at the beginning of the service.
- None of these requirements need be met if the call price cannot exceed 50p.
- The contact details of the service provider should also be clearly stated, where these are not obvious.

15.13.6   The code has detailed requirements for promotional material and call content in relation to particular types of service, including competition services (see also Chapter 5) and charitable promotions and fundraising. Promotional material for charitable promotions and for fundraising must make clear:

- the name of the beneficiary;
- either the total sum per call or the amount per minute to be paid to the beneficiary;
- any restrictions or conditions attached to the contribution to be made to the beneficiary.

15.13.7   There must be no limit to callers' contributions, and any amounts exceeding expected income must be given to the charity on the same basis. Substantiation of the benefit to the charity as a result of the promotion must be available on request.

15.13.8   Note that these arrangements are also subject to the Charities Act 1992 (see Chapters 16 and 17) and to the British Codes of Advertising and Sales Promotion (if advertised in print media, etc.), or the RA and ITC codes (if broadcast on radio and television).

15.13.9   Special rules apply to 'pay for product' services where the cost of the call exceeds £1. Prior permission from ICSTIS is required if the call cost exceeds £5 or is charged at the £1.50 per minute tariff, or is a live service. No pay for product service may be aimed at persons under 16 or promote products that may be expected to be particularly attractive to persons under 16. The call costs must also not exceed £20. See ICSTIS Guideline No 11.

15.13.10 ICSTIS has a range of sanctions to enforce compliance with its code, including fines and recommendations to network operators to pass the service provider's profits to ICSTIS or to refuse to carry a service.

15.13.11 The operation of a premium-rate service is a trading activity that should be generally run through the charity's trading company. An exception to this would be a line that delivered services as a primary purpose of the charity or that simply gave information about the charity's primary purposes. Such use would, however, be rare. It would also be possible to run the activity through the charity if the income fell within the tax relief for small-scale trading. (For more information about trading and the use of a separate company, see Chapters 10 and 22.)

15.14 The Internet

Advertisements on the Internet are subject to the British Codes of Advertising and Sales Promotion. Advertisements in any other media for Internet services or sites will be subject to the codes of practice covering those media. The International Chamber of Commerce has published Guidelines on Advertising and Marketing on the Internet, which are available on its website (www.iccwbo.org).

15.15 Aerial advertising

15.15.1 The Civil Aviation (Aerial Advertising) Regulations 1995 prohibit certain types of aerial advertisements, visible and audible. The two most common types of advertising that charities might adopt are permitted, namely:

- banners trailed behind aeroplanes;
- advertisements on captive balloons that are not more than 7 metres in any linear dimension and not more than 20 cubic metres in total area.

15.16 Direct marketing/distance selling

15.16.1 In addition to the requirements set out above, charities engaging in direct marketing and/or distance selling should consider the codes of practice issued by the following organisations:

- the Direct Marketing Association;
- the Mail Order Traders' Association;
- the National Newspapers' Mail Order Protection Scheme.

(See pp. 239, 242 and 243 for details.)

Also relevant is the Mail Order Transactions (Information) Order 1976. This states that advertisements for mail-order goods must state the name and business address of the person conducting the business.

15.16.2 Charities involved in direct mail must also pay particular attention to data-protection law, which is explained in Chapter 12.

15.16.3 This book does not deal in detail with the sale of goods (including sales of goods through direct mail). However, certain contractual and liability matters that will be relevant to such sales are considered in Chapters 11 and 13; **11.8** also deals with the requirements of the Consumer Protection (Distance Selling) Regulations 2000.

15.17 **Political advertising and campaigning**

15.17.1 Political advertising seeks to influence government or public opinion regarding laws or government decisions. This might be the sole purpose of an advertisement or it might be linked with or implied in an appeal for funds. Political advertising is governed by general charity law and under the Broadcasting Act 1990. Unless it is party political advertising, it is also covered by the British Codes of Advertising and Sales Promotion (see above).

15.17.2 Charity law does not allow a charity to exist for a political purpose, but a charity may nevertheless advertise and campaign politically to achieve its non-political purposes. This is a complex area of law; any charity intending to engage in such activities should consider carefully the Charity Commission leaflets CC9 and CC9a, which set out the limits imposed by the Charity Commission on such activities by registered charities in England and Wales, and take legal advice.

15.17.3 The essential requirements of the Charity Commission are that:
- the activity must be within the charity's objects;
- there must be a reasonable expectation that the activity will further the charity's objects to an extent that justifies the resources expended;
- views expressed must be based on a well-founded, reasoned case and expressed in a responsible way;
- information provided to the public in support of the campaign as a whole must be accurate and sufficiently full to support its position;
- if a communication medium makes it impracticable to set out the full basis of the charity's position, the charity can simply state its position, but it must be able to set out its full position if called on to do so;
- it would be unacceptable (except where the nature of the medium makes it impracticable) to seek to persuade government or the public on the basis of material that is merely emotive;
- a charity must not claim evidence of public support for its position on a political issue without adequate justification;
- a charity must not invite the public to take action in support of its position without providing them with sufficient information to enable them to decide whether to give their support;
- a charity must not provide information that it knows (or ought to know) to be inaccurate, or that has been distorted by selection to support a preconceived position;

- a charity must not promote the results of research that it knows, or ought to know, to be flawed.

15.17.4 Broadcasting Act 1990

Political advertising on commercial radio and television is controlled by the RA and ITC under the Broadcasting Act 1990. This Act states that a licensed service must not include:

- any advertisement that is inserted by or on behalf of any body whose objects are wholly or mainly of a political nature;
- any advertisement that is directed towards any political end;
- any advertisement that has any relation to any industrial dispute (other than an advertisement of a public-service nature inserted by, or on behalf of, a government department).

15.17.5 The ITC and RA codes of practice indicate that the term 'political' is to be understood in the wider sense of charity law described in **15.17.1**, and not as meaning 'party political'. That view has been upheld in the Court of Appeal in the case of a radio advertisement for Amnesty International United Kingdom that was banned. There is some doubt as to whether these provisions breach the right to freedom of expression in the European Convention on Human Rights (Amnesty took its case to the European Commission for Human Rights and reached an out-of-court settlement with the United Kingdom government), and there may be further challenges once the Human Rights Act 1998 comes into force in October 2000, both in relation to broadcasting and also to general charity law.

15.17.6 The BBC Charter and Producers' Guidelines also contain safeguards to control political content in broadcasting, but the BBC is, as mentioned above, prohibited from carrying advertising in any case (see **15.9**).

15.18 VAT

Special rules regarding VAT on advertising services and the supply of printed matter are dealt with in Chapter 20.

Summary

- There are numerous laws covering the content of advertisements, including many criminal offences ranging from recklessly making certain false statements to using other people's trade marks.
- Advertisements soliciting funds for a registered charity must state that the charity is registered.
- Billboard advertisements, flyposters, etc. must comply with planning law and highways law. There are general consents for some types of advertisements for charity events.
- Advertisements must be legal, decent, honest and truthful. The British Codes of Advertising and Sales Promotion contain detailed requirements applicable to charity advertising.
- Make sure your advertisements are checked in advance by the Copy Advice Team of the Committee of Advertising Practice.
- The Radio Authority and Independent Television Commission have codes of practice for advertising in those media.
- There are special rules for premium-rate advertising services – see the ICSTIS Code.
- Data-protection law (Chapter 12) must be considered if using telephone/fax/e-mail advertising.
- Take legal advice on the content of campaigning advertisements that seek to influence government or public opinion.
- Take legal advice if your advertising might defame anyone.

16

Commercial participators

16.1 Introduction

Part II of the Charities Act 1992 imposes controls in England and Wales on people who sell goods and services and who state that a proportion of the proceeds from such sales is to go to a charitable institution. These people are called 'commercial participators'. See **4.1** concerning the definition of a 'charitable institution'.

16.2 What is a 'commercial participator'?

16.2.1 A commercial participator is someone who encourages purchases of goods or services on the grounds that some of the proceeds will go to a charitable institution or that a donation will be made. Commercial organisations that enter into cause-related marketing (CRM) deals with charities will almost certainly be commercial participators. Charitable institutions considering CRM will need to be careful in planning and negotiating the relationship with the partner and consider:

- the legal requirements set out in the 1992 Act (covered in this chapter)
- controls on advertisements (see Chapter 15)
- taxation (see Chapter 8)
- VAT (see Chapter 20).

16.2.2 Section 58(1) defines a commercial participator as:

'*In relation to any charitable institution any person who:*

- *carries on for gain a business other than a fundraising business, but*
- *in the course of that business, engages in any promotional venture in the course of which it is represented that charitable contributions are to be given to or applied for the benefit of the institution.*'

'A charitable institution' means an organisation established for charitable, benevolent or philanthropic purposes (see **4.1**).

A number of the expressions used in this definition are defined in the Act. 'Promotional venture' is defined as 'any advertising or sales campaign or any other venture undertaken for commercial purposes'.

'Represent' means to represent:

'in any manner whatever, whether done by speaking directly or by means of a statement published in any newspaper, film or radio or television programme or otherwise'.

'Charitable contribution' means:

'in relation to any representation made by any commercial participator or other person

- *the whole or part of*
  - *the consideration given for goods or services sold or supplied by him, or*
  - *any proceeds (other than such consideration) of a promotional venture undertaken by him,*

or

- *sums given by him by way of donation in connection with the sale or supply of any such goods or services (whether the amount of such sums is determined by reference to the value of any such goods or services or otherwise).'*

16.3 Examples of commercial participators

16.3.1 Charity trading companies

The Act does not control sales by a trading company, if the trading company is owned by the charity. However, the Voluntary Services Unit of the Home Office has stated in *Charitable Fund-raising: Professional and Commercial Involvement*:

'the need for good practice in fundraising by charities, other charitable institutions and connected companies is just as strong as it is for those subject to Part II, including the need to have full regard to professional codes and other recommended practice.

Although some regard has to be made for the different circumstances where a charitable institution or its connected company undertakes direct fundraising, as far as is applicable, the Home Office (and in relation to charities) the Charity Commission strongly recommends, as a matter of good practice that these bodies follow the same requirements (e.g. for agreements and statements) as others who are subject to the requirements of Part II.' (Home Office, February 1995, p. 3)

This is only a recommendation; it is not a legal requirement, and charities do not have to follow it.

However, if a trading company owned by Charity A carries on activities for the benefit of Charities B, C, and D and makes representations concerning payments to B, C and D, then the trading company will be a commercial participator in respect of its dealings with Charities B, C and D because it is not a company owned by B, C or D.

16.3.2 Broadcast appeals

If a charity broadcasts an appeal and pays a bank to receive the donations, the bank is not a commercial participator: the bank is merely providing a paid service to the charity.

16.3.3 Affinity cards

Affinity cards are credit cards, issued by a bank, which are dedicated to a particular charity. Under this system, banks donate a percentage of the customer's monthly payments to a charity. Clearly, in this situation, the bank is:

- engaging in a business (banking) that is not a fundraising business;
- engaging, in the course of this business, in a promotional venture in which it is stating that a percentage of what the consumer spends on the card will go to a charitable institution.

In this instance, therefore, the bank is a commercial participator. (See also **8.8**.)

16.3.4 Other examples of commercial participators

- The maker of a product who prints a charity's logo on the product and states '1p will go to XYZ charity for each packet sold'.
- The event organiser (e.g. the Glastonbury Festival) who states that the net proceeds of the event will go to a charitable institution.
- The travel company that offers to pay 1 per cent of the price of a holiday to a named charitable institution.
- All CRM deals (see Chapter 8).

16.4 The need for an agreement between commercial participators and charitable institutions

16.4.1 The commercial participator must have an agreement with a charitable institution. It is unlawful for a commercial participator to state that charitable contributions are to be given to a charitable institution unless they do so in accordance with an agreement that satisfies the prescribed requirements. 'Unlawful' in this context means that the agreement is unenforceable unless it complies with the 1992 Act.

Under the regulations, the agreement between the charitable institution and the commercial participator has to be in writing and must be signed by, or on behalf of, the charitable institution and the commercial participator.

The agreement has to specify:

- the name and address of each of the parties to the agreement;
- the date on which the agreement was signed by, or on behalf of, those parties;
- the period for which the agreement is to remain in effect;
- any terms concerning termination of the agreement before the date on which the period expires;
- any terms relating to changes made to the agreement during that period.

The agreement also has to state:

- its principal objectives and the methods to be used in pursuit of those objectives;
- how the following are to be determined (depending on the individual agreement):
  - how any benefit arising from the agreement is to be divided between the charitable institutions, should there be more than one such institution that is party to the agreement; and
  - what proportion of the payment received for goods or services sold or supplied by the commercial participator is to be given to, or applied for the benefit of, the charitable institution; and
  - similarly, what proportion of any other proceeds of a promotional venture undertaken by the commercial participator is to be given to, or applied for the benefit of, the charitable institution; or
  - what sums are to be given or applied to the charitable institution by way of donations made by the commercial participator in connection with the sale or supply of any goods or services sold or supplied by him;
- what the commercial participator will be paid for fulfilling their side of the agreement, and how that sum is to be calculated.

The Charity Commission recommends that a section 60 agreement be signed by a trustee.

16.4.2 Breach

If there is no written agreement between the charity and the commercial participator that complies with the Act, only the High Court or county court may enforce any agreement between them. So, the commercial participator will not be entitled to receive any payment under a defective agreement until a court orders that the commercial participator may be paid. It is unlikely, however, that this provision will be of much use to charitable institutions, because money will normally pass from the commercial participator to the charitable institution, and not the other way round.

According to regulation 5, if a commercial participator has an agreement with a charitable institution, they must, on request and at all reasonable times, allow the institution to see any relevant books, documents or other records (in whatever form these are kept) that relate to the institution. These records must be kept in legible form. This regulation applies only to an agreement with a charitable institution and does not cover an agreement with a charity's trading company; if a trading company wishes to have such a right, it must put it in a contract.

According to regulation 6, any money due to the charitable institution has to be paid over as soon as is reasonably practicable after it has been received and in any event not later than 28 days after that receipt or some other period to be agreed with the institution. This will be impossible with most commercial arrangements. For example, once an on-pack promotion had been going for 28 days, the retailer would have to account to the charitable institution every day for that proportion of the day's sales that was due to the charity! The agreement will therefore have to override these requirements and replace them with something more commercially sensible.

The payment has to be made to the charitable institution or into a bank account that it controls.

Breach of regulations 5 and 6 is a criminal offence that gives rise to a maximum fine of £500 per offence.

16.4.3 Recommended additions to the standard requirements

The regulations offer considerable protection to charitable institutions that are entering into contracts with commercial participators. However, charitable institutions should also consider whether or not there are other clauses that should be inserted to assist them. In particular, they should consider the fact that licensing their name to a commercial organisation can give rise to a number of problems (see also Chapter 8).

Every charity entering into arrangements which associate its name with the goods and/or services provided by a third party must appreciate that there is a risk that the charity's name could be brought into disrepute through the activities of the licensee or some member of its group of companies. Modern trans-national companies have operations in many countries, and the company with which a charity has a licensing arrangement in the UK may be involved in many different industries in many parts of the world. It is impossible for the charity to check adequately on the performance of all those companies before entering into any licence.

In these circumstances, charities need to proceed with considerable caution. One suggestion is that, where a charity is licensing its name, it could require the contract to contain clauses such as the following, in addition to the requirements laid down by the regulations:

- a minimum guaranteed sum payable to the charity;
- a warranty by the licensee that neither it, nor any of its associated companies (i.e. subsidiaries or joint ventures), will at any time during the duration of the agreement do anything that could bring the reputation of the charity into disrepute;
- a termination clause allowing the charity to terminate the licence immediately if, in its reasonable opinion, its name is brought into disrepute by the licensee or its associates or if the licensee is in a material breach of any of the terms of the agreement;
- a term relating to what happens to stock bearing the charity's logo in the event of early termination of the agreement due to its breach by the licensee;
- strict controls on the use of the charity's name and logo and recognition of their trade marks;
- mutual clearance of all publicity materials and agreed wording to describe each partner and their relationship;
- an undertaking that the commercial participator will abide at all times by all relevant health, environmental and legal obligation and codes of best practice;
- interest on late payments;
- an indemnity in respect of any losses or damage suffered by the charity as a result of any action by the commercial participator.

A charity might also wish to seek other clauses such as:

- an agreement that the commercial participator will not enter into a similar arrangement with any other organisation operating in the same field as the charity for the duration of the agreement;
- an obligation on the commercial participator to segregate moneys due to the charitable institution in a separate bank account preferably marked with the name of the charity, so that, should the commercial participator go into liquidation, the moneys in the account will be deemed to be trust moneys and not part of the general assets of the commercial participator available for distribution to the general body of its creditors.

See also the ICFM/Bates, Wells & Braithwaite model contracts in Appendices 3–5.

16.4.4   For other contractual matters, consider the points set out in Chapter 11 about negotiating contracts.

16.4.5   For matters regarding taxation and VAT, consider the points made in Chapter 8.

16.5 **The need for written statements (section 60)**

16.5.1   Where a commercial participator states that it shall give charitable contributions to one or more particular charitable institutions, that statement shall be accompanied by a clear indication of:

- the name or names of the institution or institutions concerned;
- if there is more than one institution concerned, the proportions in which the institutions are respectively to benefit; and
- (in general terms) the method by which it is to be determined

    – what proportion of the 'consideration' given for goods or services sold or supplied by the commercial participator, or of any other proceeds of a promotional venture undertaken by them, is to be given to or applied for the benefit of the institution or institutions concerned; or

    – what sums by way of donations by them in connection with the sale or supply of any such goods or services are to be so given or applied,

as the case may require.

16.5.2   In almost all cases, this statement will be carried on the goods themselves, in brochures or catalogues describing the goods or services, or through point-of-sale advertising.

16.5.3   There are two different ways in which the statement can be made, as the case may require. Unfortunately, section 60(3) is not satisfactorily worded.

The first possible statement

The first possible statement is as follows:

'(in general terms) the method by which it is to be determined what proportion of the consideration given, etc.'

This could, on close analysis, be ludicrously easy to comply with. For example, a high-street retailer with its own brand of products, QuickMart, decides to give 10p to Charity X for each can of baked beans sold. The statement required under section 60(3)(c)(i) could be as general as:

'The directors of QuickMart shall meet each year in the Ritz Hotel to decide what proportion of the price paid for this can of beans will be given to Charity X, a registered charity.'

Such a statement does indicate (in general terms) the methods to be used to work out what proportion of the price of the can of beans will be given to Charity X! This is obviously ridiculous. Charitable institutions negotiating arrangements with commercial participators should be advised to ensure that the statement clearly indicates what proportion of the consideration given for the goods or services sold will be given to them.

This view is substantiated by the Home Office in their publication, *Charitable Fund-raising: Professional and Commercial Involvement*:

'*We strongly recommend that in the case of commercial participation ... or similar activities by charitable institutions or their connected companies not subject to Part II, that the exact amount going to charitable institutions is given in the statement, expressed net (i.e. after deduction of all expenses, costs, etc.): for example, "X per cent of the purchase price goes to charity Y" or "£X per item sold goes ... etc.".*

'*Where this cannot be stated exactly then a reasonable alternative is recommended, such as "A minimum X per cent ... etc.", or "It is estimated that X per cent ... etc." provided this is a reasonable statement to make and meets the requirements of the law in the particular circumstances of the case.*

'*We recommend that only where no such statement can meaningfully be made should a percentage be expressed as a gross figure. In such a case it is most important that attention is drawn in the statement to the significance of that fact, i.e. that further expenses will have to be paid, reducing the benefit that the charitable institution will receive from the donation.*'

(Home Office, February 1995, p.5)

This is not a legal requirement, but is recommended good practice. If a statement was ever scrutinised by a court, this guidance would almost certainly be considered as evidence of what constitutes a 'fair' statement.

The Home Office recommendations go beyond the express letter of the law in requiring rather more precise statements. Charitable institutions should be wary of agreeing to arrangements whereby they accept X per cent of the net profits, as this begs the question 'net of what'? If this formula is to be accepted, charitable institutions need to be very careful and thorough in agreeing what deductions can be made in order to arrive at the net-profit figure; such all-embracing phrases as 'management charges' should be avoided. However, it is sometimes very difficult for commercial participators to state precisely what proportion of the price paid will go to the charity because of the complexities of particular commercial arrangements: charities need to be realistic. In these circumstances, agreed minimum donations can be very useful.

The second possible statement

The second possible statement is as follows:

'*(in general terms) the method by which it is to be determined ... what sums by way of donation by the commercial participator in connection with the sale or supply of such goods are to be ... given.*'

The best example of this is a trading company owned by a charity. In this case, the statement could be:

'100 per cent of the taxable profits of XYZ Trading Limited are given each year by deed of covenant to XYZ Charity, a registered charity.'

Such a statement is not strictly necessary in any event because of the exemptions from the controls for companies controlled by a charitable institution. However, as already noted, the Home Office recommends that charities' trading companies do make such a statement. This is not a legal requirement but recommended practice.

Another example would be where a commercial participator states:

'ABC Corporation has agreed to give £50,000 to XYZ Charity, a registered charity. Each purchase you make helps ABC reach that target.'

Such a statement clearly gives the information of what sum (by way of donation) the commercial participator is to make in connection with the sale or supply of the goods in question.

EXAMPLES OF A SECTION 60(3) STATEMENT

a In a shop

Five per cent of the retail price of this bottle will be given to ABC Charity, a registered charity.

or

For each bottle sold, 5p will be paid to ABC Charity, a registered charity.

b A statement made on radio or TV concerning the sale of goods, for example a lawnmower

Five per cent of the price you pay for your lawnmower will be given to ABC Charity. If you pay for goods costing more than £50 by credit or debit card, you have the right to cancel your purchase within seven days of this broadcast.*

Telephone sales

If a statement under section 60(3) is made by telephone, the commercial participator must, within seven days of any payment of £50 or more to the commercial participator, give the customer the section 60(3) statement and details of the right to cancel.

*If a statement under section 60(3) is made in the course of a radio or television programme, and payment can be made by credit or debit card, the broadcast has to include details of the right to cancel. In the case of goods, any right to cancel and to have a refund paid is conditional upon the purchaser of the goods returning the goods in question and paying any administrative costs.

16.5.4   You should also consider the British Codes of Advertising and Sales Promotion (see Chapter 15).

16.5.5 Trading companies

As explained in Chapter 10, charities have to operate certain types of commercial activity through a separate, non-charitable, trading company. Most arrangements with commercial participators fall into this category (see also **8.5.4**). Charities' trading companies may well need to be involved in relationships with commercial participators. In order to comply with section 60(3) in such a case, the trading company will have to make a statement like this:

'Xp per item is paid to ABC Trading Limited, which covenants all its taxable profits to ABC, a registered charity.'

This statement is the best that can be made in order to comply with the spirit of the 1992 Act and to ensure that the charity's affairs are structured in the most tax-efficient manner.

16.6 Criminal sanctions

A commercial participator who breaches section 60(1) to (5) is guilty of a criminal offence that carries a maximum fine of £5,000 per offence.

Technically, if a retailer displayed 5,000 items of a product with a wrong statement, each item would constitute a separate offence, giving rise to a potentially huge fine. In reality, this is most unlikely to happen: these controls have been in force since March 1 1994, but no prosecutions have been brought at the time of writing.

16.7 A word of warning

The Charities Act imposes obligations on the commercial partner, but charitable institutions that are considering entering into such arrangements should be aware that the commercial partners see this as charity legislation and therefore look to the charitable institution to ensure compliance. For this reason, it is vital that fundraisers understand the legislation and take responsibility for ensuring that there is an appropriate contract and statement. If necessary, fundraisers should take legal advice, but they should do it early – before all the packaging or brochures have been designed – so that the legal requirements can form part of the design brief.

16.8 Quasi-commercial participators

One of the anomalies in Part II of the 1992 Act is that the controls on commercial participators apply only if the commercial participator claims that part of the proceeds of sale of goods or services will go to a named charitable institution. There are no controls in the Act itself on a business that seeks to sell goods or services with the inducement that part of the proceeds would go to a general charitable cause, for example 'to relieve poverty in the Third World'. Because of this oversight the regulations seek to control such activities. Regulation 7 applies to:

'any person who carries on for gain a business other than a fundraising business and who engages in any promotional venture in the course of which it is represented that charitable contributions are to be applied for charitable, benevolent or philanthropic purposes of any description (rather than for the benefit of one or more particular charitable institutions).'

For the purposes of this book, such persons are called quasi-commercial participators.

The owner of a pizza restaurant, for example, states that '£1 per pizza will be sent to the victims of the Colombian earthquake'. In these circumstances, according to regulation 7(2), the quasi-commercial participator has to ensure that a statement accompanies the representation that clearly indicates:

- the fact that charitable contributions are to be applied for those purposes and not for the benefit of any particular charitable institution;
- (in general terms) a statement similar to that required in **16.5**. In this case, the statement will be in relation to the charitable purposes rather than a charitable institution, and the statement will explain:
  - the method by which the donation is to be determined, and
  - how the charitable contributions are to be distributed between different charitable institutions.

EXAMPLE OF A STATEMENT UNDER REGULATION 7(2)

£1 per pizza sold will be applied for the benefit of children in Bosnia and not for the benefit of a particular charitable institution. The proprietor of the restaurant will decide which charitable institutions will be supported.

Breach of regulation 7(2) is a criminal offence; however, as this is laid down by statutory instrument and not by primary legislation, the maximum fine is £500.

Summary

- As fundraisers, you need to be constantly aware of the complex legal controls imposed on commercial participators. These link with tax, contract and other areas of law and practice.
- You need to make sure that you are able to spot when possible legal, contractual or tax problems may be looming, and to take early advice.
- Be aware of the definition of commercial participator: in particular, this applies to CRM deals.
- Ensure that you have proper contracts with all commercial participators.
- Do not just accept the legal minimum contract laid down by the Charities Act 1992: ask yourself whether you need greater protection.
- Commercial partners expect charities to sort out these legal issues.

17
Professional fundraisers

17.1 Introduction

Part II of the Charities Act 1992 imposes controls on commercial participators (see Chapter 16) and professional fundraisers in their relationships with charitable institutions. See **4.1** concerning the definition of a charitable institution.

These controls only apply in England and Wales. For the Scottish position, the ICFM and Scottish Council for Voluntary Organisations have issued the Scottish Code of Fundraising Practice. This seeks to provide a framework within which fundraising in Scotland can operate to achieve equivalent standards to those provided for in Part II Charities Act 1992. There is no legal obligation on professional fundraisers to follow this.

17.2 Who is a professional fundraiser?

Some charities will engage the services of consultants to help with their fundraising. Whether or not those persons are professional fundraisers will depend on what they do. A professional fundraiser is defined in section 58(1) as:

Test one

(a) 'Any person who carries on a fundraising business', in other words people who for gain specialise wholly or primarily in soliciting money, etc., for charitable institutions. This does not include charitable institutions.

or

Test two

(b) *'Any other person who for reward solicits money or other property for the benefit of a charitable institution, if he does so otherwise than in the course of a fundraising venture undertaken by a person falling within paragraph (a) above.'*

Under Test Two you are a professional fundraiser if, for reward, you solicit money, even if this is not done through a fundraising business (e.g. a business that works mainly for commercial clients but that also does some work for charitable institutions).

An appeal by an agency to ask an individual to collect money for a charity does not fall within these controls. In other words, the agency is not a professional fundraiser.

'Solicit' has a very wide meaning. Under section 58 (6), you may be soliciting when you:

- speak directly to the person being solicited (whether in their presence or not) [hence, a solicitation can be made face to face, or by telephone];
- publish a statement in any newspaper, film, radio or television programme;
- do anything else which expressly or impliedly invites or requests the payment or donation of money or other property.

The Act covers solicitations for

- money
- property.

It does not cover soliciting for volunteers to help in house-to-house or street collections or to sell raffle tickets.

17.3 'Otherwise procuring'

A fundraising business includes a business engaged in *otherwise procuring* money or other property for charitable, benevolent or philanthropic purposes. 'Otherwise procuring' could have a very wide meaning as well. When the legislation was considered in the House of Lords, the government made it clear that, in their view, these words have a very limited meaning. As Viscount Astor stated:

'the words are intended to deal with a situation where, although an appeal or a campaign is undertaken solely by a professional fundraiser, the appeal literature appears to come from the charity itself with the name and address of the fundraiser appearing, sometimes inconspicuously, as the recipient of donations and so forth. The key factor is that the fundraiser is the agent who makes the appeal and gathers in the funds. In such a case, the reference to soliciting alone would probably be inadequate because the solicitation would appear to come from the charity even if, in reality, it was from the fundraiser. The expression "procuring" is used in preference to "obtaining" in order to make it clear that the fundraiser in question must actively achieve the obtaining of funds for charitable purposes and not simply be a passive recipient by accident.'

The example cited by Viscount Astor does not have any bearing on normal fundraising practice.

It is also clear, however, that 'otherwise procuring' does not extend to cover the activities of organisations that act as agents for charities in helping them with fundraising (e.g. direct mail houses or an advertising agency that specialises in designing fundraising appeals).

17.4 **Some examples of professional fundraisers**
17.4.1 **A covenant renewal agency**

A firm that telephones covenantors to explain that their covenants have lapsed and to ask them to renew is a professional fundraiser.

The donors send no money to the agency, and you could argue that the agency is merely performing a service on behalf of the charity. However, the fact that it is being paid to solicit money for charitable purposes (i.e. soliciting the renewal of covenants) means that the agency is a professional fundraiser.

17.4.2 **Telephone appeals**

A telephone appeal for charitable donations carried out by a telemarketing organisation will amount to fundraising even if:

- the telemarketing organisation requests that all payments be made to the charity;
- the agency sends the appeal literature to a donor who responds positively to the telephone appeal and asks them to send the donation direct to the charity.

17.4.3 **Secondees**

Some organisations (e.g. banks) second their staff to work for charities. The bank continues to employ (and pay) the secondee. If the secondee solicits funds on behalf of the charity with which they are working, are they a professional fundraiser? They will be soliciting money and they will be being paid (by their employer). Does this mean that they will be soliciting money for reward? It could be that the secondee, in these circumstances, would be classified as a professional fundraiser. If so, they should make an appropriate statement (see **17.7**), but this could be useful publicity for the employer!

17.4.4 **Consultants**

A consultant is paid to advise a charitable institution about how to go about fundraising; this in itself does not make the consultant a professional fundraiser controlled by the Act, unless they solicit funds or property for the charitable institution.

17.4.5 **Incoming telephone services**

Telephone fundraising raises a number of problems. The Home Office publication, *Charitable Fund-raising: Professional and Commercial Involvement*, states on page 10:

'Incoming telephone services: if a company answers telephone calls simply to record credit card details for people who have decided to make a donation, e.g. in response to an appeal by direct mail or newspaper or television advertisement, and the donations are credited direct to the institution's (not the company's) bank

account, the company may not be a professional fundraiser. However, the distinction is a narrow one and care is needed: if, for example, the operator repeats or explains details about the appeal, even in response to a request for clarification from the caller, this may well amount to professional fundraising, and operators must therefore be able to recognise this distinction and respond appropriately in each case. Where incoming telephone services are provided by automated (e.g. computer based) answering equipment owned by a service provider and rented to an institution, then even when a solicitation is made by a person whose voice is recorded, provided that person is from the charitable institution, the service provider may not be regarded as a professional fundraiser.' (Home Office, February 1995)

17.5 Summary of exemptions from the definition of professional fundraiser

Fundraising by any of the following is exempt from the controls of Part II of the 1992 Act:

- charitable institutions
- companies connected with charitable institutions
- low-paid workers
- collectors
- celebrities.

17.5.1 Exemption for charitable institutions

The controls introduced by Part II of the 1992 Act do not apply to direct fundraising undertaken by a charitable institution. Equally, fundraising by one charitable institution on behalf of other charitable institutions (for example, the BBC's 'Children in Need Appeal' – itself a registered charity) is outside the 1992 Act.

17.5.2 Exemption for connected companies

Any company connected with a charitable institution is also exempt, provided that company is not running a fundraising business. A company is 'connected with' a charitable institution if that institution is entitled to exercise the whole of the voting power at any general meeting of the company. This means that trading companies that are wholly owned by charities (as most are) and used for putting on fundraising events are not professional fundraisers. However, if a trading company owned by Charity A undertakes fundraising for Charity B for a fee, the trading company will be a professional fundraiser – since it is receiving a reward.

17.5.3 Exemption for low-paid workers

You are not a professional fundraiser if you do not receive more than £5 per day or £500 per year as remuneration for soliciting money or other property.

Should you be paid a small fee (£500 or less) for organising or otherwise undertaking other kinds of fundraising events or activities for a charitable institution, you will also be exempt. So, for example, if you are paid £400 for organising a garden fete at which you solicit money or other property for the benefit of a charitable institution, you are not a professional fundraiser.

17.5.4 Exemption for appeals by celebrities

Section 58(2)(d) excludes from the definition of professional fundraiser any person who makes a solicitation on behalf of a charitable institution in the course of a radio or television programme.

Hence, even if a celebrity is paid to make such an appeal on behalf of a charity, they will not be a professional fundraiser.

17.6 Agreements between professional fundraisers and charitable institutions

17.6.1 According to section 59(1), 'It is unlawful for a professional fundraiser to solicit money or other property for the benefit of a charitable institution unless he does so in accordance with an agreement with the institution satisfying the prescribed requirements.'

The prescribed requirements are laid down in the Charitable Institutions (Fund-Raising) Regulations 1994 (SI 1994/3024) (the Regulations). Regulation 2 states that there must be a written agreement between the charitable institution and a professional fundraiser and that this agreement must be signed by or on behalf of the charitable institution and the professional fundraiser.

These requirements are very similar to those for commercial participators (see **16.4.1**).

17.6.2 Injunctions

The court may grant an injunction if it is satisfied that:

- a professional fundraiser is soliciting money for the benefit of a charitable institution without having entered into an appropriate agreement; and
- unless restrained, such a contravention is likely to continue or be repeated.

17.6.3 An agreement cannot be enforced if a charitable institution enters into a section 59(1) agreement with a professional fundraiser that does not comply with the prescribed requirements. In that case, the agreement can be enforced only if the professional fundraiser goes to court and wins an order to have the agreement enforced (the court will decide this). For this reason, professional fundraisers must check that all agreements with charitable institutions conform to the requirements of the regulations.

17.6.4 This is just as important for charity trustees. For example, if a charity enters into an agreement with a professional fundraiser that breaches section 59(1), the only way in which the charity could be made to keep that agreement would be through a court order (see section 58). However, the charity might nevertheless make payments under the agreement: if this was the case, could the trustees be held personally liable to reimburse the charity for payments made in breach of section 59(1), on the basis that the charity has suffered as a result of their negligence? This would be the argument: if the trustees had not been negligent (by allowing payments to be made, even though the agreement was non-enforceable), the charity could have resisted paying out under the agreement, unless payment had been sanctioned by the court.

17.6.5 In addition to the standard requirements laid down in regulation 2, regulation 5 provides that a professional fundraiser:

'shall on request, and at all reasonable times, make available to any charitable institution which is a party to an agreement with him any relevant books, documents or other records which relate to that institution.'

The records have to be kept in legible form.

According to regulation 6, as a professional fundraiser, unless you have a reasonable excuse, you have to pay over to the account of the charitable institution any money or any negotiable instrument you receive as soon after receiving it as is reasonably practicable. You have to make this payment to the charitable institution itself, or into an account in the name of the institution, not later than 28 days after you received it, unless you have agreed another period with the institution.

If you receive property other than money, then you will have to deal with it according to any instructions the charitable institution may have given for that purpose. You also have to keep such property securely until you hand it over.

Breach of regulation 5(1) or regulation 6(2) is a criminal offence that can give rise to a maximum fine of £500.

17.6.6   The requirements laid down by the regulations are the legal minimum. Charitable institutions may want to protect themselves on other issues in their dealings with professional fundraisers, by adding to those requirements:

- a penal rate of interest, should the professional fundraiser delay making payments due to the charitable institution under the fundraising agreement;
- regular meetings to monitor the fundraising appeal.

In addition, they might consider the following questions:

- Who owns the copyright in artwork or any copy produced by the professional fundraiser? (See also Chapter 21.)
- Who owns any data, for example lists of names created by the professional fundraiser? (See also Chapter 12.)
- Is the professional fundraiser under a duty of confidentiality?
- For as long as the agreement lasts, should the professional fundraiser be restrained from undertaking any work of a similar nature for any organisation operating within the same or a similar field of activity as the charitable institution?

The Charity Commission recommends that a section 59 agreement be signed by a trustee. The standard ICFM/Bates, Wells & Braithwaite professional fundraiser agreement is set out in Appendix 2 (p. 250).

17.7 The need for a written statement (section 60)

Most charities recognise that it is best if the charity, rather than a professional fundraiser, makes a solicitation. Sometimes, however, a charity cannot do this: for example, it may not have the in-house resources for a telephone fundraising appeal it is mounting. Section 60(1) of the 1992 Act requires that where a professional fundraiser solicits money or other property for the benefit of one or more particular charitable institutions, a statement shall accompany the solicitation that must clearly indicate:

- the name or names of the institutions concerned [e.g. 'XYZ charity'];
- if there is more than one institution concerned, the proportions in which the institutions are respectively to benefit [e.g. 'XYZ charity 50 per cent, ABC charity 50 per cent']; and
- (in general terms) the method by which the fundraisers' remuneration in connection with the appeal is to be determined [e.g. 'the organisers of this appeal will be paid X per cent of the proceeds of the appeal'].

An appeal made in the course of a radio or television programme may be accompanied by an announcement that payment may be made by credit or debit card. This announcement must include details of the donor's right to cancel their donation and demand a refund, providing the demand for a refund is made within seven days of the broadcast.

> EXAMPLE OF SECTION 60(1) STATEMENT
>
> **Charity appeal**
>
> For XYZ charity, a registered charity, and ABC Charity, a registered charity:
> XYZ and ABC will each receive 50 per cent of the net proceeds of this
> appeal.
> XYZ and ABC will pay Scrooge and Co, the organisers of this appeal, 10p for
> every £1 raised by the appeal.
> If you make a donation of more than £50 by credit or debit card, you have
> the right to cancel your donation within seven days of this broadcast.

17.8 The donor's right to cancel

If a potential donor indicates to you (as the professional fundraiser) that they
may give more than £50 in response to a radio or TV appeal, you must notify
the donor of their right to demand a refund if the donation is made by credit
or debit card. If you solicit a donation by telephone, you must notify the donor,
within seven days, of:

- the full details of the section 60 statement;
- the donor's right to cancel the donation within seven days and to demand a
  refund if they pay more than £50 to you.

This only applies if the payment is made to you; if the payment is made to a
charitable institution – the normal practice – this requirement does not apply,
even if it was you, the professional fundraiser, who solicited the donation. In
the case of a telephone appeal, however, the donor has the right to cancel, irrespective of how they have paid the £50 or more. In the case of a TV or radio
appeal, the right to cancel applies only if payment is made by a debit or credit
card.

If a donation is refunded to a donor, the fundraiser may deduct 'administrative
expenses reasonably incurred' in connection with the refund.

17.9 Breach of section 60 – criminal liability

Section 60 imposes a strict criminal liability on a professional fundraiser who
fails to give the statement required. The maximum fine is currently £5,000.

If you are charged with any offence under section 60, you may, in your defence,
seek to prove that you took all reasonable precautions and exercised all due diligence to avoid the commission of the offence. You will need to ensure that you
have proper procedures, adequately monitored, so that your staff comply with
the requirements of section 60. If not, you will be unable to establish that you
have taken all reasonable precautions and exercised all due diligence.

The Act is notably silent about who is responsible for its enforcement. There is no section empowering trading standards officers to assume responsibility; in the absence of such a section, it is the police who are responsible for enforcement. However, in the war against crime, breaches of the Charities Act 1992 are bound to come low down any list of priorities. Consequently, the Charity Commission is endeavouring to monitor the position and liaise with the relevant local police force.

These points apply to commercial participators (see Chapter 16).

17.10 What are the regulations concerning the right to cancel?

The controls in Part II of the 1992 Act do not apply to charitable institutions, or companies controlled by them, when raising funds for their charity. However, the government did consider applying the right to cancel in the case of donations over £50 to appeals made directly by charitable institutions. In the end it decided against this, in part because the Home Office had given financial support towards the development of a voluntary code of practice for broadcast appeals. The charities involved in broadcast appeals now include in their code a requirement that potential donors donating more than £50 should be informed in writing or by telephone of their right to cancel the donation (see Chapter 15).

Despite this, the government has reserved its position to introduce regulations to extend the statutory right to cancel to radio or television appeals made by charitable institutions or their connected companies.

Summary

- Be aware of the definition of professional fundraiser.
- Ensure that you have proper contracts with all professional fundraisers.
- Ensure that all professional fundraisers are obliged by contract to make a section 60 statement.
- Do not just accept the legal minimum contract laid down by the Charities Act 1992: ask yourself whether you need greater protection.

18 Payment methods

18.1 Introduction

This chapter deals with the issues surrounding the various, different methods by which payment can be made to your charity. Generally speaking, it is a question of following good practice rather than the law. The way in which charities receive money will be the result of different fundraising techniques:

- Gift Aid payments will be made by cheque or credit card.
- Public collections will mainly be in cash.
- Deeds of covenant, membership subscriptions and other recurring payments should, ideally, be made by standing order or direct debit.
- Individuals or companies with CAF accounts will use CAF cheques.

18.2 Controls over incoming funds – cash and cheques

Your auditor should advise you on the appropriate controls to adopt. Charity Commission guidelines suggest the following:

- For money raised from events, the Charity Commission recommends putting controls in place to record gross receipts and all costs and, for ticketed events, to keep records of tickets allocated, tickets sold, and to reconcile the two (see Charity Commission leaflet CC8, *Internal Financial Controls for Charities*).
- Incoming post should be opened at the earliest opportunity and in the presence of two responsible people.
- All incoming cheques and cash should be recorded immediately and entries verified by someone other than the person who has made the entry. It is appreciated that this may be a problem for charities that have neither premises nor paid staff. The Charity Commission suggests that, in such circumstances, donations should be sent to a central point and a book kept to record receipt of all money sent.
- You should consider rotating post-opening staff where practical.
- The security of unopened mail must also be considered.

You should take care to ensure that, once funds are received into the control of the charity, their continued security is maintained:

- Incoming receipts should be banked regularly and as soon as possible – at least weekly.
- Cash or cheques should be placed in a safe or locked cash box if they cannot be banked on the day of receipt, with keys held by a nominated officer. It is possible to obtain insurance cover for cash held in a safe or cash box up to a specified limit. This could also be considered for cash in transit.
- All incoming money should be banked gross with no amount held back for petty cash. Without banking, it becomes impossible to trace particular receipts.
- Care should be taken to identify and administer separately any restricted funds.

18.3 Transfers

18.3.1 Standing order

A standing order is when donors instruct their bank to make regular fixed payments of a set sum to your charity. You can make this easier for donors by providing a form for them to complete. Usually, charities request that the form be returned to them so that they can reference it and forward it to the donor's bank. This makes it easier to trace the donations when they are received. The donor can cancel the standing order at any time.

18.3.2 Direct debit

With direct debit, instead of the donor's bank automatically making regular payments to your charity, you have to 'request the money'. Direct debits can be for variable amounts. Again, the donor can cancel at any time. Direct debits are useful for annual membership subscriptions, which may increase from time to time. They are also useful for covenants and other committed giving, as they enable the donor to increase the sum donated without having to change a standing order, so increases can be negotiated by telephone.

In order to operate direct debits, it is necessary for the charity to make appropriate arrangements with its bank, which some banks may refuse to do in the case of small organisations. A bank also requires an indemnity from the trustees to the bank in respect of any liabilities that the bank may incur as a result of operating the direct debit system. However, it is possible to insure against the liability under the indemnity for a relatively small amount of money: you should talk to your insurance brokers about this.

18.3.3 CAF vouchers/CAF cards/CAF standing orders

These are forms of tax-efficient giving. The donor makes payments into a CAF account, either directly from their payroll so that tax relief is added back, or by Gift Aid (see Chapters 7 and 19). Donors give the charity a CAF voucher as their gift; the charity completes the CAF voucher and returns it to CAF to receive payment. The payments are donations and so cannot be used as payment for goods or services, including raffle tickets. CAF normally demands that a recipient charity be a registered charity but is prepared to waive this requirement in certain circumstances where it can establish to its own satisfaction that the recipient is established for charitable purposes.

Summary

- Be aware of the Charity Commission guidelines on internal financial controls.
- Direct debits may be difficult to set up, due to the requirements of the relevant bank.
- CAF vouchers should not be used to buy tickets for balls, raffles, etc.

19

Tax relief for donations

19.1 Introduction

19.1.1 It is possible for charities to claim back from the Inland Revenue the basic-rate income tax, currently 22 per cent (2000 figure), that has been paid on a donation by a donor, if the donor is a UK resident for tax purposes. The relief is also available for gifts to UK charities only. It is not available for gifts made to charities established under the laws of any other country, even if they are carrying out activities in the UK.

19.1.2 There are restrictions on the amount of benefits that donors can receive in return for their tax-efficient donations. The permissible benefits that donors or persons connected to them can receive are:

AGGREGATE DONATIONS IN THE TAX YEAR	AGGREGATE VALUE OF BENEFITS IN THE TAX YEAR
£0–£100	25% of the aggregate donations
£101–£1,000	£25
£1,001–£10,000	2.5% of the aggregate donations
£10,001+	£250

A person is 'connected' to a donor if the person has any of the following relationships with the donor *or* the donor's spouse:

- parents, grandparents, great-grandparents, etc.
- children, grandchildren, great-grandchildren, etc.
- brothers and sisters
- partners in a business partnership

or if the person is married to anyone falling into one of the above categories.

The benefit rules do not prevent a donor placing conditions on what the charity is to do with the money.

19.1.3 Since 6 April 2000 Gift Aid is available on gifts of cash of any amount. Gifts of assets or in kind do not qualify. The charity can obtain from the Inland

Revenue the basic rate of income tax on the value of the gift. Before 6 April 2000, the minimum gift eligible for Gift Aid was £250.

> **EXAMPLE**
>
> A donor agrees to give XYZ Charity £300.
> The donor is a basic-rate taxpayer, i.e. they pay income tax at 22 per cent.
> The donor gives XYZ Charity £300 and completes the Gift Aid form. XYZ Charity is able to recover from the Inland Revenue the basic-rate tax paid by the donor on the sum that, after deducting basic-rate income tax, equals £300. Grossing £300 up at 22 per cent equals £384. XYZ Charity receives £84 from the Inland Revenue.

19.1.4 Higher-rate tax payers

Individuals who earn more than £28,400 in a tax year pay income tax at the rate of 40 per cent on earnings above £28,400. If a higher-rate tax payer makes a Gift Aid payment, then the charity is able to recover the basic-rate income tax in just the same way as set out in **19.1.3**. In addition, however, the donor is able to obtain higher-rate tax relief on the amount of their donation. Higher-rate tax relief is the difference between the higher rate of income tax or capital gains tax (40 per cent) and the basic rate (22 per cent): in other words, 18 per cent.

> **EXAMPLE**
>
> A donor decides to give XYZ Charity £300 under Gift Aid.
> The donor is a higher-rate tax payer.
> The charity recovers £84 from the Inland Revenue as in the example at **19.1.3**. In addition, the donor is able to obtain higher-rate relief at 18 per cent on the sum of £384, that is £69. That means that their tax bill will be reduced by that amount. The net cost to the donor is therefore £300 − £69 = £231.
> So, for a cost to the donor of £231, XYZ Charity actually receives £384.

It is well worth fundraisers drawing this to the attention of individuals who are prepared to make a donation under Gift Aid. If the donor in the example above was genuinely willing to give £300 in cash, they should have agreed to give the charity £500 gross. From this, the basic-rate tax (22 per cent) will be £110, so the figure put into the Gift Aid declaration should be £390, which is the actual amount the donor will give. The charity will then recover the further £110 from the Inland Revenue. The donor will get higher-rate tax relief of 18 per cent on £500 (£90), so that the net cost to them will be £300.

19.1.5   It is worth remembering that many major businesses in the United Kingdom, such as firms of accountants and solicitors, are operated as partnerships and not as limited liability companies. This means that individual partners are responsible for their own tax bill and pay income tax as opposed to Corporation Tax (which is dealt with in **19.2**). Consequently, persuading a partnership to make a donation to a charity actually involves persuading the individual partners to make a donation under Gift Aid or deed of covenant, unless the partnership has established its own charity or the partners make tax-efficient donations to CAF and have CAF vouchers.

19.1.6   Under the new Gift Aid rules, a donor can make their declaration:

- in advance
- to cover a single donation or any number of donations
- in writing (e.g. by post, fax, electronically), or orally.

The Gift Aid declaration must contain all the information set out in the Inland Revenue's recommended form.

19.2   Corporate Gift Aid

19.2.1   Gift Aid is also available to those organisations that pay Corporation Tax: limited liability companies, unincorporated associations (but not partnerships where individual partners are responsible for their own tax bill and therefore fall into the individual category referred to in **19.1.5**) and companies established by Act of Parliament. Corporation Tax varies from 20 per cent to 30 per cent depending on the size of the company. Seek further advice from your accountant/finance team if necessary.

19.2.2   Many of the Gift Aid rules that apply to individuals apply equally to companies. Corporate Gift Aid is only available for companies that pay UK Corporation Tax.

19.2.3   As with personal Gift Aid, a corporate donor cannot receive any benefits that exceed the scale – see **19.1.2**. This rule applies if the donor is a 'close company'. A close company is defined as one that is under the control of five or fewer participators, i.e. shareholders. Classically, a private company will be a close company, although not all private companies are close companies.

A public company quoted on the stock exchange is not a close company. There are no express rules about what benefits a non-close company can receive from a charity to which that company makes a Gift Aid payment. This has led to some debate as to whether or not a charity may accord non-close companies benefits that are greater than the scale limit imposed on close companies. Individual tax inspectors do, sometimes, give varying advice about the level of benefits that can be given back in return. The safest and most prudent advice that can be given is that charities should only accord benefits that do not exceed the scale limit to corporate donors (whether close or non-close) who make charitable contributions under Gift Aid.

19.2.4   A charitable donation is not usually a tax-deductible business expense unless it is made under Gift Aid or deed of covenant. For a payment to be tax deductible, it has to be incurred wholly and exclusively in the carrying out of the company's business. Giving money to a charity is not treated as being wholly and exclusively for the purposes of business. Therefore, in order for a corporate donation to be made in a tax-efficient manner, the donation has to be made either under Gift Aid, by deed of covenant (see **19.4**) or under the special rules discussed in **8.2.2**. A payment under Gift Aid by a company is treated as a 'charge on income'. That means that, from the company's point of view, the full amount of the donation is tax deductible in computing its taxable profits.

> EXAMPLE
>
> Company ABC decides to make a Gift Aid payment of £1,000 to XYZ Charity. ABC pays corporation tax at 20 per cent.
> ABC will pay £1,000 to XYZ charity.
> ABC will claim the full £1,000 as a tax-deductible business expense when it completes its corporation tax computation at the end of corporation tax year.

19.3 Personal deeds of covenant

19.3.1   From 6 April 2000, tax relief for Gift Aid payments is available for one-off contributions to a charity of any amount (the minimum donation under Gift Aid had been £250). Before 6 April 2000, if a donor was prepared to commit to make a minimum of four annual payments under a deed of covenant, then the charity could recover basic-rate income tax on the value of the gift. In this case, there was no minimum level of donation required before a donor could enter into a deed of covenant. Now all payments under deeds of covenant are treated as Gift Aid payments. Deeds of covenant are still useful, however: they show that the donor is committed to make more than one gift, and that they may even sign a standing order.

19.3.2   The key elements of a deed of covenant are that:

- the donor must be a UK tax payer;
- the donor must commit themselves to make the payment by a valid deed of covenant – the best way to ensure this is to use the standard model approved by the Inland Revenue;
- the deed of covenant must be signed by the donor and their signature witnessed by an independent witness – this can be someone who works for the

charity that is to receive the donation but, in order to avoid any hint of undue influence, it is wiser if it is not;

■ in the case of a company, the deed should be signed on behalf of the company by two directors or one director and the company secretary;

■ technically, a witness is not needed in the case of a deed of covenant executed under Scottish Law, although it is recommended that a deed is witnessed – in Northern Ireland (but not in England, Wales or Scotland) the deed must refer to its being 'sealed', even if it is not actually sealed;

■ the donor must complete a Gift Aid declaration (see **19.1.6**) for deeds of covenant entered into after 6 April 2000;

■ the donor must not receive any benefit beyond those set out in **19.1.2**.

19.3.3 Once the charity has received the deed of covenant, it will be able to apply to HM Inland Revenue for basic-rate income tax on the value of the first instalment of the deed of covenant. This operates in just the same way as recovery of basic-rate income tax under Gift Aid, and if the donor is a higher-rate income tax payer they are able to obtain higher-rate income tax relief in the same way (see **19.1** for an explanation).

19.3.4 Fundraisers are sometimes confronted with the problem that a donor has signed up to a deed of covenant and then defaults and fails to honour the obligation to make a minimum of four payments spread over four tax years. Fundraisers may be concerned about what should be done in these circumstances. By charity law, the charity should take 'reasonable steps' to enforce the donor's obligation: this means that the charity is not obliged to spend a disproportionate amount of time or effort in seeking to enforce compliance. The Inland Revenue is very unlikely to demand repayment of the tax already paid to the charity.

19.4 Deeds of covenant – corporate donors

19.4.1 An organisation that pays Corporation Tax (see **19.2**) can make a donation to a charity under deed of covenant, but since 6 April 2000 all payments under deed of covenants are treated as Gift Aid payments.

19.4.2 Just as for individuals, a deed of covenant is a binding obligation on the part of the donor to give an agreed sum of money or a sum calculated in accordance with a fixed formula, to a charity. Certain points must be noted:

■ It is wise to use the standard form of deed of covenant prepared by the Inland Revenue.

■ Take professional advice before any changes are made to this: it is very easy to make a mistake with the deed of covenant, with potentially major implications for a tax recovery.

■ Equally, do not amend a deed without advice.

19.4.3   The mechanics of a payment under deed of covenant are identical to those under Gift Aid.

19.5   Capital Gains Tax (CGT)

Fundraisers should be aware of the concessions for gifts of capital to charities. Individuals pay CGT on their chargeable gains (i.e. capital gains that are subject to capital gains tax). Charities are exempt from CGT. If a UK taxpayer donates an asset to a charity, and the charity then sells it, any gain will be CGT-free. If on the other hand the donor sold the asset, they would have to pay CGT on the sale even if they gave the proceeds to the charity.

> **EXAMPLE**
>
> Bloggs owns a painting, currently valued at £200,000, whose base cost for CGT is £100,000. Bloggs is a higher-rate tax payer and therefore pays tax at 40 per cent.
>
> If Bloggs sells the painting for £200,000, she will pay CGT on £100,000 @ 40% = £40,000. She will receive £160,000 net.
>
> If Bloggs gives the painting to XYZ Charity, which then sells it, it will be able to receive all £200,000, CGT-free.

Under a new relief, introduced in April 2000, if a donor gives shares or securities that are quoted on a stock exchange to a charity, the donor will get two forms of tax relief:

- from CGT (as above)
- from income tax for the value of the shares.

> **EXAMPLE**
>
> Bloggs is a higher-rate tax payer, who owns shares in utterfrenzy.com, a new Internet company selling tickets to raves.
>
> She bought 1,000 shares for £1,000. They are now quoted on the Stock Exchange at £1,000 per share. She decides to give half her shares, worth £500,000, to XYZ Charity:
>
> - She will pay no CGT on the disposal to XYZ, and XYZ can sell the shares and pay no CGT.
> - She will get income tax relief on the value of the gift: £500,000 × 40% = £200,000. In other words, her income tax bill will be reduced by that amount.

19.6 **Inheritance Tax (IHT)**

Inheritance Tax (IHT) is charged at 40 per cent on the value of estates over £234,000 (2000 tax year), although there is no tax charged if property is transferred to a spouse. No IHT is charged on the value of gifts to charities. This exemption applies to both lifetime transfers and on death.

Any charity that is aware that a donor wishes to leave it a legacy should encourage the donor to have their will drawn up professionally. The Capital Taxes Offices, which deal with IHT liability, look out for gifts that are imprecise and that may fall outside the exemption.

Summary

- Charities receive the 22 per cent basic-rate income tax paid by a UK tax payer who makes a Gift Aid donation.
- UK higher-rate tax payers get an 18 per cent tax relief on their Gift Aid donations.
- Companies are given Corporation Tax relief on their Gift Aid donations.
- Since 1 April 2000 deeds of covenant are treated as Gift Aid payments.
- Gifts of assets to charities are free from Capital Gains Tax.
- Gifts to charities are not subject to Inheritance Tax.

20

Value Added Tax and fundraising

20.1 Introduction

As a general rule, Value Added Tax (VAT) has an adverse impact on charity fundraising. In the course of fundraising, many charities incur VAT that they cannot recover. This so-called 'irrecoverable' VAT costs the charity sector approximately £350 million each year (1999 figures). This chapter will help you to understand whether you must charge VAT to those who pay money to your charity and whether you can avoid paying VAT on the services you give.

VAT is effectively a sales tax. The ultimate consumer – the non-VAT-registered individual or organisation that purchases a service or product – bears all the tax. Along the business chain, businesses are charged and charge VAT on value added at each stage of the business chain. Organisations that are registered for VAT do not lose out: they get a credit for VAT paid (input VAT) and they charge customers VAT on the goods and services supplied (output VAT). They can off-set their input VAT against their output VAT and pay the difference to Customs and Excise. In effect they are tax collectors. However, for most charities, even if they are registered for VAT, VAT works differently. Most charities are not able to recover all their input VAT, because most charities do not spend all their activities undertaking zero-rated or standard-rated supplies for VAT purposes. Only if a charity does this is it able to recover all its input VAT. Donations are not subject to VAT and, in consequence, charities cannot recover input VAT incurred in connection with fundraising costs.

VAT is a complex tax, and everything hinges on the particular details relating to particular supplies of particular goods or services. Consequently it is necessary to look in great detail at fundraising activities to ascertain the VAT position.

20.1.1 Zero rating

There are some provisions in the VAT legislation that do help charities. In particular, certain supplies are zero rated. Zero rating is the best possible status under VAT legislation, because an organisation making zero-rated supplies does not have to charge output VAT to its customers but can recover input VAT. Fundraising involves a large amount of printed materials. Most supplies of printed material are zero rated.

20.1.2 Exempt supplies

By contrast, it may sound attractive for an organisation to carry on exempt supplies, but in fact it is not. With exempt supplies, although an organisation does not have to charge output VAT, it cannot recover input VAT – a position that applies to many charities.

20.1.3 'Outside the scope' of VAT

A number of charitable activities (e.g. fundraising) are 'outside the scope' of VAT: in other words, as with exempt supplies, any input VAT cannot be recovered.

20.1.4 Standard-rated supplies

If an organisation carries on standard-rated supplies, it can recover all input VAT relating to the making of those standard-rated supplies.

20.1.5 'Partial exemption status'

A number of charities carry on a mixture of standard-rated, zero-rated, exempt and outside-the-scope supplies. This means that they then have to negotiate with Customs and Excise a 'partial exemption status', by which it is agreed how much of their input VAT they can recover overall. Typically this is presented as a percentage (e.g. 30 per cent).

20.2 The VAT audit

As the government uses VAT-registered businesses as its unpaid tax collectors to collect VAT, it is not surprising that the government has wide powers to check that VAT is being collected.

The normal method of VAT audit is the control visit by the VAT officer. Most control visits are made by prior appointment, but that is a concession. VAT officers have full power to walk into business premises at any reasonable time. They can:

- inspect and check the operation of a computer;
- inspect the premises and any goods found on them;
- demand production of documents, inspect and copy them or remove them for a reasonable period.

You can demand to see a VAT officer's identification.

The Commissioners for Customs and Excise have wide powers if they consider there is a breach of the VAT legislation. They can:

- seize goods;
- sue for overdue VAT in the High Court or County Court;
- petition to bankrupt an individual or unincorporated organisation or wind up a limited company;
- with a search warrant issued by a magistrate, search premises and seize goods.

The VAT officer's powers of enforcement are much wider than the Inland Revenue's and are reminiscent of continental systems of government – which is not surprising, since VAT is a European tax, first adopted in France.

20.3 Direct-mail packs

A direct-mail pack is defined as a package of materials sent to existing or prospective supporters of a charity. A direct-mail pack normally includes a number of articles within an outer envelope, such as:

- letters requesting support
- leaflets
- donation forms
- collectors' envelopes
- window stickers.

20.3.1 How to design a VAT-free appeal leaflet

- Work out which articles qualify for zero rating (i.e. pre-printed collectors' envelopes, appeal letters, envelopes used in conjunction with appeal letters).
- Work out whether any of the items fall within the exemptions for books and leaflets (see **20.4**). If standard-rated and zero-rated printed matter is supplied together as a package for a single price, the VAT liability may be calculated according to the liability of the articles that predominate. To do this, work out whether the majority of the supplies are zero or standard rated by considering the individual items in the single package. Where a package consists of several items, but one item has far more significance than the others, the most significant article dictates the liability of the package as a whole – significance is based on which items cost the most to produce.
- If the package as a whole is zero rated, zero rating can also be applied to preparatory work on any items within the package that qualify for zero rating. If the package as a whole is standard rated, zero rating applies only to preparatory work on those articles that are eligible for zero rating.

20.4 **Printed advertising services supplied to charities**

Certain supplies of advertising services to charities are zero rated for VAT if they are:

- for fundraising purposes (e.g. seeking donations, legacies, etc., or publicising fundraising events like jumble sales, fetes, etc. and recruiting runners for the London Marathon);
- for making known the aims and objectives of the charity (e.g. advertisements that explain the need for the charity to exist, describe the activities of the charity, ask for donated goods to enable the charity to carry out its objects, list courses which it provides, etc.).

The charity must provide the supplier with a declaration that the advertisement is for a qualifying purpose. To be sure the invoice you receive has no VAT, it's best to do this when instructing the supplier to do the work.

Employee recruitment advertising is also covered by the relief, as is volunteer recruitment (including advertisements for people to work overseas at local rates of pay plus travelling expenses).

From the charity's point of view, zero rating means that it will not be charged VAT on the services supplied to it – your budget will therefore buy you 17.5 per cent more.

Zero rating under this provision covers:

- advertisements in newspapers, posters, programmes, leaflets, brochures, pamphlets, periodical or similar publications;
- advertisements on television, radio and in the cinema (but not by telephone, because those are not printed);
- pre-printed paperboard collection boxes;
- pre-printed collecting envelopes;
- pre-printed appeal letters with associated envelopes that are over-printed with an appeal request relating to that in the letter – this includes envelopes for fundraising donations;
- lapel stickers.

Zero rating does not cover supplies of printed matter such as Christmas cards, raffle tickets, calendars, banners and so on, even if used for fundraising purposes. Nor does it cover advertisements on the Internet or on repeated loop television systems (e.g. in shops or other public places).

Except for television, radio and cinema advertisements, the zero-rating relief covers all relevant services applicable to the advertising, including artwork, typesetting, placement, etc. For television, radio and cinema, only the costs of broadcasting or screening are covered. When you get an ad agency to prepare an ad for you and buy the space, you can therefore give a certificate to the agency to avoid being charged VAT on production costs.

20.5 Supplies of books, booklets, etc.

The zero-rated supplies of most significance for fundraisers are:

- books and booklets
- brochures and pamphlets
- leaflets
- newspapers.

In addition to these items, Customs and Excises will treat a number of other printed item as zero rated. Fundraisers should therefore check with their finance department or advisers on the VAT status of particular items produced for fundraising purposes (mail order catalogues and catalogues are zero rated, for example).

20.5.1 Books or booklets

To qualify for zero rating as a book or booklet, an article must:

- have several pages;
- have a cover that is stiffer than the pages (although, even without this, it might still qualify for VAT purposes as a brochure or pamphlet);
- either be bound or adapted for inclusion in a ring binder.

There is a function test. An item that has the physical characteristics of a book but whose main function is not that of a book (e.g. books of postcards and diaries) will be standard rated.

20.5.2 Brochures or pamphlets

To qualify for zero rating as a brochure or pamphlet, the article must:

- consist of either several pages fastened together or a single folded sheet;
- be designed to be held in the hand and read.

Again, there is a function test. An item that looks like a brochure or pamphlet will be standard rated if its main function is not that of a brochure or pamphlet. For example:

- Articles whose main significance lies in parts to be completed or detached as donation forms. Customs and Excise takes the view that brochures or pamphlets with more than 25 per cent of their total area for completion or detachment should be standard rated. This is, however, a rule of thumb and has not been established in law.

- Articles that do not convey information by means of text will be standard rated. It is necessary to ensure that there is some thematic link between the illustrations in order to ensure zero rating. A pamphlet full of pictures that are not linked by text will be standard rated.

20.5.3 Leaflets

In order to qualify as a leaflet, an article:

- must be limp (i.e. not printed on stiff or laminated paper or card) – if the 'paper' exceeds 180 gsm, a written ruling should be obtained from the VAT office before zero rating the article as a leaflet;
- must be designed to be held in the hand for reading by individuals rather than for general display (as would be the case, for example, with car stickers);
- should consist of a single sheet of paper not greater than A4 size, although larger publications up to A2 size can be zero rated, provided that they are printed on both sides and folded down to A4 or smaller, and that they meet other conditions;
- should be complete in itself;
- should be widely distributed;
- should convey information by means of text.

Again, if more than 25 per cent of the total area of the leaflet is for completion and detachment, Customs and Excise takes the view that the leaflet should be standard rated.

20.5.4 Journals and periodicals

To qualify for zero rating as a journal or periodical, Customs and Excise usually requires that an article:

- consist of several sheets, which are either folded or bound together;
- be published in a series at regular intervals (more frequently than once a year).

To meet the function test, an article must:

- be designed for reading and not be primarily a collection of stationery items;
- convey information primarily by means of text.
- be mainly intended to convey information and not to act as a vehicle for self-promotion.

20.6 Member subscriptions

Refer to **3.16** to consider the VAT consequences of member subscriptions.

20.7 Exploitation of a charity's name and logo

You should refer to Chapter 8 to consider the VAT consequences of a charity licensing its name and logo.

20.8 Charities, VAT and trading

Chapter 10 considered when charities can carry out commercial trading. Where charities trade in fulfilment of their primary purposes, the VAT status of those supplies will depend upon their nature. There is no general exemption from VAT for charities that undertake trading activities. The trading activities of many charities will fall within the definition of 'business supplies' for VAT even though charities do not pursue a 'profit motive'. VAT is a tax on turnover, not profit: whether VAT is payable or not will depend on the nature of what is supplied and not, normally, on the status of the supplier.

There are a number of exemptions from VAT that are significant for charities, notably education, health and welfare, and fundraising events. Charities do not have to charge VAT on the services but, equally, they cannot recover their input VAT. For answering specific queries, you should speak to your finance director, auditor or solicitor before speaking to Customs and Excise.

20.9 Supplies of advertising services by charities

Charities receiving commercial sponsorship will often promote the sponsor using the sponsor's logo, style and corporate colours. This is a form of advertising service by the charity, the VAT, direct tax and other implications of which are explained in Chapter 8.

Summary

- As a generalisation, VAT can increase fundraising costs.
- Be aware of the exemptions available in respect of certain fundraising materials.
- Plan production of fundraising materials with someone in your organisation who understands VAT.
- Be aware that licensing a charity's name will mean that VAT will have to be charged, if the charity or its trading company is registered for VAT (see Chapter 8).
- Be aware that, with VAT, the devil lies in the detail!

21

Intellectual property

21.1 Introduction

Intellectual property is the umbrella name used to describe the following types of rights.

Registered rights

- registered trade marks
- patents
- registered design rights

Unregistered rights

- passing off
- copyright
- database rights
- unregistered design rights
- moral rights
- performers' rights

'Intellectual property' is a generic term and has no fixed legal meaning. However, each of the rights listed above has strict legal meanings.

These rights are important because they give protection to such things as names, drawings, books, reports, designs, databases and some types of idea. Not all ideas can be protected. For any idea, you have to go through each of the categories listed above and see if the idea fits one or more of the categories.

There is some overlap between categories: for example, a charity's logo could potentially be protected by a registered trade mark, copyright and passing off. Equally, there are some things that do not fit into any of the categories and therefore cannot be protected: for example, a new general idea for a method of fundraising cannot usually be protected.

As a fundraiser, the ways in which you will usually come across intellectual property are:

- giving other people rights to use the charity's intellectual property such as its name and logo;
- ensuring that the charity/trading subsidiary owns all intellectual property in work done for it;
- making sure that, if you need to use a third party's intellectual property, you have the necessary permission(s) to do so;

- making sure you do not inadvertently infringe a third party's rights;
- taking action for unauthorised use of the charity's intellectual property (see **21.9**).

The key to getting these things right is knowing what is likely to be protected and knowing who is likely to own the rights.

21.2 Trade marks

21.2.1 Registered and unregistered trade marks

Most people consider a trade mark to be the name of an organisation or the name of a particular product. In terms of protection, the law draws a distinction between registered and unregistered trade marks. Registered trade marks are protected by an action for trade mark infringement. Unregistered trade marks are protected by an action for passing off (see **21.3**). There is much better protection for registered trade marks mainly because the costs of enforcing your rights are cheaper and the outcome usually more certain.

21.2.2 What can be protected as a registered trade mark?

Not everything can be protected as a *registered trade mark*, although the range is quite wide. The limits are set out in the Trade Marks Act 1994. This says 'a trade mark means any sign capable of being represented graphically which is capable of distinguishing goods or services' of one business from another. 'A trade mark may, in particular, consist of words (including personal names) designs, letters, numerals or the shape of goods or their packaging.'

As a rough rule of thumb, this means you can register names, stylised logos, slogans, your organisation's initials, even smells, colours and sounds provided that:

- what you are registering is distinctive;
- there are no marks already registered that are identical or confusingly similar.

If the mark you want to register is descriptive (e.g. 'Cycle Ride Alaska'), you will not be able to register it unless you can prove that your use of the mark means it has become distinctive of your organisation.

Some examples of trade marks registered by charities and their trading subsidiaries are:

- Cancer Research Campaign has its name and logo registered in Class 16 for, among other things, collecting boxes, paper flags and badges, publications, greeting cards and stationery.
- Scope has registrations in Class 16 for the mark 'Skychair' for use on wheelchairs and for the mark 'Beerjolais' in Class 41 for organisation of competitions relating to the transport of beer barrels!

- World Wide Fund for Nature has a number of registrations for the initials 'WWF' and the Panda logo including for charitable fundraising services (Class 36) and consultation and advisory services (Class 42).

21.2.3 What protection does it give?

When you apply to register a trade mark you have to identify on which goods or services you will be using the mark. The Trade Marks Register is divided into 42 categories (known as 'classes'), 36 of which cover different types of product, and 6 of which cover different types of service. You can register in one or more classes. The most useful ones for fundraisers are:

- Class 16   All printed matter, including leaflets, posters
- Class 25   Clothing
- Class 36   Fundraising services.

Your registration then gives you an exclusive monopoly in the UK to use the mark for the goods or services for which it is registered (see below for protection in other countries.) You can sue for infringement if anyone else:

- uses the same mark on the goods or services covered by your registration;
- uses a confusingly similar mark on the goods or services covered by your registration;
- uses the same or a confusingly similar mark on similar goods or services.

Take professional advice before alleging infringement of a trade mark. If you threaten infringement proceedings and your threat is groundless, the recipient can claim against you for any damages suffered as a result of the threat. (See **21.9** for what to do if you think your mark has been infringed.)

21.2.4 How do you register a trade mark?

You start the process by submitting a completed application form TM3 and an application fee to the Trade Marks Registry, which is part of the Patent Office (see p. 243) and deals with registrations. The Registry has offices in London, Manchester and Newport. At the time of writing, the fee to register a mark in one class is £200 with an extra £50 per additional class.

The registration process can take anything from several months to several years, and the Registry may object to all or part of your application. It is possible to submit applications yourself but, as this is a specialised area, it is worth seeking advice from a trade-mark agent or experienced solicitor who can deal with the application on your behalf. Their fees would be extra.

Consider whether any application should be in the name of the charity or its trading subsidiary – registering in the name of the charity and giving the trading subsidiary a licence is the most common way to proceed.

21.2.5 Duration of protection

If your application is successful, you are given protection from the date of your application. Protection will continue indefinitely provided that you pay the renewal fees due every ten years and that you do not allow a period of five years to elapse during which you have not used the mark.

21.2.6 Using the ® and ™ signs

The ® symbol should only be used with registered trade marks – otherwise it is a criminal offence.

In the UK, the ™ sign can be used whether or not a trade mark is registered – in the UK, the ™ sign does not have any legal meaning other than to warn third parties that you regard the mark as belonging to you.

21.2.7 Registering licences

If a trading subsidiary or a third party is going to use a charity's registered trade mark, the charity should give a non-exclusive licence and ensure that the grant of the licence is registered at the Trade Marks Registry. This improves the ability of both the charity and the trading subsidiary to sue for damages if there is any infringement by a third party.

21.2.8 Checking what is already registered

It is definitely worth checking what has already been registered not just if you are thinking of getting protection yourself but also if you want to be sure that any new name for your organisation, event or product does not infringe someone else's registration.

For a fee of £50–£100 per mark and class, the Trade Marks Registry will carry out a search for you. A cheaper alternative is to carry out searches in person at the Registry offices, but your own results may be less reliable than an official search report.

21.2.9 International protection

A UK registration does not give you any protection in other countries. As a general rule, getting international protection means filing separate applications in each country. There are two exceptions to this.

21.2.9.1 Community Trade Mark

If you want protection within Europe, you can now apply for a Community Trade Mark that gives protection for all the member countries of the European Community. These applications are dealt with at the Community Trade Mark Office in Alicante. It operates the same system of 42 classes, but the initial application fee is much more expensive (€975) and there is a further fee of €1,100 payable if the application is successful. It is not worth applying if you already know of some conflicting registered marks, as a Community application will fail completely even if there is only one conflicting mark already registered in any of the member states.

21.2.9.2 *Applications under the Madrid Protocol*

The Madrid Protocol is a treaty (agreement) that a number of countries have signed up to. Anyone owning a trade-mark registration or application in one of the signatory countries can file a separate application in Geneva which has the effect of filing simultaneous national applications in all the countries that have signed up to the treaty. At the time this book went to press, there are 42 such countries, many of them EC member states, but also including China, Korea and the Russian Federation. The fees vary depending on whether you want the application to take effect in some or all of the signatory countries.

An application under the Madrid Protocol will not automatically fail completely if there is a conflicting mark in one country – the application can continue in any other countries where there are no conflicting marks.

Applications are filed via the UK Patent Office, from which application forms, up-to-date lists of fees and a full list of signatory countries may be obtained.

21.3 Passing off
21.3.1 What is protected by passing off?

Passing off is an action to protect goodwill and reputation. It prevents a third party from trading off your established reputation. Passing off can be used to protect unregistered trade marks, such as your organisation's name or a name for an event or product. Passing off also protects the way a product is packaged and can even prevent advertising campaigns being copied. One of the classic passing-off cases was brought by Jif against a competitor who started selling lemon juices in plastic containers shaped like lemons.

Two recent examples of passing-off cases involving charities are:

- the British Diabetic Association obtaining an injunction to prevent a new charity from calling itself the British Diabetic Society;
- the Royal British Legion obtaining an injunction to prevent a record company from selling a remembrance album called 'Poppies' and bearing a picture of a poppy.

21.3.2 How does protection arise?

Passing-off protection applies whether or not you have any other registered rights. To win a court case, you need to show:

- goodwill or reputation in a name, logo or 'get-up' – for some charities this may be difficult to prove, particularly if a name is descriptive or used by a number of organisations;

- a misrepresentation by a third party that is likely to confuse the public – the key part here is that there must be some likelihood of confusion: the more different the other party's activities, the harder it can be to prove likelihood of confusion;
- actual or likely damage – the charity needs to show it is likely to lose out financially, or that its reputation could be damaged.

21.3.3 Who has the right to bring a claim?

Only the person with the reputation can bring the claim. Charities will need to assess whether the charity or the trading subsidiary (as will be the case in some instances) should bring the claim.

21.3.4 Cost

Bringing a passing-off action can be very expensive. This is because proving the first element requires detailed evidence of reputation, and proving the second element usually requires market research surveys to show the public is likely to be confused. In the recent passing-off case brought by the British Diabetic Association (mentioned above), BDA is reported to have spent approximately £450,000 on legal fees.

21.4 Copyright

21.4.1 What is protected by copyright?

Copyright is an incredibly useful right because of the range of works it protects. The legal definition of what it protects is:

- *'original literary, dramatic, musical or artistic works;*
- *sound recordings, films, broadcasts or cable programmes;*
- *the typographical arrangement of published editions.'* (Copyright, Designs and Patents Acts 1988)

In practice, this means copyright protects:

- books, articles, reports, magazines, posters, leaflets and most written pieces of work;
- designs and drawings – this includes most stylised logos;
- photographs, paintings, sculptures;
- music and lyrics;
- plays and screenplays;
- recordings of music, film, videos and television programmes;
- computer programs and some databases (this is on the basis that they are 'literary works'!) ;
- the way books, newspapers and other publications are typeset.

As a general rule, copyright does not protect names and ideas.

21.4.2 How does protection arise?

The joy of copyright is that you do not have to register anything for copyright protection to arise. The protection arises automatically when an original piece of work is created.

In practice, you should keep original drafts marked with the name of the author and the date the draft was created, so that you can refer back to the draft to prove the date the work was created. Other steps you can take, but do not have to take, include:

- posting a copy of the completed work to yourself by registered post – if you leave the envelope unopened, this is a way of proving the work existed at a particular date;
- lodging a copy of the completed work at a bank or solicitors.

21.4.3 Extent of protection

Owning copyright in a piece of work gives you the right to prevent third parties from copying 'the whole or any substantial part'. Your remedies for unauthorised copying (or infringement) are an injunction and damages.

What if someone has only copied part of the work? You then have to assess whether what they have copied is enough to be 'substantial'. There is no legal definition of what 'substantial' means, and in each case it is a question of degree. The quality of what has been copied is as important as the quantity.

> **TWO EXAMPLES OF RECENT CASES**
>
> - In a case relating to band music, an extract of 1 minute from a 4-minute piece of music was held to be infringement. It was relevant that the 28 bars of music copied constituted the main theme of the piece.
> - In a recent case relating to the hit song 'Macarena', a judge held that even copying just 7.5 seconds of music could amount to infringement.

In most cases, you should seek professional advice on whether or not copying amounts to infringement.

21.4.4 Duration of protection

For most copyright works, protection lasts for 70 years from the end of the year in which the author died.

For any film made between 1 August 1989 and 1 January 1996, copyright lasts for 50 years from the year in which the film was made. But for films made since 1 January 1996, copyright lasts for 70 years from the end of the year in which the principal director, author, author of the dialogue or composer of original music dies, whichever is the later.

21.4.5 Who owns copyright?

The person who creates the copyright work usually owns the copyright, so that:

- copyright in a book belongs to the author;
- copyright in a design belongs to the designer;
- copyright in a film or sound recording belongs to the person who makes the necessary arrangements for making the recording;
- copyright in a photograph belongs to the photographer;
- copyright in a computer-generated work belongs to the person who made arrangements to create the work.

21.4.6 Work done by employees

Copyright in work done by employees belongs to their employer, provided the work was within the normal course of their employment. For example, if a fundraiser designs a poster for a fundraising event, this would usually be in the course of their employment, and the employer would own copyright. However, if the Finance Director offered one of her drawings to be used for the charity's Christmas card, it is unlikely that doing the drawing would be treated as part of her employment, and the employer would not own copyright.

21.4.7 Work done by non-employees, such as volunteers and consultants

Unless agreed otherwise, copyright in work done by non-employees will belong to them. This is the case even if the work was commissioned and paid for by the charity. If a charity expects to own copyright in commissioned work, it has to agree this specifically with the consultant and should record their agreement either in a letter or written agreement.

The same rule will apply to volunteers. You should ask volunteers working on important projects to sign a deed assigning copyright in their work to the charity.

21.4.8 Use of the © symbol

There is no legal requirement to use the © symbol. However, using it is a clear way of telling third parties that the author or publisher claims copyright. The usual practice is to use © followed by the name of the copyright owner and the year the work was created. For example, in the case of this book, © Bates, Wells & Braithwaite 2000.

21.4.9 Use of copyright works

There are some situations in which it is not an infringement to reproduce a third party's copyright. These include:

- making a single copy of a published work for research or private study;
- use of some copyright works for educational purposes, such as copying text for teaching purposes or performing a play.

21.5 **Patents and designs**

Patents and designs are not something that most fundraisers will ever need to worry about – they mainly provide protection to industrial products and processes. They do not protect:

- general fundraising ideas
- names.

As patents and designs are not things most fundraisers are likely to come across, the following paragraphs give you no more than a thumbnail sketch of what they protect and the duration of protection. For further information, contact the Patent Office and ask for one of their free brochures, or seek professional advice.

21.5.1 **What do patents and designs protect?**

Patents protect inventions that are capable of industrial application. A patent must be novel (i.e. the product or method it protects must not have been made or used before) and must involve an 'inventive' step (i.e. the invention must not be an obvious development from what has been done before). For example, medical charities might use patents to protect new scientific processes or drugs.

Registered designs protect 'features of shape, configuration, pattern or ornament applied to an article by an industrial process, being features which in the finished article appeal to and are judged solely by the eye'. For example, registered designs protect wallpaper designs and car radiators. Registered designs have to be novel.

Unregistered designs protect original features of shape or configuration (whether internal or external) of the whole or part of an article. For example, design right has been held to protect the diagonal ribs on the surface of a hot water bottle (which protect the skin of the user from coming too close to the hottest part of the bottle).

21.5.2 **How is protection obtained?**

- **Patents** – by application to the UK Patent Office. There is no initial filing fee, but there are fees for certain stages of the registration process.
- **Unregistered designs** – protection arises automatically.
- **Registered designs** – by application to the Design Registry. There is an initial filing fee, currently £60.

21.5.3 **Duration of protection**

- Patent protection lasts for 20 years from the date of grant, assuming you continue to pay the annual renewal fees. The renewal fees increase each year to make it expensive for patent owners to maintain protection for the full 20 years.

- Unregistered design rights' protection lasts for 10–15 years.
- Registered design protection lasts for up to twenty-five years, provided five-yearly renewal fees are paid.

21.5.4 Ownership

Ownership of patents is determined by who filed the patent application: this may not necessarily be the inventor. Inventions made by employees will usually belong to their employers, but employees have rights to apply for compensation if a patent is of 'outstanding benefit to the employer'.

Registered and unregistered design rights are owned by the person who created the design except for works:

- commissioned and paid for by someone else (in which case, the person commissioning and paying for the design owns the rights);
- created by employees (as a general rule, the design rights for such works are owned by the employers).

21.6 Database rights

Since 1 January 1998, there has been a new protection for databases. This arises from the Copyright and Rights in Databases Regulations 1997. One consequence of the regulations being so new is that there is little case law to help interpret how they will work in practice. For the moment this means there are a number of grey areas, for example when protection arises and what amounts to infringement.

21.6.1 What is protected?

A database right protects the contents of a database provided 'there has been a substantial investment in obtaining, verifying or presenting the contents of the database' (Copyright and Rights in Databases Regulations 1997). 'Substantial' can either be in terms of quantity or quality or both. There have not been any cases to test what 'substantial' means. If you are not sure whether your database would qualify for protection, take advice. Even if it does not qualify for database rights, it may have some protection under copyright.

The right gives the owner the right to prevent unauthorised reproduction of 'substantial' parts of the database. In a case decided under copyright law, use of 12 per cent of a database was treated as use of a substantial part. The right may also be infringed by repeated extraction or use of small parts of the database.

Charities often feel very possessive about donor names that they have either bought or generated themselves from mailings. Intellectual property rights do not protect individual names: the closest intellectual property comes to protecting individual names is this database right, but even this does not give protection to just one name in a database. The amount copied has to be substantial to give rise to a claim. However, any unauthorised use of names may be a breach of data protection regulations – see Chapter 12.

21.6.2 How does protection arise?

Protection arises automatically – there is no need to register anything.

21.6.3 Duration of protection

Protection lasts for 15 years from the end of the calendar year in which the database was completed. If a database is updated, each time the changes are 'substantial' a new database right will arise. Therefore, provided a database is revised substantially at least every 15 years, it could potentially be protected indefinitely. To prove an updated database qualifies for a new right:

- keep a list of the amendments made;
- keep a copy of the database both before and after updating.

You can then refer back to these if you need to prove the amendments were 'substantial'.

21.6.4 Who owns the right?

Unless agreed otherwise, the right is owned by the person or organisation that took the initiative in 'obtaining, verifying or presenting the database and assumed the risk of investing in the making of the database'. There are several exceptions to this, the most important being that, where a database is made by an employee in the course of their employment, the employer owns the database rights.

If outside consultants or volunteers are going to help create or update a database, it is a good idea to get them to agree in writing that any database rights are owned by the charity or trading subsidiary.

21.7 Moral rights

'Moral rights' is a collective term used to describe four new rights introduced by the Copyright Designs and Patents Act 1988. They are rights that arise in addition to the other rights mentioned above and were introduced to give some permanent rights to the original creators of certain types of artistic works.

The rights are:

- The author of a copyright work has the right to be identified as its author.
- The author of a copyright work has the right not to have their work subjected to derogatory treatment.

- Any person has the right not to be falsely named as the author of a piece of work.
- Any person who commissions a photograph or film for private and domestic purposes has the right to prevent copies being issued to the public.

These rights cannot be assigned but they can be waived. Any waiver must be in writing.

There are two important points to note:

- The rights are fairly narrow and do not give the author or creator of a piece of work unlimited rights to dictate how their work should be treated.
- Employees do not have any of these rights – they only apply if the work is done by a non-employee.

21.8 Performers' rights

Individual performers have rights in some situations to object to exploitation of their performances or to object to recordings being made of their performances. If a fundraising event is going to be filmed or recorded, you should take advice about getting consents from all participants.

21.9 Dealing with disputes

21.9.1 Disputes about intellectual property and who has rights to do what usually involve getting specialist legal advice. Before you do that, make sure you have thought about the following and collected together all relevant documents:

- What rights do you have? Have you got the proof?
- What has the other party done to infringe your rights? If they have done something similar but not identical, have any members of the public been confused? Gather as much information as possible.
- What do you know about the other party's legal status, business activities and resources? This information can help make a provisional assessment of whether the other party has the money to defend litigation or will be more willing to reach an amicable solution.
- What risks do you run if you threaten infringement? Remember you could expose your organisation to a claim if threats of patent or trade mark infringement are unjustified.

If no alternative to litigation appears possible, the trustees should follow a special procedure to get approval from the Charity Commission (known as applying for a Beddoes Order) before beginning litigation.

21.9.2 Disputes with other charities

The courts are unlikely to be sympathetic to disputes between charities. In the British Diabetic Association case (see **21.3**), the judge was highly critical of two charities litigating and said 'a passing-off action by one charity against another is on the face of it … a deplorable, even scandalous thing to occur [except] if a so-called charity is set up as a fraud or a scam, and uses a large part of its funds for private gain and should be stopped – either by the Charity Commissioners or by the Court.'

Your first step should be to establish your rights and then try to agree an amicable solution. Litigation should be very much a last resort.

21.10 Contract clauses covering intellectual property

A 'licence' gives permission to a third party to use intellectual property. An 'assignment' transfers ownership. In any arrangement involving licensing intellectual property or the creation of intellectual property, you should consider having clauses to cover the following:

- Is any party licensing a registered trade mark? If so, record details of the registration number.
- If any party is giving permission to use its name or logo, attach samples in a schedule.
- For both the above, record the limits of the permission granted (e.g. use in UK only, use for the purposes of the contract only, any material bearing the name or logo to be approved in advance).
- If any party is allowing the other access to its copyright material, then record the terms upon which permission is given.
- If new materials will be created during the course of the contract, record who will own copyright – ideally, this will be the charity. Where work under a contract has already started, make sure this clause covers not just future work but also all work done already.
- If the charity will own all rights, put an obligation on the other party to do all necessary things to give the charity proof of ownership of its rights.
- If the other party insists on owning copyright, try to get an irrevocable royalty-free licence for the charity to use the copyright material for any purpose whatsoever.
- Obtain a guarantee (known as a warranty) that materials supplied by the other party are original and do not infringe any third party's intellectual property rights.
- If payment is in instalments, say that rights in all work done up to the date of payment belong to the charity once the instalment is paid.

Summary chart

WHAT DO YOU WANT TO PROTECT?	HOW PROTECTED
Name of charity	<ul><li>registered trade mark</li><li>passing off (if substantial reputation)</li><li>register working names at Charity Commission</li></ul>
Charity's logo	<ul><li>registered trade mark</li><li>passing off (if substantial reputation)</li><li>copyright</li></ul>
Slogan	<ul><li>registered trade mark</li><li>passing off (if substantial reputation)</li></ul>
Fundraising ideas	No protection for general ideas, but:<ul><li>name may be protected by registered trade mark or passing off</li><li>printed materials such as leaflets, posters would be protected by copyright</li></ul>
Names of donors/funders	<ul><li>No protection for a single name but a collection of names may be protected under the database right</li></ul>

22

Trading companies

22.1 Introduction

Chapter 10 considered the legal implications of a charity carrying out a trade itself and discussed how a charity may undertake some small or minor non-primary-purpose trading without running the risk of breaking charity law or being confronted with a tax bill. However, each case will depend on its facts, and it is dangerous to generalise.

There may well come a point when it is necessary to set up a separate trading company (see **10.11**). Charities and their advisors need to keep a sense of balance around this. In one case, a city farm (which was a charity) owned a cow, whose milk it sold. The Charity Commission told the charity that this 'trading' activity would have to be run through a separate, non-charitable trading company! It could have been argued perfectly reasonably that:

- the trade was ancillary so far as charity law was concerned and thus within the charity's constitutional capacity;
- if there were any profits, after a proper apportionment of overheads had been taken into account, these were so small or even non-existent as to be within the *de minimis* exemption (see **10.10**).

There will, however, come a point for some charities when they have to set up a trading company in order to avoid the taxation of profits derived from commercial trading or fundraising activities. Alternatively, a charity may carry out charitable trading or fundraising activities that it decides to put into a separate trading company in order to isolate the risk. This is a perfectly reasonable strategy. Many commercial organisations spread risk by having a large number of separate subsidiary companies, each of which undertakes a different activity. If one business fails, this will not jeopardise the financial position of the whole group (unless cross-guarantees have been given).

A charity may also consider establishing a trading company as a VAT-saving scheme (e.g. to set up a design-and-build company when undertaking construction of a new building).

The Charity Commission and Inland Revenue both recognise and approve the establishment of separate for-profit trading companies.

22.2 How to establish a trading company

A trading company will normally be established as a company limited by shares. A company limited by shares has a share capital. For example a company may have a share capital of £100 divided into 100 shares of £1 each. Each £1 share gives the owner of that share a stake in the company as well. If 100 shares are issued, the holder of one share owns 1 per cent of the company's wealth. By owning a share, a shareholder 'shares' in the wealth of the company with the other shareholder – hence the term. It is normal for a trading company established by charity to be wholly owned by the charity, although this is not necessary.

22.3 Investment powers

Before a charity can decide whether to invest any money in a trading company, either by purchasing shares, or by loan, it must check that it has the necessary constitutional powers. Many charities are established with very limited powers of investment, which confine them to the investments sanctioned by the Trustee Investments Act 1961. If a charity's investments powers are limited to the 1961 Act, then trustees cannot purchase shares in a private limited company such as a trading company: it will be necessary to obtain the consent of the Charity Commission to extend the powers of investment. The limitations on investments contained in the Trustee Investments Act are due to be repealed for trusts, but not charitable companies, and the Charity Commission is now willing to sanction charities expanding their investment powers.

22.4 Trustees' duties when investing in a trading company

Having established that they have the power to invest in the trading company, the trustees must exercise the duty of care required of them if they wish to do so. This applies regardless of whether the trustees are thinking of supporting the trading company by buying shares in it or by making a loan.

22.4.1 The duty of care

Under Common Law, trustees have to exercise reasonable care and skill in acting as trustees – trustees can take fewer risks than if they were investing their own money.

22.4.2 **The need for diversification**

Section 6(1) of the Trustee Investments Act 1961 states:

'In the exercise of his powers of investment, a trustee shall have regard:

- *to the need for diversification of investments of the trusts insofar as is appropriate to the circumstances of the trust;*
- *to the suitability to the trust of investments of the description of the investment proposed and of the investment proposed as an investment of that description.'*

In other words the trustees must ensure that they are not putting too many eggs in one basket!

This duty applies to all trustees, including charity trustees, and to any exercise of the power of investment; it does not just apply to investments made in the categories stipulated in the 1961 Act for narrow and wider-range investments.

The Trustee Bill 2000 (which is not in force at the time of going to print) repeals this section of the Trustee Investments Act but introduces a new duty of care, including a duty to consider the need for diversification of investments.

22.4.3 **The need not to take risks**

In addition to this statutory duty, case law imposes a general duty of care on all trustees, including charity trustees. The first requirement is that a trustee should avoid investments of a hazardous or speculative nature. As a generalisation, when investing the charity's money, trustees have to act prudently and not as they would act when acting for themselves (when they might take a risk).

22.5 **The decision to invest**

Like any prudent businessperson contemplating an investment, charity trustees must ensure that they are provided with sufficiently detailed information to allow them to make a sound and proper decision as to whether or not to invest. Such information may well include:

- market research (unless it is a question of a charity hiving off a business that it has already built up);
- a proposed budget showing projected capital and on-going expenditure and income;
- a cash-flow forecast for at least two years;
- a business plan showing how it is proposed to develop and market the business;
- an analysis of working capital requirements.

The trustees should consider this information carefully and in detail, mindful of their duty to act in accordance with their various obligations. The minutes of the trustees' meeting should record the terms of any resolution to invest and refer to the documents that the trustees have reviewed in reaching their decision. Those documents should be annexed to the minutes, so that, if the trustees' decision to invest is ever challenged, contemporary evidence will be available to justify the trustees' action. The wording of the resolution should be carefully drawn up – it should not commit the charity to financing the trading company open-endedly. It is worth considering taking advice from a suitably qualified professional advisor.

22.6 How to invest

22.6.1 Loans

Once the trustees have decided in principal to invest in a trading company, they must then decide how to structure that investment.

It is normal practice for the charity's investment to take the form of a loan. Although the Charity Commission is on record as recommending that charities should obtain finance for their trading companies from commercial sources, in reality most charities provide their trading companies with working capital. The Charity Commission has recognised this to a degree by drawing up guidelines that charities should adhere to when lending money to a trading company. These guidelines state that the charity should:

- charge a proper rate of interest;
- take security for the loan;
- lay down terms for repayment of the loan.

Proper rate of interest

Charities should make sure that they charge a proper rate of interest on loans to trading companies. They should not make them interest free. An interest-free loan could put at jeopardy any Gift Aid payment between the trading company and the charity whereby the trading company pays its taxable profits over to the charity tax free (see **22.10**). The interest payable to the charity should be physically paid by a cheque that is drawn on the trading company's account and credited to the charity's account. It is not sufficient to do this by an internal accounting exercise. The rate of interest charged should reflect the risk that the charity is taking and should be higher than the rate that a normal commercial lender would charge.

Security for the loan

The Charity Commission requires that the trading company execute a charge or mortgage in favour of the charity to secure the loan. The charge will be over all the trading company's assets – thus, it should be a fixed charge over any land, buildings, plant, machinery, intellectual property rights and so on, together with a floating charge over stock and other items that change in the course of trade. This security may be more apparent than real, as in many cases the assets of a trading company may amount to very little other than some unsold stock and debts due. The reason for taking a charge is that, if the trading company should be unable to meet its liabilities, the charity will be able to appoint a receiver who can sell the items subject to the charge and pay the proceeds of sale to the charity, thus cutting out the other creditors' claims.

Repayment of the loan

The repayment of loans made by charities to trading companies can be fraught with difficulty. The Charity Commission requires that, when a loan is sanctioned, the trustee should stipulate repayment terms. Usually the loan is repayable on demand, but repayment is rarely demanded. The problem with the repayment of a loan is that it comes out of taxable profits: most trading companies pay all their taxable profits over to the parent charity and therefore do not retain profits. Consequently they do not have the available monies to pay off the loan.

Qualifying expenditure and loans

Before making a loan to a trading company, charity trustees must consider whether or not the loan constitutes 'qualifying expenditure' for the purposes of section 505(3)(Tax Act 1988). This is a further reason why trustees should take appropriate professional advice when considering setting up a trading company and investing in it.

22.7 How to invest in a trading company: purchase of shares

By and large, most charities finance their trading company through loans. Purchasing a large amount of shares in a trading company is not seen as a good idea: the holders of shares are paid out last on the liquidation of a company whereas, if the charity makes a loan and takes a charge, it will be a preferential creditor (see **22.6**).

22.8 **The relationship between a charity and a trading company**

Charities must bear in mind at all times that trading companies are separate legal entities distinct from the charity, and the relationship between the two organisations should be at arm's length. This means in practice that the charity should give no subsidy whatsoever to the trading company for sharing facilities, equipment or staff, and so on. The charity should ensure that it recovers the proper cost of any of its assets used by the trading company, which should include not only direct costs (e.g. salaries) but also indirect costs (e.g. a proper attribution of overheads). A charity should charge on a regular basis. This may well demand sophisticated apportionments of:

- employees' time (where an employee works for both organisations);
- overheads (probably based on square footage);
- the use of equipment (e.g. monitoring how much each organisation uses the photocopier).

The management charge should be structured on a cost-recovery basis only.

It may be necessary to charge VAT on the management charge. This will depend on the level of VATable turnover of the charity, whether it is registered for VAT and whether the charity and the trading company are members of the same VAT group.

Not all the trustees should be directors of the trading company, and vice versa. It is prudent to have at least one trustee who is not a director and one director who is not a trustee, so as to provide an independent perspective on each board, which will help guard against conflicts of interest.

In maintaining the relationship between charity and trading company the following points should be borne in mind at all times:

- The charity and trading company must have separate bank accounts.
- Separate minutes should be kept of meetings of the board of directors of the trading company and those of the trustees of the charity, even if the two boards meet on the same day.
- The trading company's notepaper should contain the following information:
  - its registered name (not the charity's)
  - its registered office
  - its place of incorporation
  - its registered company number (not the charity's)
  - the names of either all the directors or none of them.

22.9 Trading agreement between charity and trading company

In order to ensure that the relationship between the charity and its trading company is clear, it is recommended that there is a master agreement between the two to regulate their relationship. The topics that an agreement should cover will vary in each case, but broadly speaking it is sensible to consider such items as:

- a licence of the charity's name and logo on a non-exclusive basis – this will allow the trading company to exploit the charity's name and logo for commercial purposes (e.g. on CRM deals; see Chapter 8) – the payment for use of the charity's name and logo should be structured as an annual payment;
- use of the charity's mailing list (but note the controls under the Data Protection Act; see Chapter 12) – the payment for use of the mailing list should be structured on a cost-recovery basis only, otherwise any surplus made on it will be taxable in the charity's hands;
- terms for use of the charity's facilities (e.g. premises, staff, computers, machinery, etc.) and what charge is to be made, again on a cost-recovery basis;
- provisions concerning accounting, inspection of books, etc.;
- termination – it should be borne in mind that the Charity Commission requires that all arrangements whereby charities license their name to commercial third parties be kept under review and that charities retain the right to terminate.

22.10 Stripping out the profits from a trading company

Trading companies owned by charities will be subject to the normal Corporation Tax rules and will pay tax on taxable profits. However, if the trading company can reduce its taxable profits by paying them away to the charity that controls the trading company, the position changes. There will then be less or no Corporation Tax payable, depending on the amount of taxable profits remaining in the trading company at its financial year end.

A trading company can avoid any Corporation Tax liability by paying all its taxable profits over Gift Aid (see Chapter 19). The payment can be made within nine months of the financial year end of the trading company, provided the trading company is owned 100 per cent by the charity. These arrangements whereby a charity's trading company avoids paying Corporation Tax and pays its profits over to the charity tax free are accepted by the Inland Revenue and the Charity Commission as legitimate, despite the fact that they are a form of tax avoidance.

Summary

- Consider if any fundraising activities require the establishment of a trading company.

- Does your charity have the power to establish a trading company? Check the constitution!

- Is there sufficient information available for the trustees concerning the establishment of a trading company?

- Should investment be by loan or by shares?

- Ensure that Charity Commission requirements for loans are met.

- Make sure there is a trading agreement between the charity and company, and that it is implemented.

- How are the company's profits paid to the charity?

23

Criminal offences and the impact of the criminal law on fundraising

23.1 Introduction

Criminal offences can be inadvertently committed by fundraisers or businesses that are genuinely collecting for a charity but fail to comply with the detail of charity legislation. There are also more serious offences committed by fraudulent fundraisers.

23.2 Public collections

23.2.1 Street collections

In England and Wales, failure to comply with the Police, Factories, etc. (Miscellaneous Provisions) Act 1916 is an offence giving rise to a fine not exceeding £200.

In Northern Ireland, failure to comply with the Collections in Streets or Public Places Regulations 1927 is an offence. The maximum penalty is a fine not exceeding £2 or more for the first offence; in the case of a second or subsequent offence the maximum fine is £5.

In Scotland the maximum penalty for a breach of the Public Charitable Collections (Scotland) Regulations 1984 is:

- £25 in respect of each offence by a collector;
- £50 in respect of each offence by the organiser of the collection.

23.2.2 House to House Collections Act 1939 (England and Wales)

- Promoting an unlicensed collection can result in imprisonment for a term not exceeding six months or a fine not exceeding £1,000, or both.
  In Northern Ireland this offence can result in a maximum fine of £100 and six months' imprisonment, or both.

- A collector carrying out an unauthorised collection is liable on summary conviction to a fine not exceeding £500 or three months' imprisonment, or both.
  In Northern Ireland this can result in a £5 fine for a first conviction or, in the case of a second or subsequent conviction, imprisonment for a term not exceeding three months or a fine not exceeding £25, or both.

- Any person who breaches any regulations under the Act is liable to a fine not exceeding £200.
  In Northern Ireland this offence can lead to a fine not exceeding £5.

- Any person guilty of using an unauthorised badge is liable on conviction to imprisonment for a term not exceeding six months or to a fine not exceeding £1,000, or both.
  In Northern Ireland this offence can lead to imprisonment for a term not exceeding six months or to a fine not exceeding £100, or both.

- Any person who fails to give their name on demand to a police officer is liable to a fine not exceeding £200.
  In Northern Ireland this offence leads to a fine not exceeding £5.

- Any person who knowingly or recklessly makes a false statement in any material particular when supplying information under the Act is liable to imprisonment for a term not exceeding six months or to a fine not exceeding £1,000, or both.
  In Northern Ireland conviction for this offence leads to imprisonment for a term not exceeding six months or a fine not exceeding £100, or both.

23.3 Charities Act 1992 Part II

Professional fundraisers or commercial participators will have committed a criminal offence giving rise to a maximum fine not exceeding £5,000 if they fail to:

- make the statement required under section 60 (see Chapters 16 and 17);
- mention the right to a refund in respect of donations of £50 or more under section 60(4)(c) (see Chapters 16 and 17);
- give information about the cooling-off period under section 60(5).

All of the following can result in a maximum fine not exceeding £500:

- Failure by a professional fundraiser or commercial participator to make available on request and at all reasonable times its books, documents or other records relating to an agreement with a charitable institution.

- Failure on the part of a professional fundraiser or commercial participator to transmit money to the charitable institution within 28 days of receiving it, or such other later date as agreed.
- Failure by a quasi-commercial participator (see Chapter 16) to make the appropriate statement required under the regulations.

23.4 Lotteries

If the lotteries legislation is contravened, then, under section 13 of the Lotteries and Amusements Act 1976, the promoter of that lottery and any other person who is party to the contravention is guilty of a criminal offence. These particular points are worth noting:

- Any 'other person' could be the charity as well as 'any director, manager, secretary or other similar officer' if the offence was committed with the person's consent, compliance, or is attributed to any neglect.
- The penalty is a fine up to a maximum of £5,000 or a term of imprisonment up to a maximum of two years or a fine plus imprisonment.
- The Gaming Board has wider powers to revoke a licence including if 'any lottery promoted on behalf of the society within the last five years has not been properly conducted'.

23.5 Misrepresenting charity status

It is an offence under section 63(1) of the Charities Act 1992 to solicit money by making out that an organisation is a registered charity when it is not.

The current maximum fine for this offence is £1,000. Prosecution would be by the police.

23.6 Theft

Collecting money in the name of a charity and not passing the money to the charity amounts to theft. This was established in the case of R v. Wain. The facts in this case were that Mr Wain raised £2,800 for Telethon Trust. He paid the money into a bank account in the name of Scarborough Telethon Trust, then transferred the money to his own account and wrote cheques from his account to the charity: the cheques bounced.

This was a particularly clear case. The police could use the dishonoured cheques as evidence that Mr Wain had used charity money for his own purposes.

It may be harder in other situations to encourage the police to prosecute, but the relevant legislation to refer to is section 5(3) of the Theft Act 1968, which states:

'Where a person receives property from or on account of another and is under an obligation to the other to retain and deal with that property or its proceeds in a particular way, the property or proceeds shall be regarded (as against him) as belonging to the other.'

The maximum punishment for theft is seven years' imprisonment. The Theft Act also creates other offences of:

- obtaining property by deception;
- obtaining pecuniary advantage by deception;
- obtaining services by deception.

23.7 **Rogues and vagabonds**

The Vagrancy Acts 1824–1935 are still in force and create the following offences:

- Begging or gathering alms amounts to a criminal offence of being an idle and disorderly person.
- Gathering or collecting alms, or endeavouring to procure charitable contributions under false or fraudulent pretence, is liable to conviction as a rogue and vagabond.

If a person convicted as a rogue and vagabond is caught collecting for charity again, they are liable to conviction as an incorrigible rogue!

The maximum punishment for this offence is a fine of £200.

23.8 **False trade descriptions**

There are offences under the Trade Descriptions Act 1968 of applying a false trade description. This has been held to include an unauthorised fundraiser's use of a charity's logo on a leaflet soliciting donated goods. Each local authority or district council has a Trading Standards department, which enforces the Trade Descriptions Act.

The maximum penalty for applying a false trade description is either an unlimited fine, or imprisonment for up to two years, or both.

23.9 **Unauthorised use of a registered trade mark or copyright**

The Trade Marks Act 1994 created several new criminal offences of unauthorised use of a registered trade mark, the maximum penalties for which are a fine, imprisonment for up to ten years, or both.

There are similar criminal offences for the unauthorised reproduction of copyright works.

23.10 Data protection

See Chapter 12.

23.11 Telephone Privacy Regulations

See Chapter 12.

23.12 Offences by corporate bodies

A number of Acts of Parliament provided that, if a corporate body (such as a company) commits a criminal offence, any director, manager, secretary or other officer can also be found guilty and punished. This applies if the offence is committed with the consent of, or connivance of, or is attributable to any neglect by, the individual.

In particular, this applies to:

■ Part II Charities Act 1992
■ the House to House Collections Act 1939
■ the House to House Charitable Collections Act 1952
■ the Data Protection Act 1998
■ the Trade Descriptions Act 1968
■ the Trade Marks Act 1994
■ the Copyright, Designs and Patent Act 1988.

However, it also applies to many other statutes.

Summary

Criminal liabilities can arise in connection with fundraising under:

■ Public collections legislation on collectors and promoters
■ Charities Act 1992 Part II on commercial participators and professional fundraisers
■ Lotteries legislation
■ Charities Act 1993
■ Theft Act
■ Vagrancy Acts
■ Trade Descriptions Act
■ Copyright law
■ Data protection legislation.

Reference section

Glossary and definitions

agreement	another word for contract
ASA	Advertising Standards Authority
branch	a sub-section of the charity, typically covering a specific region of the country
CAP codes	the British Codes of Advertising and Sales Promotion
cause-related marketing (CRM)	the use of a charity's name or logo by a company in co-operation with the charity to promote the company's business and to benefit the charity
charitable institution	an organisation set up to carry out charitable, benevolent or philanthropic purposes
charity	an organisation set up to carry out exclusively charitable purposes
company limited by guarantee	an organisation with limited liability whose members 'guarantee' payment of £1 in the event of its insolvent liquidation – used as a way of establishing not-for-profit organisations
consideration	the price payable for goods or services (whether paid in money or in kind)
contract	a legal document laying out the terms and conditions of an agreement
copyright	the right of an author to prevent his or her original work being copied – normally lasts for 70 years from the date of death of the author
deed	a document that is sealed
de minimis	a minimal or inconsequential amount – in tax law it means the small amount of income that a charity can earn from non-primary-purpose trading without risk of incurring a tax liability on any profit
donation	a gift (of money, goods or time) to a charity that carries no strings
exempt supply	a supply of goods and services that does not attract VAT and where the supplier cannot recover any input VAT

ex-gratia payment	a payment by a charity that is made without a legal obligation (e.g. a payment to top up a retired employee's pension)
grant	a gift of money
grant-giving trust	a charity established to support other charities
Great Britain	England, Wales and Scotland
ICFM	the Institute of Charity Fundraising Managers
input VAT	VAT that a charity is charged by organisations which supply it with VATable goods or services
intellectual property	property that is created by thought (e.g. trade marks, copyright and patents)
irrecoverable VAT	VAT that the charity cannot claim back, either because it is not registered for VAT or because the VAT has been incurred in connection with an exempt supply
ITC	Independent Television Commission
lottery	a promotion where the prizes are distributed by chance and where there is a contribution to enter
non-primary-purpose trading	trading that does not further the charity's objects
objects	the charity's reason for being, as stated in the objects clause in its constitution
OFTEL	the regulatory body of the telephone industry
output VAT	VAT that a charity charges to organisations to which the charity supplies goods or services
permanent endowment	a gift that stipulates that only the income can be spent; the capital must be saved
primary-purpose trading	trading that furthers the charity's objects
quasi-commercial participator	a business that states that part of the proceeds of sale of goods or services will go to a charitable cause (rather than a charitable institution)
RA	Radio Authority
raffle	a more popular name for a lottery
restricted funds	money that has been raised for a specific purpose – legally, it must be spent on those purposes
service-level agreement	a document laying out the expected service between a charity and an agency

trade mark	a sign that distinguishes an organisation (e.g. a logo) – a trade mark can be registered or unregistered
unincorporated association	an organisation without limited liability, whose members elect a management committee or are responsible for its administration
United Kingdom	the United Kingdom of Great Britain and Northern Ireland
vicarious liability	where an individual or organisation is responsible for the acts or omissions of another person (e.g. an employer who is responsible for the acts of his or her employee)
zero-rated supply	a supply of goods or services where the supplier does not charge output VAT but can recover input VAT (e.g. printed materials)

Useful addresses

Active Community Unit
Home Office
Horseferry House
Dean Royal Street
London
SW1P 2AW
tel.: 020 7217 8803

Adult Disadvantage Policy Division
Department for Education and Employment
Room N8
Moorfoot
Sheffield
S1 4PQ
tel.: 0114 259 3000

Advertising Standards Authority
Brook House
2 Torrington Place
London
WC1E 7HW
tel.: 020 7580 5555
website: www.asa.org.uk

Bates, Wells & Braithwaite
Cheapside House
138 Cheapside
London
EC2V 6BB
tel.: 020 7551 7777
website: www.bateswells.co.uk
e-mail: @bateswells.co.uk

BBC Appeals Office
Room 214
Henry Wood House
3 & 6 Langham Place
London
W1A 1AA
tel.: 020 7765 4595
website: www.bbc.co.uk/info/bbc/app/index.shtml/

British Board of Film Classification
3 Soho Square
London
W1V 6HT
tel.: 020 7439 7961
e-mail: webmaster@bbfc.co.uk
website: www.bbfc.co.uk

Broadcasting Advertising Clearance Centre
200 Grays Inn Road
London
WC1X 8HF
tel.: 020 7843 8256

Broadcasting Standards Commission
5–8 The Sanctuary
London
SW1P 3JS
tel.: 020 7233 0544
e-mail: bsc@bsc.org.uk
website: www.bsc.org.uk

Broadcasting Support Services
BSS London
Union House
Shepherd's Bush Green
London
W12 8UA
tel.: 020 8735 5000
website: www.bss.org.uk

Business in the Community
135 Shepherdess Walk
London
N1 7RR
tel.: 0870 600 2482

Centre for Voluntary Sector Development
81 Cornwall Gardens
London
SW7 4AZ
tel.: 020 7881 9270
e-mail: mail@cvsd.org.uk

Charity Commission
Second Floor
20 Kings Parade
Queens Dock
Liverpool
L3 4DG

Harmsworth House
13–15 Bouverie Street
London
EC4Y 8DP

Woodfield House
Tangier
Taunton
Somerset
TA1 4BL

General information for all three sites: 0870 3330123
website: www.charity-commission.gov.uk

Charities Aid Foundation

Kings Hill
West Malling
Kent
ME19 4TA
tel.: 01732 520000
website: www.cafonline.org

Civil Aviation Authority

CAA House
Rm T506
45–59 Kingsway
London
WC2B 6TE
tel.: 020 7379 7311
fax: 020 7832 6692
website: www.caa.co.uk

Committee of Advertising Practice

tel.: 020 7235 7020
fax: 020 7580 4072
website: www.cap.org.uk

Data Protection Commissioner

Wycliffe House
Water Lane
Wilmslow
Cheshire
SK9 5AF
tel.: 01625 545745
website: www.dataprotection.gov.uk

Department of Health

Richmond House
79 Whitehall
London
SW1A 2NS
tel.: 020 7210 4850
website: www.doh.gov.uk

Department of Health and Social Security Northern Ireland

Castle Court
Royal Avenue
Belfast
BT1 1SB
tel.: 090 336 000

Department of Social Security

Richmond House
79 Whitehall
London
SW1A 2NS
tel.: 020 7712 2171
website: www.dss.gov.uk

Department of Trade and Industry

1 Victoria Street
London
SW1H OET
tel.: 020 7215 5000
website: www.dti.gov.uk

Direct Marketing Association

(for Telephone Preference Service and Mailing Preference Service)
Haymarket House
1 Oxenden Street
London
SW1Y 4EE
tel.: 020 7321 2525
website: www.dma.org.uk

The Directory of Social Change

24 Stephenson Way
London
NW1 2DP

Federation House
Hope Street
Liverpool
L1 9BW

Publications and subscriptions
tel.: 020 7209 5151
fax: 020 7209 5049

Marketing and research
tel.: 020 7209 4422
    0151 708 0136

Courses and conferences
tel.: 020 7209 4949
    0151 708 0117

Charity fair
tel.: 020 7209 4949
    020 7209 1015 (exhibitors)
website: www.dsc.org.uk
e-mail: info@dsc.org.uk

Employment Service

Level 3
Rockingham House
123 West Street
Sheffield
S1 4ER

Financial Services Authority

25 The North Colonnade
Canary Wharf
London
E14 5HS
tel: 020 7676 1000
website: www.fsa.gov.uk

Gaming Board for Great Britain

Berkshire House
168–173 High Holborn
London
WC1V 7AA
tel.: 020 7306 6200
website: www.gbgb.org.uk

Health & Safety Executive

Caerphilly Business Park
Caerphilly
CF83 3GG
tel.: 0870 1545500
website: www.hse.gov.uk

HM Customs & Excise

New King's Beam House
22 Upper Ground
London
SE1 9PJ
tel.: 020 7620 1313
website: www.hmce.gov.uk

Independent Committee for the Supervision of Standards of Telephone Information Services

177 High Holborn
3rd Floor
Alton House
London
WC1V 7AA
tel.: 020 7240 5511
website: www.icstis.org.uk

Independent Television Commission

33 Foley Street
London
W1W 7TH
tel: 020 7255 3000
e-mail: publicaffairs@itc.org.uk
website: www.itc.org.uk

Inland Revenue

Somerset House
The Strand
London
WC2A 1LB
tel.: 020 7438 6622
website: www.inlandrevenue.gov.uk

Inland Revenue Offices for Charity Matters

Scotland
Charity Section
Inland Revenue
FICO (Scotland)
Trinity Park House
South Trinity Road
Edinburgh
EH5 3SD

Northern Ireland (dealt with in Liverpool)
Inland Revenue
FICO
St Johns House
Merton Road
Bootle
Merseyside
L69 9BB

Institute of Charity Fundraising Managers

Central Office
Market Towers
1 Nine Elms Lane
London
SW8 5NQ
tel.: 020 7627 3436
website: www.icfm.org.uk

Liquor, Gambling and Data Protection Unit

Home Office
50 Queen Anne's Gate
London
SW17 9AT
tel.: 020 7273 3108
website: www.homeoffice.gov.uk

The Lotteries Council

c/o Honorary Secretary
Windermere House
Kendal Avenue
London
W3 0XA
tel.: 01457 872988

Mail Order Traders' Association

40 Waterloo Road
Berkdale
Southport
PR8 2NG
tel.: 01704 563787

National Council for Voluntary Organisations

Regents Wharf
8 All Saints Street
London
N1 9RL
tel.: 020 7713 6161
website: www.ncvo-vol.org.uk
e-mail: ncvo@ncvo-vol.org.uk

National Newspapers' Mail Order Protection Scheme

16 Tooks Court
London
EC4A 1LB
tel.: 020 7269 0520

The Patent Office and Trade Marks Registry

Concept House
Cardiff Road
Newport
NP10 8QQ
tel.: 0845 9500505

Harmsworth House
13–15 Bouverie Street
London
EC4Y 8DP
(does not take telephone enquiries)

Commercial Library
Central Library
St Peter's Square
Manchester
M2 5PD
tel: 0161 234 1993
website: www.patent.gov.uk

Performing Right Society

29–33 Berners Street
London
W1P 4AA
tel.: 0845 300 8060

Phonographic Performance Ltd

1 St James' Street
London W1R 3HG
tel.: 020 7534 1000

Radio Advertising Clearance Centre

46 Westbourne Grove
London
W2 5SH
tel.: 020 7727 2646
website: www.crca.co.uk

Radio Authority
Holbrook House
14 Great Queen Street
London
WC2B 5DG
tel.: 020 7430 2724
website: www.radioauthority.org.uk

Scottish Council for Voluntary Organisations
18–19 Claremont Crescent
Edinburgh
EH7 4QD
tel.: 0131 556 3882
website: www.scvo.org.uk

Scottish Executive Justice Department
Civil Law Division
Saughton House
Broom House Drive
Edinburgh
EH11 3XD
tel.: 0131 244 3458

Smee & Ford Ltd.
2nd Floor
St Georges House
195–203 Waterloo Road
London
SE1 8UX
tel.: 020 7928 4050
website: www.smeeandford.co.uk

Voluntary Service Unit
Home Office
Room 1382
50 Queen Anne's Gate
London
SW1H 9AT

The Welsh Council for Voluntary Action
Baltic House
Mount Stuart Square
Cardiff Bay
Cardiff
CF10 5FH
tel.: 029 2043 1700

Fundraising Special Interest Groups

Corporate Fundraisers Network

Martin Bishop
Marie Curie Cancer Care
tel.: 020 7599 7777

Covenant Marketing Group

Kate Storey
Centre for Voluntary Sector Development
tel.: 020 7881 9271

Events Managers Forum

Jane Higgins
Terence Higgins Trust
tel.: 020 7816 4616

Legacy Marketing Group

Maggie Thomas
Amnesty International
tel.: 020 7814 6223

Lotteries Discussion Group

Kate Storey
Centre for Voluntary Sector Development
tel.: 020 7881 9271

Payroll Giving Forum

Brian Robbins
South West Charitable Giving
tel.: 01822 810094

Voluntary Sector Customer Care Forum

Helen Smith
National Asthma Campaign
tel.: 020 7704 5885

Appendices

Appendix 1 Standard form of agreement between charity and consultant

N.B. This draft is a model form and ICFM recommends it be adapted for individual circumstances, in which case appropriate professional advice should be taken.

AGREEMENT

Dated the   day of   200

BETWEEN [1][*name of charity*] whose registered charity number is [ ] (and a registered company number [ ]) whose office/[registered office] is at

[   ] fax number   ('the Charity') (1) and [*name of CONSULTANT*] of [address]

fax number   ('Consultant') (2)

Background

The Charity wishes to raise funds for its charitable purposes namely [*insert details of the principal objectives*].

The Charity wishes to contract with Consultant to raise or collect funds on behalf of the Charity in accordance with the terms of this Agreement.

NOW IT IS HEREBY AGREED AND DECLARED:

1   Definitions

In this Agreement the following words and phrases shall have the following meanings:

'the Data'   all lists of names and/or other details of supporters of the Charity in whatever form supplied to or held by the Consultant

'the Services'   the Consultancy services to be rendered by Consultant under this Agreement as detailed in Clause 2.1.

The masculine gender shall be deemed to include all other genders and vice versa.

2   Advice

2.1   The Consultant will advise the Charity on [*specify fundraising events and types of fundraising to be advised on*][2]

[1]State the full name of the Charity including its registered charity number and all other details if it is a registered company as well; charities are formed in many ways and if the Charity is an unincorporated association or a trust, technically the Agreement should be entered into under the names of the trustees or the names of the members of the Management Committee by the phrase '*as Trustees of the XYZ Charity*'. This does not apply if the Charity has been incorporated under the Charities Act 1993 in which case it can enter into the Agreement in its corporate name without naming the trustees even though it does not have the benefits of limited liability.

[2]Specify clearly the area of activities to be undertaken by the Consultant. The following provides an indication of possible methods:

- soliciting donations;
- sponsorship and gifts in kind;
- promotional schemes;
- deed of covenant and Gift Aid;
- payroll giving;
- corporate giving;
- trust giving;
- special events;
- advertising;
- lotteries;
- promotion of legacies.

2.2 The Consultant shall give priority to the provision of the Services at all reasonable times and shall use its best endeavours to promote the interests of the Charity and shall faithfully and diligently perform its duties and exercise such powers consistent with them which shall from time to time be necessary in connection with the fulfilment by it of its obligations under this Agreement.

2.3 The Consultant shall do nothing to bring the name or reputation of the Charity into disrepute in any manner whatsoever.

3 Meetings and reports

3.1 The Consultant and the Charity will hold regular meetings at [   ]. The purpose of such meetings will be for the Consultant to report progress and discuss future plans and for the Charity to review the Consultant's performance.

3.2 In addition to attending such meetings, the Consultant will provide to the Charity a written progress report every [   ] months while this Agreement is in force.

3.3 Either party may by written notice to the other require the holding of a special meeting to discuss any urgent or exceptionally important matter.

4 Period of Agreement

4.1 This Agreement will commence on the   day of   200   and shall continue for a period of [   ] months unless terminated earlier under this clause[3].

4.2 Either party may at any time terminate this Agreement by giving the other [   ] months' notice in writing.

4.3 The Charity shall be entitled to terminate this Agreement forthwith if:

4.3.1 the Consultant does anything which in the reasonable opinion of the Charity brings or in its opinion is reasonably likely to bring the Charity's reputation into disrepute; or

4.3.2 a resolution is passed for the voluntary or compulsory liquidation of the Consultant or a Receiver is appointed over all or part of its business or being an individual has a bankruptcy petition presented against him or her.

4.4 Notwithstanding termination of this Agreement, Clauses 6.2, 6.3, 6.4 and 6.7 and 8 shall survive termination. Clause 2.6 shall survive termination of this Agreement (however terminated) for a period of three years from the date of termination.

5 Remuneration

5.1 In consideration of the provision by Consultant of the Services the Charity will pay to Consultant a fee of [amount/method of calculation/dates of payments] upon receipt of Consultant's invoice[4]. All sums stated are exclusive of VAT (if any) due on Consultant's fees.

5.2 All reasonable subsistence, travelling and other expenses incurred by Consultant in the execution of its obligations under this Agreement will be reimbursed in full within [   ] days of receipt of a written request to that effect by Consultant to the

[3]It is best not to agree to a long-term agreement unless under 4.2 the notice period is very short. Otherwise the Charity could find itself locked into long-term and expensive fundraising arrangements with little reward.

[4]The Charity Commission has expressed its concern with payment on a commission basis and prefers fundraisers to be paid a fixed fee.

Charity provided that the Charity shall not be liable to indemnify Consultant for any expense in excess of [£] without such expenditure having been approved in writing in advance by the Charity[5].

6   Copyright and Data Protection

6.1   The copyright in all art work, copy and any other work capable of being subject to copyright produced or created by Consultant at the specific request of the Charity shall vest in the Charity.

6.2   All art work and hard copy of such copyright material shall be handed over by Consultant to the Charity within 14 days of the termination of this Agreement and at any time on the request of the Charity during the currency of this Agreement.

6.3   The Consultant undertakes with the Charity to maintain all the Data in a complete and accurate manner including all appropriate details of donors to the Charity recruited as a result of Consultant's activities and to hand over a hard copy and a computer disk of that Data each month to the Charity. On termination of this Agreement Consultant shall hand over to the Charity all copies of the Data (in whatever form). Consultant undertakes that it shall not deal in, exploit or use in any manner whatever the Data whether during the currency of this Agreement or after its termination save in accordance with the terms of this Agreement.

6.4   The Consultant irrevocably appoints the Charity to be its attorney or agent in its name and on its behalf to do all such acts and things and to sign all such deeds and documents as may be necessary in order to give the Charity the full benefit of the provisions of this Agreement and in particular but without limitation Consultant agrees that with respect to any third party a certificate signed by any duly authorised officer of the Charity that any act or thing or deed or document falls within the authority hereby conferred shall be conclusive evidence that that is the case[6].

6.5   The Consultant warrants and represents to the Charity that any copyright works or documents created by it pursuant to this Agreement or by its personnel or sub-contractors will not infringe the intellectual property rights of any third party whatsoever.

6.6   The Consultant undertakes to abide at all times by the Data Protection Act 1984 and all other relevant legislation and regulations in relation to the discharge by it of it obligations under this Agreement.

6.7   The Consultant hereby undertakes with the Charity that if it commissions any manipulative software to be used in conjunction with the Data that it shall procure that the Charity shall be granted by the licensor a perpetual free licence to use such software in the event of the termination of this Agreement.

7   Indemnity

The Consultant agrees to indemnify the Charity in respect of any costs, claims, loss or liability whatsoever suffered by the Charity (including reasonable legal costs and disbursements) as a result of any breach by Consultant of any of the terms of this Agreement.

---

[5]It is best to specify a fairly low threshold concerning expenses as some charities have found that they have incurred very considerable liabilities in respect of expenses incurred by Consultants.
[6]This clause is vital. Without it the Charity cannot force Consultant to hand over copyright in material created by Consultant in conjunction with this Agreement or lists of Data.

8   Confidentiality

8.1   The Charity agrees with the Consultant and the Consultant with the Charity to treat as secret and confidential and not at any time for any reason to disclose or permit to be disclosed to any person or persons or otherwise make use of or permit to be made use of any information relating to Consultant's or the Charity's business affairs or finances (as the case may be) where knowledge or details of the information was received as a result of this Agreement.

8.2   The conditions of confidence referred to in this clause shall not apply to any confidential information which:

8.2.1   is in the possession of and is at the free disposal of the Charity or the Consultant or is published or is otherwise in the public domain prior to receipt of such information by the Charity or Consultant; or

8.2.2   is or becomes publicly available on a non-confidential basis through no fault of the Charity or the Consultant; or

8.2.3   is received in good faith by the Charity or the Consultant from a third party who on reasonable enquiry by the Charity or the Consultant claims to have no obligations of confidence to the Consultant or the Charity in respect of it and imposes no obligations of confidence upon the Charity or Consultant.

9   General

9.1   The Consultant agrees to abide by the code or codes or practice issued from time to time by the Institute of Charity Fundraising Managers.

9.2   The Consultant agrees that for the duration of this Agreement it shall not undertake any work of a similar nature for any charity which operates in the same or similar fields of activity as the Charity.

9.3   This Agreement shall be governed by and construed in accordance with the laws of England.

9.4   Neither party shall be liable for any breach of any term of this Agreement which is the result of any cause beyond the reasonable control of the party in breach.

9.5   Any notice may be served by either party upon the other by sending it by post in a pre-paid recorded delivery or registered post or by telex or facsimile transmission addressed to such other party at its address above and any notice so sent shall be deemed to have been received within 72 hours of posting or 24 hours if sent by telex or facsimile transmission to the correct number of the addressee.

AS WITNESS the hands of the parties hereto

SIGNED by
for and on behalf of
Charity[7]

SIGNED by
for and on behalf of
Consultant

---

[7]The agreement should be signed by a Trustee.

Appendix 2 Standard form of agreement between charity and professional fundraiser

N.B. This draft is a model form and ICFM recommends it be adapted for individual circumstances, in which, appropriate professional advice should be taken.

AGREEMENT

Dated the   day of   200

BETWEEN [1][*name of charity*] whose registered charity number is [ ] (and a registered company number [ ]) whose office/[registered office] is at [   ] fax number ('the Charity') (1) and [*name of professional fundraiser*] of [*address*] fax number

('PFR') (2)

Background

A   The Charity wishes to raise funds for its charitable purposes namely [*insert details of the principal objectives*].

B   The Charity wishes to contract with PFR to raise or collect funds on behalf of the Charity in accordance with the terms of this Agreement.

NOW IT IS HEREBY AGREED AND DECLARED:

1   Definitions

In this Agreement the following words and phrases shall have the following meanings:

'the Bank Account'	the account in the name of the Charity with .... Bank Plc at .... account number .... sort code .... or such other account as the Charity shall from time to time designate
'the Data'	all lists of names and/or other details of supporters of the Charity in whatever form supplied to or held by PFR
'the Services'	the services to be rendered by PFR under this Agreement

The masculine gender shall be deemed to include all other genders and vice versa.

2   Method of Fundraising

2.1   PFR will observe all rules of law, by-laws and regulations relevant to fundraising and in particular will comply in all respects with the provisions of the Charities Act 1992, and the Charitable Institutions (Fund-Raising) Regulations 1994 and will ensure that all employees of PRF make the statement required under Section 60(1) Charities Act 1992.

2.2   The methods of fundraising to be used will include [e.g telemarketing; direct mail and [*events*]][2]. PFR undertakes with the Charity to obtain its prior written approval if it wishes to use any other method of raising or collecting funds.

2.3   PFR shall require that all donors draw cheques and other such items in favour of the Charity.

---

[1]State the full name of the Charity including its registered charity number and all other details if it is a registered company as well; charities are formed in many ways and if the Charity is an unincorporated association or a trust, technically the Agreement should be entered into under the names of the trustees or the names of the members of the Management Committee by the phrase '*as Trustees of the XYZ Charity*'. This does not apply if the Charity has been incorporated under the Charities Act 1993 in which case it can enter into the Agreement in its corporate name without naming the trustees even though it does not have the benefits of limited liability.

2.4 All cash, cheques and donations of whatever kind received by PFR pursuant to this Agreement shall be paid into the Bank Account within three days of receipt. If PFR breaches this clause it shall pay to the Charity interest on the sum due calculated at the rate of 4% above the base rate for the time being of the Bank from the date when payment should have been made to the date of actual payment.

2.5 All gifts in kind received by PFR and the originals of all executed covenants, Gift Aid certificates and other documentary evidence of gifts or promises shall be handed over to the Charity within 14 days of receipt.

2.6 PFR undertakes to keep proper records of all the matters in a clear and legible form specified in Schedule 1. PFR hereby grants to the Charity and its officers or duly authorised agents at any time during office hours on not less than 24 hours' written notice to PFR (save in case of emergencies) all necessary access to inspect all or any of the records or other items held by PFR (including records kept in a computerised form) which relate to this Agreement. The Charity may take such copies of such documents and records as it thinks fit at its reasonable expense.

2.7 PFR shall give priority to the provision of the Services at all reasonable times and shall use its best endeavours to promote the interests of the Charity and shall faithfully and diligently perform its duties and exercise such powers consistent with them which shall from time to time be necessary in connection with the fulfilment by it of its obligations under this Agreement.

2.8 PFR shall do nothing to bring the name or reputation of the Charity into disrepute in any manner whatsoever.

3 Meetings and reports

3.1 PFR and the Charity will hold regular meetings at [   ]. The purpose of such meetings will be for PFR to report progress and discuss future plans and for the Charity to review PFR's performance.

3.2 In addition to attending such meetings, PFR will provide to the Charity a written progress report every [   ] months while this Agreement is in force.

3.3 Either party may by written notice to the other require the holding of a special meeting to discuss any urgent or exceptionally important matter.

4 Period of Agreement

4.1 This Agreement will commence on the   day of   200   and shall continue for a period of [ ] months unless terminated earlier under this clause[3].

---

[2]Specify clearly the area of activities to be undertaken by the PFR. The following provides an indication of possible methods:

- soliciting donations;
- sponsorship and gifts in kind;
- promotional schemes;
- deed of covenant and Gift Aid;
- payroll giving;
- corporate giving;
- trust giving;
- special events;
- advertising;
- lotteries;
- promotion of legacies.

[3]It is best not to agree to a long-term agreement unless under 4.2 the notice period is very short. Otherwise the Charity could find itself locked into long-term and expensive fundraising arrangements with little reward.

4.2   Either party may at any time terminate this Agreement by giving the other [ ] months' notice in writing.

4.3   The Charity shall be entitled to terminate this Agreement forthwith if:

4.3.1   PFR fails to pay any sum due to the Charity after the due date; or

4.3.2   PFR does anything which in the reasonable opinion of the Charity brings or in its opinion is reasonably likely to bring the Charity's reputation into disrepute; or

4.3.3   a resolution is passed for the voluntary or compulsory liquidation of PFR or a Receiver is appointed over all or part of its business or being an individual has a bankruptcy petition presented against him or her.

4.3.4   Notwithstanding termination of this Agreement, Clauses 6.2, 6.3, 6.4 and 6.7 and 8 shall survive termination. Clause 2.6 shall survive termination of this Agreement (however terminated) for a period of three years from the date of termination.

5   Remuneration

5.1   In consideration of the provision by PFR of the Services the Charity will pay to PFR a fee of [*amount/method of calculation/dates of payments*] upon receipt of PFR's invoice[4]. All sums stated are exclusive of VAT (if any) due on PFR's fees.

5.2   All reasonable subsistence, travelling and other expenses incurred by PFR in the execution of its obligations under this Agreement will be reimbursed in full within [ ] days of receipt of a written request to that effect by PFR to the Charity provided that the Charity shall not be liable to indemnify PFR for any expense in excess of [£] without such expenditure having been approved in writing in advance by the Charity[5].

6   Copyright and Data Protection

6.1   The copyright in all art work, copy and any other work capable of being subject to copyright produced or created by PFR at the specific request of the Charity shall vest in the Charity.

6.2   All art work and hard copy of such copyright material shall be handed over by PFR to the Charity within 14 days of the termination of this Agreement and at any time on the request of the Charity during the currency of this Agreement.

6.3   PFR undertakes with the Charity to maintain all the Data in a complete and accurate manner including all appropriate details of donors to the Charity recruited as a result of PFR's activities and to hand over a hard copy and a computer disk of that Data each month to the Charity. On termination of this Agreement PFR shall hand over to the Charity all copies of the Data (in whatever form). PFR undertakes that it shall not deal in, exploit or use in any manner whatever the Data whether during the currency of this Agreement or after its termination save in accordance with the terms of this Agreement.

6.4   PFR irrevocably appoints the Charity to be its attorney or agent in its name and on its behalf to do all such acts and things and to sign all such deeds and documents as may be necessary in order to give the Charity the full benefit of the provisions of this Agreement and in particular but without limitation PFR agrees that with respect to any third party a certificate signed by any duly authorised officer of the

---

[4] The Charity Commission has expressed its concern with payment on a commission basis and prefers fundraisers to be paid a fixed fee.

[5] It is best to specify a fairly low threshold concerning expenses as some charities have found that they have incurred very considerable liabilities in respect of expenses incurred by PFRs.

Charity that any act or thing or deed or document falls within the authority hereby conferred shall be conclusive evidence that that is the case[6].

6.5 PFR warrants and represents to the Charity that any copyright works or documents created by it pursuant to this Agreement or by its personnel or sub-contractors will not infringe the intellectual property rights of any third party whatsoever.

6.6 PFR undertakes to abide at all times by the Data Protection Act 1984 and all other relevant legislation and regulations in relation to the discharge by it of it obligations under this Agreement.

6.7 PFR hereby undertakes with the Charity that if it commissions any manipulative software to be used in conjunction with the Data that it shall procure that the Charity shall be granted by the licensor a perpetual free licence to use such software in the event of the termination of this Agreement.

7 Indemnity

PFR agrees to indemnify the Charity in respect of any costs, claims, loss or liability whatsoever suffered by the Charity (including reasonable legal costs and disbursements) as a result of any breach by PFR of any of the terms of this Agreement.

8 Confidentiality

8.1 The Charity agrees with PFR and PFR with the Charity to treat as secret and confidential and not at any time for any reason to disclose or permit to be disclosed to any person or persons or otherwise make use of or permit to be made use of any information relating to PFR's or the Charity's business affairs or finances (as the case may be) where knowledge or details of the information was received as a result of this Agreement.

8.2 The conditions of confidence referred to in this clause shall not apply to any confidential information which:

8.2.1 is in the possession of and is at the free disposal of the Charity or the PFR or is published or is otherwise in the public domain prior to receipt of such information by the Charity or PFR; or

8.2.2 is or becomes publicly available on a non-confidential basis through no fault of the Charity or PFR; or

8.2.3 is received in good faith by the Charity or PFR from a third party who on reasonable enquiry by the Charity or PFR claims to have no obligations of confidence to the PFR or the Charity in respect of it and imposes no obligations of confidence upon the Charity or PFR.

9 General

9.1 PFR agrees to abide by the code or codes or practice issued from time to time by the Institute of Charity Fundraising Managers.

9.2 PFR agrees that for the duration of this Agreement it shall not undertake any work of a similar nature for any charity which operates in the same or similar fields of activity as the Charity.

9.3 This Agreement shall be governed by and construed in accordance with the laws of England.

9.4 Neither party shall be liable for any breach of any term of this Agreement which is the result of any cause beyond the reasonable control of the party in breach.

[6]This clause is vital. Without it the Charity cannot force PFR to hand over copyright in material created by PFR in conjunction with this Agreement or lists of Data.

9.5   Any notice may be served by either party upon the other by sending it by post in a pre-paid recorded delivery or registered post or by telex or facsimile transmission addressed to such other party at its address above and any notice so sent shall be deemed to have been received within 72 hours of posting or 24 hours if sent by telex or facsimile transmission to the correct number of the addressee.

AS WITNESS the hands of the parties hereto

SCHEDULE 1

1   Details of records to be maintained by Professional Fundraiser:

2   Daily record of cash and/or other property received.

3   Daily record of credits paid into the Bank Account[7].

4   Daily record of all expenses to be charged in accordance with clause 5.2.

SIGNED by

for and on behalf of

Charity[8]

SIGNED by

for and on behalf of

PFR

[7]The details here are by illustration only and are not exhaustive.
[8]The agreement should be signed by a Trustee.

Appendix 3 Standard form of two-party agreement

N.B. This draft is a model form and ICFM recommends it be adapted for individual circumstances, in which, appropriate professional advice should be taken.

AGREEMENT

DATED the   day of   200

BETWEEN

[1][Charity] [Registered Charity No] whose head office [Registered Office] is at

[   ] [CRN No.   ] ('Charity') ; and

[Commercial Participator] [of] [whose registered office is at] [CRN No.   ] ('CP')

Background

A   The Charity is the beneficial owner of the Name and Logo and wishes to licence CP to exploit them.

B   This Agreement is entered into to comply with the Act and the Regulations.

1   Definitions

In this Agreement the following words and phrases shall have the following meanings unless the context otherwise requires:

'the Act'	the Charities Act 1992
'Logo'	the logo of the Charity details of which appear in Schedule 1 (which is a registered trade mark no.)
'Name'	[*Charity*] (which is a registered trade mark no.)
'Product'	the details of the product/services which appear in Schedule 2
'the Regulations'	The Charitable Institutions (Fund-Raising) Regulations 1994
'Royalty'[2]	[% of the recommended retail price/ p per Product sold]
'Term'[3]	The period of ....
'Territory'[4]	[ ]

2   The purpose of this Agreement is to raise funds for the Charity by [*state the method by which this will be achieved*].[5]

[1]State the full name of the Charity including its registered charity number and all details if it is a registered company as well; charities are formed in many ways and if the Charity is an unincorporated association or a trust, technically the Agreement should be entered into under the names of the trustees or the names of the members of the Management Committee by the phrase '*as Trustees of the XYZ Charity*'. This does not apply if the Charity has been incorporated under the Charities Act 1993 in which case it can enter into the Agreement in its corporate name without naming the trustees even though it does not have the benefits of limited liability. [2]The description of the royalty will inevitably vary widely and the precise definition needs to be put in. The Charity Commission has indicated that it does not think it is appropriate to state '*All net profits from the promotion go to XYZ Charity*' or similar phrases although such a phrase will comply with Section 60(3)(c) Charities Act 1992. That is because it is inherently impossible to determine in advance whether or not there will be any net profits. It is better if possible to agree a fixed price per item to be paid over or a fixed percentage of the price of the product or service. [3]If the Agreement is capable of lasting more than one year, then it is possible to use this Two-Party Agreement provided all the charity is doing is licensing its name and/or Logo. If more than this is to be done (e.g. licensing data) or if the agreement will last for less than a year, then it is necessary to use either the Tripartite Agreement Version A or B (Appendices 4 and 5). [4]State the area, e.g. United Kingdom of Great Britain and Northern Ireland. [5]State the method by which the Agreement will be carried out, e.g. the sale of baked beans bearing XYZ Charity's logo.

3   Appointment of Licensee

In Consideration of the undertakings given by CP in this Agreement, the Charity hereby appoints CP as its non-exclusive licensee to use the Name and Logo in connection with the Product in the Territory for the Term on the terms of this Agreement.

4   Obligations of CP

CP undertakes with the Charity that it shall:

4.1   not bring the Name or the Logo into disrepute in any way whatsoever and that none of its activities or those of any subsidiary or holding company are or will be inimical to the activities of the Charity;[6]

4.2   promote the sales of the Product throughout the Territory to the best of its abilities;

4.3   create and manage the design artwork print and manufacture of the Product and all advertising materials relating thereto but on condition that it shall obtain the prior written approval of the Charity (which approval shall not be unreasonably withheld or delayed) to all materials which bear the Name and/or Logo;

4.4   be responsible for the production promotion marketing and distribution of the Product and to that end may enter into such reasonable agreements as it shall think fit so as to fulfil its obligations under this Agreement;

4.5   ensure that the Product shall be of good quality and comply in all respects with all relevant statutory standards and shall contain the statement:
'[*pence per Product*] is paid to the [*name of Charity*] (a registered charity number).[7]
and shall not use the Name and Logo in any other manner whatever without the prior written consent of the Charity (such consent not to be unreasonably withheld or delayed).

4.6   keep separate, legible and detailed books of account and records relating to the production, promotion and sales of the Product and shall allow the Charity, its employees agents and professional advisers to inspect audit and take copies of any such books of account, VAT records, bank statements and other records of CP.

4.7   pay all moneys due to the Charity from the CP from time to time into a separate bank account in the CP's name and marked '[*name of charity*] Trust Account'[8]

4.8   promptly pay to the Charity any sums revealed as having been underpaid as a result of an inspection pursuant to 4.6 plus interest at 4% over Barclays Bank Plc's base rate for the time being calculated from the date payment should have been made to the date of actual payment.[9]

4.9   pay the reasonable professional costs of inspection under 4.8 in full if it has made an underpayment of at least 10% of the sums due;

---

[6]The Charity Commission has given considerable detailed advice in its Annual Report for 1991 Paragraphs 106 and 107 concerning the commercial exploitation of charities' names and logos and reference should be made to this if a charity finds difficulty in negotiating this clause.

[7]This clause is necessary to ensure the Commercial Participator abides by its obligations under Section 60(3)(c) Charities Act 1992 in respect of the statement concerning its activities.

[8]This clause gives greater protection to the Charity. If it is honoured, it prevents CP using the Charity's cash for CP's working capital requirements and if CP goes into insolvent liquidation the monies due to the Charity will not form part of the CP's assets to be shared among its creditors.

[9]The rate of interest is not laid down by statute and is a matter of commercial negotiation.

4.10   provide details to the Charity of the sales of the Product [monthly] [quarterly] [by 'x' date] and of the Royalty due.[10]

4.11   arrange that the statements of royalty prepared under this Agreement are audited by its auditors each year and that a copy of such certificate is promptly given to the Charity.[11]

4.12   maintain product liability insurance at all times in respect of the Product for a minimum cover of £.....................[12]

4.13   abide at all times with Part II of the Charities Act 1992 and in particular will state on all notices, advertisements and other documents soliciting funds for the Charity the fact that the Charity is a registered charity and its registered charity number.

5   The Royalty

5.1   CP shall pay to the Charity the Royalty on [   ] plus VAT as an annual payment as referred to in Section 348 (1) Income and Corporation Taxes Act 1988.[13]

5.2   Prior to the payment of an instalment of Royalty CP shall advise the Charity of the amount due and the Charity shall promptly render a VAT invoice to CP in respect of the instalment.

6   Termination

6.1   The Charity shall be entitled to terminate this Agreement forthwith if:

6.1.1   CP fails to pay any sum due to the Charity after the due date and the Charity has given CP 30 days' written notice requiring it to pay and CP has failed to pay in the 30-day period;

6.1.2   CP does anything which in the reasonable opinion of the Charity brings or is reasonably likely to bring the Name or Logo or reputation of the Charity into disrepute;[14]

6.1.3   a resolution is passed for the voluntary or compulsory liquidation of CP or a receiver is appointed over all or part of its business or if CP is an individual, has a bankruptcy petition presented against him or her.

6.2   If the Charity terminates this Agreement under 6.1 CP will no longer be authorised to use the Name and Logo and will cease immediately the distribution and sale of all existing Products bearing the Name and/or Logo.

6.3   Subject to the Charity's right to terminate under 6.1. this Agreement shall last for the Term. On termination under this sub-clause CP shall have the right to sell all existing copies of the Product which bear the Name and/or Logo as if termination had not taken place and in accordance with this Agreement it shall account to the

---

[10]In a short-term promotion it may only be possible to have the details of the sales paid over and the payment made at the end of the promotion. But on a promotion that is to last for more than one year, the Charity should demand at the very least quarterly payments and details of sales.

[11]This may be difficult to negotiate because of the costs involved. Charities are recommended to try to obtain this as it gives further protection to their position.

[12]Whether or not product liability insurance is necessary will depend on the products involved. Clearly there is little risk to members of the public from the sale of Christmas cards but the position could well be different with electrical goods and if a charity was seen to endorse a product which then caused injury, there is a remote possibility that the Charity could be sucked into litigation and the presence of product liability insurance would be extremely useful in such an instance.

[13]Before any charity enters into an agreement whereby monies are paid as an annual payment, it should seek appropriate professional advice from its solicitors or accountants.

[14]This clause is vital and ties in with note 7.

Charity for all Royalty payments in respect of such sales and the rights of the Charity under this Agreement shall continue during that period.

6.4　　Notwithstanding termination of this Agreement clauses 4, 5 and 9 shall survive termination.

7　　Indemnity

7.1　　CP agrees to indemnify the Charity in respect of any costs, claims, loss or liability whatsoever suffered by the Charity (including reasonable legal costs and disbursements) as a result of any breach by CP of any of the terms of this Agreement.

8　　Exclusive Agreement

8.1　　CP undertakes with Charity for the duration of this Agreement that it will not enter into a similar agreement relating to the Product or any similar product or services with any other charitable institution.

8.2　　The Charity undertakes with CP that for the duration of this Agreement it will not enter into a similar agreement with any other party in respect of a product or services which is similar to the Product, other than an agreement with a trading company of which the Charity owns at least 50% of the issued voting shares.

9　　Confidentiality

The Charity agrees with CP and CP with the Charity to treat as secret and confidential and not at any time for any reason to disclose or permit to be disclosed to any person or persons or otherwise make use of or permit to be made use of any information relating to CP's or the Charity's business affairs or finances (as the case may be) where knowledge or details of the information was received during the period of this Agreement.

The obligations of confidence referred to in this clause shall not apply to any confidential information which:

9.1　　is in the possession of and is at the free disposal of the Charity or CP or is published or is otherwise in the public domain prior to the receipt of such information by the Charity or CP; or

9.2　　is or becomes publicly available on a non-confidential basis through no fault of the Charity or CP; or

9.3　　is received in good faith by the Charity or CP from a third party who on reasonable enquiry by Charity or CP claims to have no obligations of confidence to the CP or the Charity in respect of it and imposes no obligations of confidence upon the Charity or the CP.

10　　General

10.1　　This Agreement is personal as between the parties and CP can only assign the benefit of this Agreement with the Charity's prior written consent but CP may appoint sub-licensees provided that it has obtained the Charity's prior written consent to the grant of a sub-licence (not to be unreasonably withheld or delayed) and CP shall remain liable for all its obligations hereunder as if it had not appointed a sub-licensee.

10.2　　No amendment or addition to this Agreement shall be made unless made in writing and executed by the parties.

10.3　　The parties are not partners nor joint venturers nor is CP entitled to act as nor to represent itself as agent for the Charity nor to pledge the Charity's credit.

10.4   This Agreement shall be governed by the laws of England and Wales.

10.5   Neither party shall be liable for any breach of any term of this Agreement which is the result of any cause beyond the reasonable control of the party in breach.

10.6   Any notice to be served on either of the parties shall be sent by pre-paid recorded delivery or registered post or by telex or facsimile transmission to the address above (or such other address as may be advised from time to time) and shall be deemed to have been received within 72 hours of posting or 24 hours if sent by telex or facsimile transmission to the correct number of the addressee.

AS WITNESS the hands of the parties.

SCHEDULE 1
Details of the Logo

SCHEDULE 2
Details of the Product[15]

SIGNED by
for and on behalf of the
Charity[16]

SIGNED by
for and on behalf of
CP

---

[15]State in full detail of the product or services which is the subject matter of the Agreement, e.g. cans of baked beans; package holidays; Christmas cards.
[16]The Agreement should be signed by a Trustee.

Appendix 4 Standard form of tripartite agreement
Version A – Lasts more than one year

N.B. This draft is a model form and ICFM recommends it be adapted for individual circumstances, in which case appropriate professional advice should be taken.

AGREEMENT

DATED

BETWEEN

1 [1][Charity] [Registered Charity No] whose head office [Registered Office] is at [ ] [CRN] fax number ('Charity'); and

2 [Trading Company] [CRN] whose registered office is at [ ] fax number ('TC'); and

3 [Commercial Participator] [of] [whose registered office is at] [CRN] fax number ('CP')

BACKGROUND

A TC is wholly owned by the Charity (and covenants all its taxable profits to the Charity)

B The Charity is the beneficial owner of the Name and Logo and has licensed TC to exploit the Data and in particular to grant sub-licences.

C CP is a commercial participator in relation to the Charity as defined in Section 58 of the Act.

D This Agreement is entered into to comply with the Act and the Regulations.

NOW IT IS AGREED AS FOLLOWS

1 Definitions

In this Agreement the following words and phrases shall have the following meanings unless the context otherwise requires:

'the Act'   the Charities Act 1992

'Data'   all lists of names and/or other details of supporters of the Charity in whatever form supplied to or held by CP

'Logo'   the logo of the Charity details of which appear in Schedule 1 [and which is registered as a trade mark no.   ]

'Name'   [Charity] [and which is registered as a trade mark no.   ]

'Payment'   the payment to TC for use of the Data

'Product'[2]   the products/services details of which appear in Schedule 2

---

[1]State the full name of the Charity including its registered charity number and all details if it is a registered company as well; charities are formed in many ways and if the Charity is an unincorporated association or a trust, technically the Agreement should be entered into under the names of the trustees or the names of the members of the Management Committee by the phrase '*as Trustees of the XYZ Charity*'. This does not apply if the Charity has been incorporated under the Charities Act 1993 in which case it can enter into the Agreement in its corporate name without naming the trustees even though it does not have the benefits of limited liability.

[2]State in full detail the product or services which is the subject matter of the Agreement, e.g. cans of baked beans; package holidays; Christmas cards.

[3]The description of the royalty will inevitably vary widely and the precise definition needs to be put in. The Charity Commission has indicated that it does not think it is appropriate to state 'All net profits from the promotion go to XYZ Charity' or similar phrases although such a phrase will comply with Section 60(3)(c) of the Charities Act 1992. That is because it is inherently impossible to determine in advance whether or not there will be any net profits. It is better if possible to agree a fixed price per item to be paid over or a fixed percentage of the price of the product or service.

'Regulations'   the Charitable Institutions (Fund-Raising) Regulations 1994
'Royalty'[3]   [% of the recommended retail price/   p per Product sold]
'Term'[4]   the period of ....
'Territory'[5]   [   ]

In this Agreement the masculine gender includes all other genders and vice versa.

2   The purpose of this Agreement is to raise funds for the Charity by
            [state the method by which this will be achieved][6].

3   Appointment of Sub-Licensee

In consideration of the undertakings given by CP in this Agreement, the Charity hereby appoints CP as its non-exclusive sub-licensee to use the Name and Logo on the Product and TC hereby appoints CP as its non-exclusive sub-licensee to use the Data in both cases in the Territory for the Term on the terms of this Agreement.

4   Obligations of CP

CP undertakes with the Charity and TC that it shall:

4.1   not bring the Name or the Logo into disrepute in any way whatsoever and that none of its activities or those of any subsidiary or holding company are or will be inimical to the activities of the Charity[7];

4.2   promote the sales of the Product throughout the Territory to the best of its abilities;

4.3   create and manage the design artwork print and manufacture of the Product and all advertising material relating thereto but on condition that it shall obtain the prior written approval of the Charity (which approval shall not be unreasonably withheld or delayed) to all materials which bear the Name and/or Logo;

4.4   be responsible for the production promotion marketing and distribution of the Product and to that end may enter into such reasonable agreements as it shall think fit so as to fulfil its obligations under this Agreement;

4.5   ensure that the Product shall be of good quality and comply in all respects with all relevant statutory standards and shall contain the statement:
            '[pence per Product] is paid to [Name of Charity] (a registered charity number
)[8]

4.6   keep separate, legible and detailed books of account and records relating to the production, promotion and sales of the Product and shall allow the Charity, its employees agents and professional advisers to inspect audit and take copies of any such books of account, VAT records, bank statements and other records of CP;

[4]The Agreement must be capable of lasting more than one year. If it is not, then it is necessary to use the Tripartite Agreement Version B.
[5]State the area, e.g. United Kingdom of Great Britain and Northern Ireland.
[6]State the method by which the Agreement will be carried out, e.g. the sale of baked beans bearing XYZ Charity's logo.
[7]The Charity Commission has given considerable detailed advice in its Annual Report for 1991 Paragraphs 106 and 107 concerning the commercial exploitation of charities' names and logos and reference should be made to this if a charity funds difficult in negotiating this clause.
[8]This clause is necessary to ensure the Commercial Participator abides by its obligations under Section 60(3)(c) Charities Act 1992 in respect of the statement concerning its activities.

4.7   promptly pay all moneys due to the Charity from the CP from time to time into a separate bank account in the CP's name and marked '[name of Charity] [name of Commercial Participator] Trust Account'[9];

4.8   promptly pay to the Charity any sums revealed as having been underpaid as a result of an inspection pursuant to 4.6 plus interest at 4% over Barclays Bank Plc's Base Rate for the time being calculated from the date payment should have been made to the date of actual payment[10];

4.9   promptly pay the reasonable professional costs of inspection under 4.6 in full if it has made an underpayment of at least 10% of the sums due;

4.10   promptly provide details to the Charity of the sales of the Product [monthly] [quarterly] [by 'x' date] and of the Royalty due[11];

4.11   arrange that the statements of Royalty prepared under this Agreement are audited by its auditors and that a copy of such certificate is promptly given to the Charity[12];

4.12   maintain product liability insurance at all times in respect of the Product for a minimum cover of £....................[13];

4.13   keep confidential all Data disclosed to it by TC and to use it only for the purpose of this Agreement and on termination of this Agreement (for whatever reason) to hand over promptly all copies of the Data to TC;

4.14   abide at all times with the Part II of the Charities Act 1992 and the Data Protection Act 1984 and in particular will state on all notices, advertisements and other documents soliciting funds for the Charity the fact that the Charity is a registered charity and its registered charity number.

5   The Royalty

5.1   CP shall pay to the Charity the Royalty on [   ] plus VAT as an annual payment as defined in Section 348(1) Income and Corporation Taxes Act 1988[14].

5.2   CP shall pay to TC the Payment on   plus VAT.

5.3   Prior to the payment of an instalment of Royalty or Payment CP shall advise the Charity and TC of the amount due and the Charity and TC shall each promptly render VAT invoices to CP in respect of the respective instalments.

6   Termination

6.1   The Charity and/or TC shall be entitled to terminate this Agreement forthwith if:

---

[9]This clause gives greater protection to the Charity. If it is honoured, it prevents CP using the Charity's cash for CP's working capital requirements and if CP goes into insolvent liquidation the monies due to the Charity will not form part of the CP's assets to be shared among its creditors. This clause will be difficult to agree. Many CPs will oppose it.

[10]The rate of interest is not laid down by statute and is a matter of commercial negotiation.

[11]In a short-term promotion it may only be possible to have the details of the sales paid over and the payment made at the end of the promotion. But on a promotion that is to last for more than one year, the Charity should demand at the very least quarterly payments and details of sales.

[12]This may be difficult to negotiate because of the costs involved. Charities are recommended to try to obtain this as it gives further protection to their position.

[13]Whether or not product liability insurance is necessary will depend on the products involved. Clearly there is little risk for members of the public from the sale of Christmas cards but the position could well be different with electrical goods and if a charity was seen to endorse a product which then caused injury, there is a remote possibility that the Charity could be sucked into litigation and the presence of product liability insurance would be extremely useful in such an instance.

[14]Before any charity enters into an agreement whereby monies are paid as an annual payment it should seek appropriate professional advice from its solicitors or accountants.

6.1.1   CP fails to pay any sum due to the Charity or TC after the due date and the Charity and/or TC has given CP 30 days' written notice requiring it to pay and CP has failed in the 30-day period[15]; or

6.1.2   CP does anything which in the reasonable opinion of TC or the Charity brings or in the opinion of TC or the Charity is reasonably likely to bring the Name or Logo or reputation of either TC or the Charity into disrepute; or

6.1.3   a resolution is passed for the voluntary or compulsory liquidation of CP or if a receiver is appointed over all or part of its business or if CP is an individual has a bankruptcy petition presented against him or her

6.2   If TC or the Charity terminate this Agreement under 6.1 CP will no longer be authorised to use the Name and Logo and Data and will cease immediately the distribution and sale of all existing Product bearing the Name and Logo and cease to use the Data.

6.3   Subject to TC's and the Charity's right to terminate under 6.1 this Agreement shall last for the Term. On termination under this sub-clause CP shall have the right to sell all Product bearing the Name and Logo and use the Data until such Product has been sold and for no other purpose as if termination had not taken place and it shall promptly account to the Charity for all Royalty payments in respect of such sales and to TC for use of the Data in accordance with this Agreement and the rights of TC and the Charity under this Agreement shall continue during that period.

6.4   Notwithstanding termination of this Agreement clauses 4, 5 and 7 shall survive termination.

7   Indemnity

7.1   CP agrees to indemnify TC and the Charity in respect of any costs, claims, loss or liability whatsoever suffered by TC or the Charity (including reasonable legal costs and disbursements paid by either) as a result of any breach by CP of any of the terms of this Agreement.

8   Exclusive Agreement

8.1   CP undertakes with the Charity and TC that for the duration of this Agreement it will not enter into a similar agreement relating to the Product or any similar product or service with any other charitable institution.

8.2   TC and the Charity each undertake with CP that for the duration of this Agreement neither will enter into a similar agreement with any other party in respect of a product or service which is similar to the Product, other than an agreement with a trading company of which the Charity owns at least 50% of the issued voting shares.

9   Confidentiality

TC and the Charity agree to treat as secret and confidential and not at any time for any reason to disclose or permit to be disclosed to any person or persons or otherwise make use of or permit to be made use of any information relating to CP's business affairs or finances where knowledge or details of the information was received pursuant to this Agreement. The obligations of confidence referred to in this clause shall not apply to any confidential information which:

9.1   is in the possession of and is at the free disposal of the TC or the Charity or is published or is otherwise in the public domain prior to the receipt of such information by the Charity or TC; or

[15]This clause is vital and ties in with note 7.

9.2 is or becomes publicly available on a non-confidential basis through no fault of TC or the Charity; or

9.3 is received in good faith by TC and/or the Charity from a third party who on reasonable enquiry by TC or the Charity claims to have no obligations of confidence to CP in respect of it and imposes no obligations of confidence upon TC or the Charity.

9.4 The obligations imposed by this clause on TC and the Charity shall apply *mutatis mutandis* to CP.

10 General

10.1 This Agreement is personal as between the parties and CP can only assign the benefit of this Agreement with the Charity's and TC's prior written consent but CP may appoint sub-licensees provided that it has obtained the Charity's and TC's prior written consent to the grant of a sub-licence (not to be unreasonably withheld or delayed) and CP shall remain liable for all its obligations hereunder as if it had not appointed a sub-licensee.

10.2 No amendment or addition to this Agreement shall be made unless made in writing and executed by the parties.

10.3 The parties are not partners nor joint venturers nor is CP entitled to act as nor represent itself as agent for TC or the Charity nor to pledge the TC's or the Charity's credit.

10.4 Neither party shall be liable for any breach of any term of this Agreement which is the result of any cause beyond the reasonable control of the party in breach.

10.5 This Agreement shall be governed by the laws of England and Wales.

10.6 Any notice to be served on any of the parties shall be sent by pre-paid recorded delivery or registered post or by telex or facsimile transmission to the address above (or such other address as may be advised from time to time) and shall be deemed to have been received within 72 hours of posting or 24 hours if sent by telex or facsimile transmission to the correct number of the addressee.

AS WITNESS the hands of the parties

SCHEDULE 1
Details of the Logo

SCHEDULE 2
Details of the Product

SIGNED by
for and on behalf of the
Charity[16]

SIGNED by
for and on behalf of the
Trading Company

SIGNED by
for and on behalf of the
Commercial Participator

[16]This Agreement should be signed by a Trustee.

Appendix 5 Standard form of tripartite agreement
Version B – Lasts less than one year

N.B. This draft is a model form and ICFM recommends it be adapted for individual circumstances, in which case appropriate professional advice should be taken.

AGREEMENT

DATED

BETWEEN

(1)   1[Charity] [Registered Charity No] whose head office [Registered Office] is at

[   ] [CRN   ] fax number

('Charity') ; and

(2)   [Trading Company] [CRN   ] whose registered office is at

[   ] fax number   ('TC'); and

(3)   [Commercial Participator] [of] [whose registered office is at][CRN   ] fax

number   ('CP')

BACKGROUND

A   TC is wholly owned by the Charity (and covenants all its taxable profits to the Charity)

B   The Charity is the beneficial owner of the Name, Logo and Data and has licensed TC to exploit them and in particular to grant sub-licences.

C   CP is a commercial participator in relation to the Charity as defined in Section 58 of the Act.

D   This Agreement is entered into to comply with the Act and the Regulations.

NOW IT IS AGREED AS FOLLOWS

1   Definitions

In this Agreement the following words and phrases shall have the following meanings unless the context otherwise requires:

'the Act'   the Charities Act 1992

'Data'   all lists of names and/or other details of supporters of the Charity in whatever form supplied to or held by CP

'Logo'   the logo of the Charity details of which appear in Schedule 1[and which is registered as a trade mark no.   ]

'Name'   [Charity][and which is registered as a trade mark no.   ]

'Product'[2]   the products/services details of which appear in Schedule 2

'Regulations'   the Charitable Institutions (Fund-Raising) Regulations 1994

'Royalty'[3]   [% of the recommended retail price/   p per Product sold]

'Term'[4]   the period of ....

'Territory'[5]   [   ]

In this Agreement the masculine gender shall include all other genders and vice versa.

[1]State the full name of the Charity including its registered charity number and all details if it is a registered company as well; charities are formed in many ways and if the Charity is an unincorporated association or a trust, technically the Agreement should be entered into under the names of the trustees or the names of the members of the Management Committee by the phrase 'as Trustees of the XYZ Charity'. This does not apply if the Charity has been incorporated under the Charities Act 1993 in which case it can enter into the Agreement in its corporate name without naming the trustees even though it does not have the benefits of limited liability.

2   The purpose of this Agreement is to raise funds for the Charity via TC by [state the method by which this will be achieved][6].

3   Appointment of Sub-Licensee

In consideration of the undertakings given by CP in this Agreement, TC hereby appoints CP as its non-exclusive sub-licensee to use the Name and Logo on the Product and to exploit the Data in the Territory for the Term on the terms of this Agreement.

4   Obligations of CP

CP undertakes with the Charity and TC that it shall:

4.1   not bring the Name or the Logo into disrepute in any way whatsoever and that none of its activities or those of any subsidiary or holding company are or will be inimical to the activities of the Charity[7];

4.2   promote the sales of the Product throughout the Territory to the best of its abilities;

4.3   create and manage the design artwork print and manufacture of the Product and all advertising material relating thereto but on condition that it shall obtain the prior written approval of TC (which approval shall not be unreasonably withheld or delayed) to all materials which bear the Name and/or Logo;

4.4   be responsible for the production promotion marketing and distribution of the Product and to that end may enter into such reasonable agreements as it shall think fit so as to fulfil its obligations under this Agreement;

4.5   ensure that the Product shall be of good quality and comply in all respects with all relevant statutory standards and shall contain the statement:

[pence per Product] is paid to TC which covenants all its taxable profits to [name of Charity] (a registered charity number   )[8];

4.6   keep separate, legible and detailed books of account and records relating to the production, promotion and sales of the Product and shall allow TC, its employees agents and professional advisers to inspect audit and take copies of any such books of account, VAT records, bank statements and other records of CP;

4.7   promptly pay all moneys due to TC from it into a separate bank account in CP's name and marked '[name of TC] Trust Account'[9];

---

[2]State in full detail the product or services which is or are the subject matter of the Agreement, e.g cans of baked beans; package holidays; Christmas cards.

[3]The description of the royalty will inevitably vary widely and the precise definition needs to be put in. The Charity Commission has indicated that it does not think it is appropriate to state 'All net profits from the promotion go to XYZ Charity' or similar phrases although such a phrase will comply with Section 60(3)(c) Charities Act 1992. That is because it is inherently impossible to determine in advance whether or not there will be any net profits. It is better if possible to agree a fixed price per item to be paid over or a fixed percentage of the price of the product or service.

[4]If the Agreement is capable of lasting more than one year, then it is possible to use the Two-party Agreement or Tripartite Agreement Version A (Appendix 4).

[5]State the area, e.g. United Kingdom of Great Britain and Northern Ireland.

[6]State the method by which the Agreement will be carried out, e.g. the sale of baked beans bearing XYZ Charity's logo.

[7]The Charity Commission has given considerable detailed advice in its Annual Report for 1991 Paragraphs 106 and 107 concerning the commercial exploitation of charities' names and logos and reference should be made to this if a charity finds difficulty in negotiating this clause.

[8]This clause is necessary to ensure the Commercial Participator abides by its obligations under Section 60(3)(c) Charities Act 1992 in respect of the statement concerning its activities.

[9]This clause gives greater protection to the TC. If it is honoured, it prevents CP using the TC's cash for CP's working capital requirements and if CP goes into insolvent liquidation the monies due to the TC will not form part of the CP's assets to be shared among its creditors.

4.8   promptly pay to TC any sums revealed as having been underpaid as a result of an inspection pursuant to 4.6 plus interest at 4% over Barclays Bank Plc's base rate for the time being calculated from the date payment should have been made to the date of actual payment[10];

4.9   promptly pay the reasonable professional costs of inspection under 4.6 in full if it has made an underpayment of at least 10% of the sums due[11];

4.10   promptly provide details to TC of the sales of the Product [monthly] [quarterly] [by 'x' date] and of the Royalty due[12];

4.11   arrange that the statements of Royalty prepared under this Agreement are audited by its auditors and that a copy of such certificate is promptly given to TC[12];

4.12   maintain product liability insurance at all times in respect of the Product for a minimum cover of £......................[13];

4.13   keep confidential all Data disclosed to it by TC and to use it only for the purpose of this Agreement and on termination of this Agreement (for whatever reason) to hand over promptly all copies of the Data to TC;

4.14   abide at all times with the Part II of the Charities Act 1992 and the Data Protection Act 1984 and in particular state on all notices, advertisements and other documents soliciting funds for the Charity the fact that the Charity is a registered charity and the Charity's registered charity number.

5   The Royalty

5.1   CP shall pay to TC the Royalty on [   ] plus VAT.

5.2   Prior to the payment of an instalment of Royalty CP shall advise TC of the amount due and TC shall promptly render a VAT invoice to CP in respect of the instalment.

5.3   TC undertakes with CP that it will donate all its taxable profits for the financial period(s) to which this Agreement relates to the Charity.

6   Termination

6.1   TC shall be entitled to terminate this Agreement forthwith if:

6.1.1   CP fails to pay any sum due to TC after the due date and TC has given CP 30 days' written notice requiring it to pay and CP has failed to pay in the 30-day period[14]; or

6.1.2   CP does anything which in the reasonable opinion of TC or the Charity brings or in the opinion of TC or the Charity is reasonably likely to bring the Name or Logo or reputation of either TC or the Charity into disrepute; or

6.1.3   a resolution is passed for the voluntary or compulsory liquidation of CP or a receiver is appointed over all or part of its business or if CP is an individual has a bankruptcy petition presented against him or her.

---

[10]The rate of interest is not laid down by statute and is a matter of commercial negotiation.

[11]In a short-term promotion it may only be possible to have the details of the sales paid over and the payment made at the end of the promotion. But on a promotion that is to last for more than one year, the Charity should demand at the very least quarterly payments and details of sales.

[12]This may be difficult to negotiate because of the costs involved. Charities are recommended to try to obtain this as it gives further protection to their position.

[13]Whether or not product liability insurance is necessary will depend on the products involved. Clearly there is little risk for members of the public from the sale of Christmas cards but the position could well be different with electrical goods and if a charity was seen to endorse a product which then caused injury, there is a remote possibility that the Charity could be sucked into litigation and the presence of product liability insurance would be extremely useful in such an instance.

[14]This clause is vital and ties in with note 7.

6.2   If TC terminates this Agreement under 6.1 CP will no longer be authorised to use the Name and Logo and the Data and will cease immediately the distribution and sale of all existing Product bearing the Name and Logo and cease to use the Data.

6.3   Subject to TC's right to terminate under 6.1 this Agreement shall last for the Term. On termination under this sub-clause CP shall have the right to sell all existing Product bearing the Name and Logo and use the Data until such Product has been sold and for no other purpose as if termination had not taken place and it shall promptly account to TC for all Royalty payments in respect of such sales in accordance with this Agreement and the rights of TC and the Charity under this Agreement shall continue during that period.

6.4   Notwithstanding termination of this Agreement clauses 4, 5 and 7 shall survive termination.

7   Indemnity

CP agrees to indemnify TC and the Charity in respect of any costs, claims, loss or liability whatsoever suffered by TC or the Charity (including reasonable legal costs and disbursements paid by either) as a result of any breach by CP of any of the terms of this Agreement.

8   Exclusive Agreement

8.1   CP undertakes with the Charity and TC that for the duration of this Agreement it will not enter into a similar agreement relating to the Product or any similar product or service with any other charitable institution.

8.2   TC and the Charity each undertakes with CP that for the duration of this Agreement neither will enter into a similar agreement with any other party in respect of a product or service which is similar to the Product, other than an agreement with a trading company of which the Charity owns at least 50% of the issued voting shares.

9   Confidentiality

TC and the Charity agree to treat as secret and confidential and not at any time for any reason to disclose or permit to be disclosed to any person or persons or otherwise make use of or permit to be made use of any information relating to CP's business affairs or finances where knowledge or details of the information was received pursuant to this Agreement. The obligations of confidence referred to in this clause shall not apply to any confidential information which:

9.1   is in the possession of and is at the free disposal of TC or the Charity or is published or is otherwise in the public domain prior to the receipt of such information by the Charity or TC; or

9.2   is or becomes publicly available on a non-confidential basis through no fault of TC or the Charity; or

9.3   is received in good faith by TC and/or the Charity from a third party who on reasonable enquiry by TC or the Charity claims to have no obligations of confidence to CP in respect of it and imposes no obligations of confidence upon TC or the Charity.

9.4   The obligations imposed by this clause on TC and the Charity shall apply *mutatis mutandis* to CP.

10   General

10.1   This Agreement is personal as between the parties and CP can only assign the benefit of this Agreement with Charity's and TC's prior written consent but CP may appoint sub-licensees provided that it has obtained Charity's and TC's prior written consent to the grant of a sub-licence (not to be unreasonably withheld or delayed) and CP shall remain liable for all its obligations hereunder as if it had not appointed a sub-licensee.

10.2   No amendment or addition to this Agreement shall be made unless made in writing and executed by the parties.

10.3   The parties are not partners nor joint venturers nor is CP entitled to act as nor represent itself as agent for TC or the Charity nor to pledge the TC's or the Charity's credit.

10.4   Neither party shall be liable for any breach of any term of this Agreement which is the result of any cause beyond the reasonable control of the party in breach.

10.5   This Agreement shall be governed by the laws of England and Wales.

10.6   Any notice to be served on any of the parties shall be sent by pre-paid recorded delivery or registered post or by telex or facsimile transmission to the address above (or such other address may be advised from time to time) and shall be deemed to have been received within 72 hours of posting or 24 hours if sent by telex or facsimile transmission to the correct number of the addressee.

AS WITNESS the hands of the parties.

SCHEDULE 1
Details of the Logo

SCHEDULE 2
Details of the products

SIGNED by
for and on behalf of the
Charity[15]

SIGNED by
for and on behalf of the
Trading Company

SIGNED by
for and on behalf of the
Commercial Participator

---

[15]This Agreement should be signed by a Trustee.

References and other useful publications

References

Business in the Community (1998) 'The Cause Related Marketing Guidelines'. London: BitC.

Charity Commission (1999) *Internal Financial Controls for Charities* (leaflet CC8). Taunton: Charity Commission.

Health & Safety Executive and the Charities Safety Group (1999) *Charity and Voluntary Workers* (HSG192) Bootle: HSE.

Home Office Voluntary Services Unit (1995) *Charitable Fund-raising: Professional and Commercial Involvement – a guide for practitioners about professional and commercial fund-raising, particularly under part II of the Charities Act 1992*. London: The Stationery Office.

Publications available from the ICFM

Codes of Practice

Charity Challenge Events

House to House Collections

Payroll Giving

Reciprocal Charity Mailing

The Scottish Code of Fundraising Practice

Telephone Recruitment of Collectors

UK Charity Challenge Events

Guidance Notes

Acceptance/refusal of donations

The management of static collection boxes

The use of chain letters as a fundraising technique

Useful publications available free of charge from the Patent Office

Registering a Trade Mark

Trade Marks – Search and Advisory Service

Copyright

Patent Protection

How to Prepare a UK Patent Application

Design Registration

Publications available from the Directory of Social Change

Adirondack, S. and Sinclair Taylor, J. (1996, 2nd edn 2001) *The Voluntary Sector Legal Handbook*.

Hinde A. and Kavanagh, C. (1998, 2nd edn 2001) *The Health and Safety Handbook*.

Sayer, K. (2000) *A Practical Guide to VAT for Charities and Voluntary Organisations*, 2nd edn.

Ticher, P. (2000) *Data Protection for Voluntary Organisations*.

Index

accounting 2.2.11
    after house-to-house collections 4.4.10
advertisements 3.6
    aerial 15.15
    and British Codes of Advertising and
        Sales Promotion 15.6
    cinema 15.6.1, 15.12
    and criminal liability 15.2
    display of public notices 15.3
    e-mail 15.6.1
    and intellectual property rights 15.4
    Internet 15.6.1, 15.14
    misleading 15.1
    political 15.1.8, 15.17
    postal appeals 3.10
    radio 15.8, 15.9
    showing registered charity status 1.7
    telephone and fax 15.6.1, 15.13.2–11
    television 15.7, 15.9
    and VAT 2.2.12, 8.2.1, 8.3, 8.4.3, 20.4
    see also sponsorship
Advertising Standards Authority (ASA)
    12.9.4, 15.6.1, 15.6.9–13
aerial advertisements 15.15
affinity cards 8.5.1, 8.7, 16.3.3
agencies:
    collection 4.9.2
    covenant renewal 17.4.1
    donor recruitment 7.7–7.9
    volunteer recruitment 4.8.3, 17.2
agency charities 7.6.1, 7.6.3
air travel 6.10.3
alcohol licences 6.6.4
alms, collecting 23.7
almshouses 10.3
annual ball tickets, sale of 10.2
appeals:
    broadcast 3.14, 15.7–15.11, 16.3.2
    celebrities' 17.5.4
    disaster 1.5
    failed 1.4.3
    telephone 3.11, 17.4.2, 17.8
    VAT-free leaflets 20.3.1
    wording of documents 1.4.2–5, 3.7
'assignments' 21.10
Astor, Viscount 17.3

bank-deposit advertisements 15.2.6
banks:
    as commercial participators 16.3.2, 16.3.3
    and internal accounting 2.2.11
    secondments 17.4.3
begging 23.7
books/booklets, zero-rated 20.5, 20.5.1
breach of contract 2.2.10, 11.5, 15.1.7
Brightman, Mr Justice 1.4.6
British Diabetic Association 21.3.1, 21.9.2
British Red Cross Society 1.5, 1.10.1, 7.11,
    15.6.6
British Union for the Abolition of
    Vivisection 3.16.5
broadcasting *see* radio; television
Broadcasting Act (1990) 15.17.4
Broadcasting Advertising Clearance Centre
    15.7.15
Broadcasting Standards Commission 15.11
brochures, zero-rated 20.5.2
Building Societies Act (1987) 15.2.7
Business in the Community: 'The Cause
    Related Marketing Guidelines' 8.5.1
businesses *see* companies

CAF *see* Charities Aid Foundation
Cancer Research Campaign 21.2.2
CAP codes 3.10.1
Capital Gains Tax 19.5
car-boot sales *see* events
care services 10.3
carol singing 4.3.9
cash:
    insuring 14.12
    recording 18.2
    and security 18.2
catalogues, selling through 10.11
cause-related marketing 1.6, 8.1, 8.5
    see also affinity cards
celebrities, appeals by 17.5.4
chain letters 3.10.2, 15.2.10
challenge events:
    participants as professional fundraisers
        6.12
    and refund of entry fees 6.12.1
    see also events; overseas challenge events